PROJECT REPORT PREPARATION:
HOSPITALITY MANAGEMENT AND TOURISM DEVELOPMENT

Project Report Preparation:
Hospitality Management and Tourism Development

Dr. Jagmohan Negi
and
Gaurav Manoher

Aman Publications
New Delhi

Published by
Rajiv Jain for Aman Publications
LG-4A, Ganpati Bhawan,
4675-B/21, Ansari Road,
Darya Ganj, Delhi - 110002
PH: 23255012, 23282127
E-mail: sshjbs@yahoo.com

First Published 2010

ISBN–81–8204–055-8
ISBN–978-81–8204–055-7

SOLE DISTRIBUTOR
JINDAL BOOK SERVICES
LG-4A, Ganpati Bhawan,
4675-B/21, Ansari Road,
Darya Ganj, Delhi - 110002

Jacket Designed by :
S.M. Graphics

Printed by:
Abhinav Prints, Delhi - 110041

Preface

Preparation of a research project is one of the most important subjects in the learning process of students undergoing for quality professional profession and academic education. The subject is gaining due weightage and many universities; colleges and institutions of professional training all over the globe have incorporated it as one of the main subject in their curriculum. Research students face lot of constraints in understanding techniques of preparation and presenting a good project report. Therefore an attempt has been made to provide them systematic guidelines in a most understandable language.

A study of the book will familiarize them with the basic concepts and techniques of report writing systematically and sequentially. The book aims to enable the researchers to learn and understand techniques, procedures and mechanism of writing the research report for academic as well as business purpose. The researcher would be able to systematically apply the conceptual knowledge, to the practical situations, utilize his/her skills for proper use, presentation and commutation of data, analysis, interpretation findings and conclusion thereof in a well-structured format. The book covers the basic steps for report preparation and presentation. The structure and contents of the book are so designed so as research writer proceeds thus enable his/her to organize and write the report with full confidence.

The book has been divided into fourteen chapters including specimen of a typical project report. These topics introduce about the concepts, Importance of research writing, critical in sights regarding selecting a suitable topic for study, approval of the synopsis, organization of the report, collection of data, analysis and interpretation, findings and fundamental conclusions, report presentation, use of diagram and graphics, oral presentation and publication of report.

Typical examples of project synopsis have been provided to enable researcher to acquire skills of writing the project synopsis. This guidance will assists in developing a synopsis.

Selection of an appropriate research topic is quite difficult task. Therefore, lists of 269 projects study topics have been suggested along with the techniques of drafting and forwarding a selected topic for study. These topics are based on primary studies and case studies and selected diagnostic studies. One may decide and select any appropriate topic for the project study using this part of a reference. Topics on diagram and graphic have been dealt in detail as diagrammatic and graphic presentation enhance the beauty of the research project and enrich the work conducted by the research scholar.

Sample project reports in the form of case study have been incorporated in chapter 14. This study would make the research students to critically understand sequence of chapters, chapter material and application of theoretical input in preparation and presentation of the report.

We are thankful to all institutes, colleges, universities and research organizations, authors and writers whose ideas, data and reports have been helpful in the preparation of this book.

Special thanks to the management of different Schools of Hospitality and Tourism and World Hospitality Research and Development to provide an opportunity to complete this work. The authors also acknowledge the work of students and many others whose ideas have been incorporate in this book for the benefits of the students, scholars of the future generation. We appreciate and welcome comments and suggestions from all the readers.

AUTHORS

Contents

List of Figures

List of Tables

About the authors

Prof. Jagmohan Negi is *a* distinguished Professor in International Hospitality Management and Development. He held many responsible positions such as National Advisor-Hospitality Management and Tourism Development, Executive Director in Swiss Institute of Tourism & Hotel Management, Professor and Director at World Centre for Hospitality & Tourism Research and Development in Amity School of Hospitality, Director National Council for Hotel Management as well as Research Professor in the Institute of Hotel Management, New Delhi.

He is a reputed author of numbers of articles and books on various aspects of this newly emerging hospitality and tourism disciplines. He has more than 38 years of experience in research, training, teaching, project development and administration. He has developed and designed a numbers of hospitality and tourism related curriculums for undergraduate and postgraduate education and hospitality research centre which have been acknowledged, approved and accepted in many universities, colleges, and research and training institutions both in India as well as abroad.

He is also a reputed guest professor and member of academic councils, board of studies and research committees in numbers of universities and colleges, and is presently associated with national and international bodies such as World Tourism Organization, UNDP, ILO, International Culinary Foundation and Himalayan Tourism and Recreation in Mountains.

Gaurav Manoher is a reputed global leadership management expert and an adventure traveller with world-wide experience in travelling countries such as Japan, South Korea, China, United States of America, Germany, France, United Kingdom, Hungary, Hong Kong and many places of his own country of birth i.e., India. With his in-depth knowledge and experience of internationally managed multinational corporations he has acquired the techniques of the modern management and its application, analysis, critical examination and review in terms of regional environment. He is one of the founder members of international reputed Himalayan Tourism and Recreation in Mountains, an organization dedicated for the sustainable development.

Preparation of a research project is one of the most important subjects in the learning process of students undergoing for quality professional profession and academic education. The subject is gaining due weightage and many universities, colleges and institutions of professional training all over the globe have incorporated it as one of the main subject in their curriculum. Research students face lot of constraints in understanding techniques of preparation and presenting a good project report. Therefore an attempt has been made to provide them systematic guidelines in a most understable language.

A study of the book will familiarize them with the basic concepts and techniques of report writing. The book aims to enable the researchers to learn and understand techniques, procedures and mechanism of writing the research report for academic as well as business purpose. The researcher would be able to systematically apply the conceptual knowledge, to the practical situations, utilize his/her skills for proper use, presentation and commutation of data, analysis, interpretation findings and conclusion thereof in a well structured format. The book covers the basic steps for report preparation and presentation. The structure and contents of the book are so designed so as research writer proceeds systematically and sequentially, thus enable his/her to organize and write the report with full confidence.

About the book

The book has been divided into fourteen chapters including specimen of a typical project report. These topics introduce about the concepts, importance of research writing, critical in sights regarding selecting a suitable topic for study, approval of the synopsis, organization of the report, collection of data, analysis and interpretation, findings and fundamental conclusions, report presentation, use of diagram and graphics, oral presentation and publication of report.

Typical examples of project synopsis have been provided to enable researcher to acquire skills of writing the project synopsis. These guidance will assists in developing a synopsis.

Selection of an appropriate research topic is quite difficult task. Therefore, a list of 269 project study topics have been suggested along with the techniques of drafting and forwarding a selected topic for study. These topics are based on primary studies and case studies and selected diagnostic studies. One may decide and select any appropriate topic for the project study using this part of a reference. Topics on diagram and graphic have been dealt in detail as diagrammatic and graphic presentation enhance the beauty of the research project and enrich the work conducted by the research scholar.

Sample project reports in the form of case study have been incorporated in chapter 14. This study would make the research students to critically understand sequence of chapters, chapter material and application of theoretical input in preparation and presentation of the report.
We are thankful to all institutes, colleges, universities and research organizations, authors and writers whose ideas, data and reports have been helpful in the preparation of this book.

Special thanks to the management of different Schools of Hospitality and Tourism and World Hospitality Research and Development to provide an opportunity to complete this work. The authors also acknowledge the work of students and many *others* whose ideas have been incorporate in this book for the benefits of the students, scholars of the future generation. We appreciate and welcome comments and suggestions from all the readers.

AUTHORS

1

Project Report : An Introduction

Research project report is a problem-solving approach addressing a question that is considered to be felt need. It is an orderly investigation of a defined problem using scientific methods to gather representative evidence and draw logical unbiased conclusions. Each of the major components of the hospitality and tourism industry relies upon research found in several segments of the industry. The four major segments are:

1) Academic institutions,
2) Associations within the field,
3) Industry businesses, and
4) Government at local, state and central levels.

Research may be defined as the objective and systematic method of finding solution to the problem i.e.,

1) Systematic collection,
2) Recording,
3) Analysis,
4) Interpretation, and
5) Reporting of information.

It refers to the systematic method consisting of enunciating the problem, collecting facts of data, analyzing the facts critically and reaching conclusions based on them, invariably given specially in a published research report or thesis.

1) Report should be written in a concise and objective style in simple language. Avoid vague expressions such as 'it seems', 'there may be', and like ones.
2) Charts and illustrations in the main report should be used only if they present the information more clearly and more forcibly.
3) Calculated 'confidence limits' must be mentioned and the various constraints experienced in conducting the survey may as well be stated.

A research expects to contribute to the knowledge of hospitality and tourism industry. In selecting research question, the ability to contribute to the industry should be one of your primary concerns. Some students have been successful in making contact which help them to land jobs in the industry. The students have been assisted in obtaining scholarship and grants. In some cases corporate houses sponsor the project work through the awarding of grants and scholarship before the thesis is written. Therefore, one should be encouraged to look beyond the immediate goal of completing a degree programme and select a project topic that will not only be of interest to them, but to industry employers and scholarship award granters as well.

Why people take themselves to research? This is the main question. The possible motives of your may be either one or more of the following desires:

1) To get a research degree along with the consequential benefits.
2) To face the challenge in solving the unsolved problem.
3) To get intellectual joy of doing creative work.
4) To be of service to the society.
5) To get respectability.

The motivation will, however, determine to a considerable extent the nature, quality, depth and duration of research.

Project report or dissertation forms a part of the curriculum of hospitality and tourism education. In the hospitality and tourism, project report may be defined as a form of communication that would provide feedback to the organisation to facilitate decision making. A project report prepared for a course is one of the most important requirements as far as assessment procedure is concerned. This is because a dissertation brings into application several of the aspects dealt within the programme. Its demonstrates the skills of the researcher to investigate and critically examine the problem under investigation and its various solutions in a systematic, methodical and scientific manner in order to present a logical solution. It is an invaluable exercise in written communication. Through this process researcher is able to know the competencies of writing skills, presentation skills and analytical skills. In fact many students learn a lot of written/business communication skills through the preparation of the project work.

Qualities of a Researcher

1) Strong writing skills
2) Strong analytic skills
3) Strong verbal skills
4) A professional appearance
5) Good grades
6) Strong quantitative skills
7) Potential new business development skills
8) A grade degree/training
9) Good schools
10) Management skills
11) Guest handling skills
12) A national reputation

13) Expertise in hotel/tourism/ catering industry

14) Expertise in specific methodology.

A project work being a part of the overall assessment, a satisfactory standard is essential to successfully complete the programme. Generally, the project work is considered equal to more than normal papers (*i.e.*, may be of 100 to 300 marks). More weightage is given to practical work and actual case studies are assigned in the project work. The standard of report in terms of contents and aesthetics plays a vital role during evaluation. These reports are sent to experts for evaluation and comments.

The original work is a necessity. If the project is substandard and does not meet desired norms, the researcher is likely to be at a loss, however well he or she may have done in other aspects of hospitality and tourism curriculum. The author of the project must knows what is required in the preparation of project report. He or she must be able to produce a standard and satisfactory document.

A student may opt to select an existing problem of an organisation as a project study. The management of hotel or organisation expects a solution of the problem through this study. The organisations expects solutions through this study for improving productivity or they hope the research findings will enable them to make some improvement at work. They expect to draw more benefit from such studies.

A student investigates into the problem and suggests a viable and economical solution to the issues of concern. The research may enhance the reputation of the researcher in the eyes of the senior management and this work may help him or her to get an entry into that organisation. On the other hand a poor quality report could create an opposite effect.

A project work should be taken up as a challenge. One can master the art of writing a project report. A researcher would feel confident of tackling any problem situation at work, thereby improving his or her ability and reputation as a problem solving manager.

The institute/school/university which runs the hospitality courses also benefits as its helps in up-dating and expansion of the knowledge of the faculty members about the current working situation and issues.

The Purpose of Project Work

1) To provide opportunity to research scholars to apply the theoretical concepts to practical actual problem situations.

2) To enhance the skills of the researcher for gaining handsome knowledge about real life situations.

3) To transform the students from research to problem solving managers.

4) To equip researcher with the tools and techniques of gathering, selecting, sorting and analysing the information for relevant use in practice.

5) Make students logical thinkers and apply the conceptual knowledge in a meaningful way.

A project work is intended to be original research provided it is based on data that are original to the author and not secondary. Questionnaire is intended to be completed by along number of experts in the field being studied. It is a reaction survey. Statistics drawn from the survey form the foundation for conclusions.

Types of Research

1) Applied and Fundamental Research

Research can be either applied research or it may be fundamental research. An applied research aims at finding a solution for an immediate problem facing a society whereas research of latter type is primarily concerned with generalisations and with the formulation of a theory. Fundamental research at times is also known as basic research.

2) Conclusion and Decision Oriented

Research can also be classified as conclusion oriented and decision oriented. While doing conclusion oriented research, you as a researcher is free to pick up a problem, redesign the enquiry as you proceeds along and is prepared to conceptualize as you wishes. Decision oriented research is always for the need of a decision maker and the researcher in this case is not free to embark upon research according to his own inclination. Operations research is an example of decision oriented research.

3) Motivation Research

Research (or a search for knowledge) can be relating to quantitative phenomena or it can be relating to qualitative phenomena. Concerning quantitative phenomena, research can be done through the use of statistical methods. Now, let us discuss some of the points concerning motivation research which is more associated with qualitative phenomena.

Various behavioral sciences such as psychology, sociology, cultural anthropology etc. are concerned with investigating the reasons for human behaviour. Specialists in these disciplines may undertake what are commonly known as Depth Interviews, which are designed to discover underlying motives and desires. In fact, depth interviews (or qualitative interviews or unstructured informal interviews) are designed to explore needs, desires and feelings of the respondents. Such interviews require great skill on the part of the interviewer and at the same time take considerable time. Besides, in such studies there are difficulties in establishing the right degree of confidence and also in interpreting the qualitative information obtained. Thus, motivation research is difficult and relatively more expensive, as such group interviews rather than individual interviews are more common while conducting motivation research in practice.

Techniques of Motivation Research

Amongst the various techniques employed in motivation research some important one are as follows:

1) ***World association test.*** These tests are used by psychologists to extract information regarding such words which have maximum association. In this sort of test an informant is asked to answer quickly the first word that occurs to him after hearing a stimulus word. The same idea is exploited in marketing research to find out the quality that is mostly associated to a brand names possessing one or more of these.

2) ***Sentence completion tests.*** These tests happen to be an extension of the technique of word association tests. Under this, informants may be asked to complete a sentence (such as: persons who wear **khadi** are . . .), to find association of **khadi** clothes with certain personality characteristics

3) ***Story completion tests.*** Such tests are a step further wherein the researcher may contrive stories instead of sentences and ask the informants to complete them.
4) ***Verbal projection tests***. There are the tests wherein the respondent is asked to comment on or to explain what other people do. For example, why do people smoke? Answer may reveal the respondent's own motivations.
5) ***Pictorial techniques.*** There are several pictorial techniques. One of the most common pictorial technique is that in which people are asked to describe what they perceive in two symmetrical ink blots. Another pictorial technique tasks the form of a series of cartoons with words inserted in 'balloons' above. The respondent is asked to put his own words in an empty balloon space. In other words, respondents may be shown certain picture and asked to make meaning out of it. The technique is also known as Thermally Apperception Test.
6) ***Quizzes, tests and examinations.*** There are also a techniques of extracting information regarding specific ability of candidates indirectly. In this procedure, long as well as short questions are framed to test through them the memorising and analytical ability of candidates.

Limitation of Motivation Research

'Depth interview' method has been criticised on several grounds which reflects the limitations of motivation research. The following limitations are noteworthy:

1) The findings are not quantified;
2) Small samples are usually used and thus, they fail to provide meaningful conclusions';
3) Individual reactions in group situations are very much conditioned by the structure and behaviour to the group;
4) It is really very difficult to know whether the investigation into the reasons for behaviour do really indicate a certain motive.

Inspite of the above states limitations, motivation research has been successfully applied to problems such as product design, package design, advertising, service facilities and pricing. Hence, motivation research is important in business and industrial problem where human behaviour matters a lot. Valuable motivation research can be carried out provide structured questions are used and that necessary training and directions are given by experienced psychologists.

References

1) Gupta, A.K., (ed.) *Methodology of Economic Research.*
2) Ferber, Robert and Verdoorn, *Research Methods in Economics and Commerce.*
3) Sharma, H.D. and Mukherji, S.P., *Research in Economics and Commerce, Methodology and Sources*.
4) Gopal, M.H., *Introduction to Research Procedure in Social Sciences.*
5) Labovitz, S. and Hagedorn, R., *Introduction to Social Research.*

2

Selecting a Research Problem

There are some issues of great relevance while making the choice of the subject of project for study:

1) It should, preferably, be related to solving a hospitality and tourism problem.
2) It must have hospitality and tourism content.
3) It must be from the researcher's area of interest.

A subject of problem may be technical in nature but it must have human implications- to make it a hospitality problem e.g.

1) A comprehensive case study : covers single organisation multi-functional area, problem formulation analysis and recommendations.
2) An Inter-organisational study:
   a) Inter-hotel comparison.
   b) Survey of hotel management practices and issues.
3) A field research study.

Basic Steps in Research Design Process

Below are given seven basic steps you should follow in planning and designing a research project:

Step-I	Define the research project	: Specify the information required to help solve the management problem.
Step-II	Specify the approximate value	: Determine the maximum that can be spent for information on the project, using either budget rates or the expected value approach.
Step-III	Select the data collection method	: Determine whether secondary data or a survey will produce the required data and choose the form of the selected method to use.

Step-IV	Select the measurement technique	:	Determine whether and how to use questionnaire attitude scales, observation and/or projection and/or projective techniques.
Step-V	Select the sample	:	Determine who and how many respondents or objects to measure.
Step-VI	Select the analytical approach	:	Determine the appropriate means that the data provide the required information.
Step-VII	Specify the time and financial cost	:	For each research approach develop time and financial cost estimates.
Step-VIII	Prepare the research proposal	:	Summarise the results of the preceding seven steps in the form of a research proposal.

There could be many problems which are managerial in nature having no technical contents at all. Such problems would be dealt with differently as compared to a problem having technical and managerial content. The example presented in Fig. 2.1 below highlight the above points.

The project study may be from any one of the types given in Fig. 2.1 and 2.2 (for guidelines only).

A Title of a Project Report

Suppose the Food and Beverage Division of ABC Hotel has provisions to prepare a number of different cuisines. The problem is to standardise the cuisines and recipes. *This is a technical problem and has to be dealt with purely on that basis.*

However, if in standardising there are going to be a new training needs for the operators or it affects the technical staff of the kitchen, these constitute a difficult problem, which needs to be solved at the same time. Include this aspect, and the project becomes acceptable. In addition, issues like costing, financial techniques/savings and inventory may be incorporated.

Therefore project study can be stated as:

Standardisation of Indian cuisines and recipes and determining the training needs for kitchen operations.

Fig: 2.1 A Typical Sample of a Title of a Project Report

Selecting the Subject

The first step of the project work is to select an appropriate topic for the project study. The topic selected shall have justified treatment if it belongs to the researcher's area of interest. A researcher can also possess more than one area of interest. There could be more than one topic in each areas of interest. A researcher should adopt the following procedure to arrive at a proper selection of the subject:-

1) Discuss critically with colleagues about merits and demerits, relevance and irrelevance *etc.*, of the subject

   Or

2) Discuss with seniors and try to eliminate less important topics to narrow down the choice.
3) Take the help of your research guide.

The second step of the project work is to ensure that:

1) The hotel or organisation, which you select, will support you in proceeding on the work
2) The necessary access is available to information required.
3) The executives are ready to exchange to information required.
4) The information or data required can be interfaced with statistical formula.

Ideally, the guide should select the topic himself, as this topic will be the one, which he or she fully knows and is keen to tackle. In such situation he or she will be handling the subject with enthusiasm and shall be in a position to motivate the researcher.

A Title of a Research Project

Provision of hygiene safety and standards in food project in a food and beverage unit could be dealt purely as a technical exercise. But when *a project is to be dealt with management implication, for example, the effect of providing food safety standard on the management and beverage staff on the operators and rate of work and the implications of any safety regulations.*

The project study can be stated as:

"Effect of providing hygiene and safety regulation on operators on rate of productivity taken with in food and beverages units."

Fig: 2.2 A Typical Sample of a Title of a Research Project

The involvement and approval of the guide from the conception stage is important. His or her cooperation will be required in helping to check on the progress of the report his/her advice from time to time, when necessary, particularly on specialised areas, is very important.

Sometimes due to uncooperative or apathetic attitude of the senior manager/guide, the researcher's task becomes difficult. But you must learn to manage and do every bit to foster the involvement of the guide/manager. Sometimes you may feel embarrassed due to the attitude of the guide (he or she may be genuinely interested in your work) and think of changing the guide in the mid-course of project. This is unhealthy practice. Avoid such situations.

1) Always involve the guide in your work
2) Respect the guide
3) Earn the trust of the guide
4) Learn to be empathetic.

Project Research Study Topics

Here are some selected and typical topics for the project reports on hospitality and tourism Industry. About 269 project studies have been listed in the areas of marketing, finance, human resource development and information technology. The projects suggested relate to primary research or diagnostic case studies. Researcher can select a topic with slight modification by taking the help of this reference material.

Sample Topics of Project Report for Hospitality and Tourism Industry

1) Planning, feasibility & *marketing* of fast food operations
2) Planning, organising and *marketing* of food festivals
3) Product positioning in deluxe hotels
4) Pre-independence status and post-independence growth of the hospitality industry in India
5) A comparison between hotel housekeeping & hostel housekeeping
6) Comparative study of air catering *kitchens and kitchen in five* star hostels in private sector
7) Availability of *human resources* at present and its proposed demand by Indian hotel industry by the year 2010 ad
8) Study and comparison of housekeeping in hotels and hospitals
9) Labour legislations applicable to hotels and a critical study analysis of *trade unions.*
10) *Role of front office in enhancing room revenues of hotels*
11) *Comparative study of hospital kitchen* and a kitchen in a hotel kitchen
12) Marketing of five star hotels through image *building*
13) *Off-premises* catering' - a detailed study
14) Planning and opening of a *restaurant*
15) *Strategic positioning of a hotel through marketing*
16) *Analysis of sales* of alcoholic beverages in five star hotels
17) A study and comparison of *sales* of different five star hotels
18) *Feasibility* of a five star deluxe hotel in Delhi metro
19) A study of Indian desserts and comparison between classical Indian *dessert* and Indian desserts
20) Critical analysis of *quality control* procedures in food production in hospitality industry.
21) 'The butter flies' restaurant and analysis
22) Feasibility study and *market survey* and opening of 3-star hotels in new Delhi
23) Inter-hotel comparison and its relevance in context of Indian hospitality industry
24) Systems analysis for *accommodation* management
25) Hoteliering in post-liberation era
26) Menu engineering, its importance & analysis

27) Decor of a theme restaurant
28) A critical study and analyses of Rajasthan cuisine
29) Role of travel agencies in increasing hotel *revenue* by providing impetus to tourism
30) Kitchen planning and management

31) Guest/*customer* satisfaction in hospitality.
32) Service auditing in hotels of five star standard in relation to *guest satisfaction* and productivity
33) Comparative study of managing sales of five-star hotels and various other units.
34) Safety and *security system* in a five-star hotel
35) Evaluation of manual v/s *computerization* of front office operation
36) Time management in relation to *front office*
37) Energy conservation in hotels
38) Mushrooms and its uses in preparation of cuisine
39) Feasibility of opening a fast food *restaurant*
40) *Interpretation and analysis of guest needs*

41) *A scientific approach to effective storage system in hotels*
42) *Comparative consumption of Indian and foreign brand of alcoholic beverages* and F & B control systems in various five-star hotels
43) A study of *information* needs to top management in five-star hotels
44) Sugar craft and its future in confectionery business
45) Food *festivals* in context with sales & marketing
46) Comparison of domestic *airlines*: the food and service provided by them
47) Computer based material management & human resource management of a hotel
48) Analysis & measurement of *guest satisfaction* in hotels
49) Amelioration of *curriculum* for hotel management schools.
50) Banquets sales – "research approach"

51) A study of Chinese *cuisine*
52) *Sales administration in a deluxe hotel*
53) *A comparative study of pricing strategy* followed by leading hotel chains of India
54) Guidelines for a *pre-project activities* of a new five star hotel in India
55) All about *coffee shops* planning and operation
56) Discotheques and its contribution in enhancing marketing and hotel sales
57) Study of consumer *behaviour* in the hospitality industry
58) Influence of western *cuisine on* Indian sweets
59) Critical study of motels & study of *feasibility* of ideal hotels

60) Impact of tourism on the economic development of the state of Rajasthan

61) Opening a three-star hotel - *legal requirements*, equipments, systems, finances, human resources etc.

62) Dishes hitherto not popular yet exotic from north-eastern region of India

63) Marketing strategies for budget hotels in India

64) Labour problem of five-star hotel of Delhi – an analytical study

65) Requirement and procurement of various *licences* needed for a new hotel project

66) Procurement, and sources of supply of *equipment & furnishing* for housekeeping department of a five-star hotel in Delhi

67) Equipment (heavy duty & light) needed for the kitchen of a five star hotel - their specifications and sources of supply in Delhi

68) Scope of *budget hotels* in different states of India

69) Food & beverage control analysis of fast food operation; a comparative study of Nirulas, Wimpys and Macdonalds

70) Study of *airlines base* kitchens in Delhi with reference to their layout and planning

71) Facility planning for a *Japanese restaurant* serving 200 covers. (Layout, design, equipment, menu and pricing)

72) Time management in food and beverage production and service

73) A comprehensive study of Sikkimese *cuisine* with traditional recipes and service of food

74) Advertising service in hospitality industry

75) Khajuraho existing tourism *infrastructure* and scope of further development

76) Discotheques in Delhi and their future scope

77) Elements of guest *satisfaction* in accordance with effective marketing

78) *Adventure tourism* and its impact on Indian economy

79) Designing a front *office management* computerized system

80) Survey of night clubs and other entertainment clubs in Delhi

81) Consequences of *environment* degradation - trends in the tourism industry

82) A comparative analysis of bar control in a five-star hotel

83) Marketing of beverages for *sales* enhancement

84) Control in food service and its implementation in hotel schools

85) Cost control *system* followed in various five star hotels

86) *Tourism* & hotel industry in India

87) *Banquet* sales & marketing

88) Problems & prospects of *tourism* in India

89) Hotel *image* & profile - the key to success

90) Dynamics of *tourism* in the state of Haryana

91) Marketing of *food festival* in five-star hotels
92) Potential of *budget hotels* in India
93) Comparative analysis of *advertising strategies* in five-star hotels
94) Selection *training* & development of professionals in hospitality industry
95) Enterprizing into five-star hotel
96) Comparative study of *laundry operations* & layout
97) State banquets
98) A step towards standardization of Indian recipes
99) Establishment of bread making unit with special reference to nutrition & hospital catering
100) An era from paper to micro chip - a revolution in printing technology

101) Computers & its application in the present hotel scenario
102) Role of *spices* in Indian cookery
103) Madhya Pradesh India's heart beckon
104) Concept of nutrition & health; its application in the hospitality industry
105) Research project on sherry its preparation and scope for marketing
106) A study of the management trainee programs conducted by the major chains
107) Domestic *tourism* in India : a detailed study for promotion of hospitality and tourism
108) The role of public *relations* in *marketing systems* of a hotel
109) Pre-planning & *feasibility study* for opening a hotel in new Delhi
110) Planning and designing a *restaurant*

111) Target 2020 - marketing hotels into the thirties
112) Redesigning of the lobby of a hotel
113) Re-designing and reorganising stores and store system for a hotel school
114) Sikkimese *cuisine - a detaileed study and analyses*
115) Procurement & sources of housekeeping
116) Indian cuisine and lesser known dishes
117) Bar control in hotels
118) Herbs & spices and their use and importance in preparation of food
119) Human research development & training program for hospitality employees
120) Beer manufacturing and marketing in India

121) *Chinese* restaurant - planning, designing and operation
122) A selective study of Indian *sweets* & breads

123) India as a tourist potential in global market
124) *Kitchen equipment* procurement for a deluxe hotel having 150 guest room capacity
125) Industrial catering
126) *Time management in hotel business*
127) *Establishing Japanese restaurant*
128) *Railway* catering
129) *Safety* & security in hotels
130) *Energy* conservation in hotels

131) *Menu* merchandising
132) Brand awareness and guest behaviour of branded alcoholic beverages (select any brand of alcoholic beverages)
133) Indian *hospitality industry* 2020
134) Launch of a *budget hotel* in a competitive environment: a post launch case study
135) Analysis of *marketing* strategies of three fast food chains in India
136) Quantitative approach in hotel marketing
137) Launching of networking in *tourism and travel*
138) *Study of export of processed foods from India and its potential-till 2020*
139) *Brand positioning* of deluxe hotels in a metropolitan city
140) Segmenting *handicraft* markets and export strategies of handicrafts

141) New product launch in food and *beverage* market: Issues and lessons
142) *Brand preferences* of consumers regarding star luxuries and measuring their impact
143) Future of multinational hotel *chains* in India - a report
144) Flexible tour *packaging* - its scope and areas of use
145) Brand perception of luxury accommodation and strategies to improve image
146) Market study on product's brand *influx* influence in hospitality industry
147) International hotel chains in India and their *marketing* strategies
148) *Marketing* strategies for food-beverages. (Select any other familiar product)
149) *Communication* strategies in hospitality industry: a case study
150) *Marketing* strategies for a new hotel product launch: a case study

151) *Buying process* of prospective tourists and its influence on small hotels
152) A comparative *market analysis* of budget hotels and guest preferences
153) Consumer perception in the premium branded hospitality and buying decision factors
154) Measuring buyers *brand attitude* towards brand comprehension and brand awareness, of luxury hotel services in different demographic segments

155) *Brand attitude* towards various category of hotels and their impact on market potential
156) Marketing of security equipment and hotel perception about their system
157) *Consumer perception* of five star luxury hotels and its influence on decision making
158) Foreign *tourists* and their purchase behaviour
159) Guest attitude towards *alcoholic beverage* and their impact on sales
160) Identification of attributes required in the sales *force of* tourism industry to make effective sales

161) Comparative study of market *strategies* of service industries
162) Relationship marketing and its relevance in credit card
163) Credit cards market *in India*
164) *Using public relations to promote hospitality: a case study*
165) *Understanding service delivery gap in the domestic airline industry*
166) *Tourism planning* and development issues and their impact on Indo-Asian/European tours
167) *Pricing services* - issues and practices
168) *Credit cards* scenario in India : present and future
169) People's role in operational efficiency of national *airlines* and international airlines
170) *Computerisation* of operation in hotels and its impact on productivity

171) *Event management* and its future in India
172) A classification and study of *creative appeals* followed for different food & beverages product categories
173) *Advertising hotel* services on internet: issues and future potentials
174) Measuring effectiveness of *advertisements* campaign of hotel chains
175) Tourism *market*: segments and potential 2020
176) A comprehensive study of the foreign exchange and its and marketing segmentation
177) *Vendor selection* - a case analysis
178) *Marketing food* and beverages products
179) *Value chain* analysis of a international chain hotel giant
180) *Quality systems* in middle class hotels sector and areas of improvement

181) *Planning and control* of major international hotel chains using computerised systems
182) Safety management in a hospitality : a case study
183) Competitive advantage through *technological innovation* in hospitality industry: a case study
184) Using project management to implement *modernisation of hotel* property
185) Evaluating performance of public *sector hotels* : a case study
186) A comprehensive study of *materials handling* equipments with reference to logistics management in a hotel

187) A study of *logistics* of a courier *company*

188) Impact of liberalization on hospitality industry (a case study)

189) Foreign exchange market in *tourism and travels*

190) Budgeting system and marketing strategies of a hotel chain

191) Comparative analysis of selected tourist *market* and opportunity for a new entrant

192) Venture *capital* and its scope in travel and tourism industry India

193) Financial incentives and its impact on *labour productivity* : a study of a hotel

194) Project evaluation and *appraisal system* in a hotel : a case study

195) Financial *accounting system* and financial performance of a hotel (select an organisation)

196) *Networking* in a hotel : acceptance and advantages

197) *Computerised* inventory management and its application in a hotel

198) *Portfolio* management in hotel industry

199) Revitalising small hotel with focus on cost reduction

200) Risk *reduction* in international tourism trade

201) Working *capital* management in hotel industry : a comparative case study

202) *A beach resort* : appraisals and recommendations

203) *Management* of change in a traditional hotel

204) *Computerisation* in hotel industry and its effect on employees morale : a case study

205) *Compensation* survey of hotel industry

206) *Absenteeism* and its impact on production and productivity in the hospitality industry

207) *Human resources development* and its impact on organisational effectiveness in a hotel

208) Organisation structure and *control mechanism* in the hotel industry

209) Using *computers* in shut-down management and its acceptance by employees - a case study

210) Study of *job satisfaction* of employees of a hotel

211) *Computerisation* of operation in hotels and its impact on productivity

212) *Job conditions* and welfare schemes : a case study of a hotel

213) *Recruitment* and selection policy of a hotel : a case study

214) Use of information technology in personnel management of a hotel

215) *TQM :* a tool for productivity enhancement

216) *Quality circles* and its effectiveness in hotels : a case study

217) *Designing a human resources planning* model for the hospital industry

218) *Manpower planning* in the hotel industry : Issues and benefits

219) Role of *computers* in human resource management in a hotel

220) Organisational climate and *leadership* in hotel : a comparative study

221) *Job dissatisfaction* and stress syndrome in hotel : a case study

222) Identification of training needs and development of a *training manual*

223) *Human resources development* strategies and industrial relations : a case study

224) *Human resources development* as a tool for enhancing organisational effectiveness : a case study

225) Planning and identifying *human resources development* intervention for solving organisational problems: a case study

226) Organisation restructuring : *strategies and actions* : a case study

227) Strategic organisational restructuring for turn-around : a case study

228) Role of human resources development in total quality management

229) Managerial performance *appraisal* system in entertainment industry

230) Management training needs for the hotel industry

231) *Absenteeism* prevention in a hotel

232) Indian managers and their skill *development* in liberalised hotel environment

233) *Grievance* procedure in a hotel organisation : a case study

234) *Stress* management and its impact on productivity : a case study

235) *Performance appraisal* systems and areas for augmentation : a case study

236) *Motivating* marketing sales executives in a hotel : a case study

237) *Personnel policies* in hospitality and tourism service : issues and practices

238) *Reward system* and its impact on productivity improvement : a case study

239) Competitive hotel business through information technology

240) Information technology applications in hospitality and tourism : a comparative study

241) How did information technology help? - a case study of a hotel

242) Information technology and automation : impact of its adoption in a hotel organisation

243) Material management information system and its contribution to productivity : a case study

244) Computerised maintenance management system and its impact on downtime management

245) Information technology and work force interface

246) ERP and its role in sales, cost and services management : a case study

247) Information technology as a competitive edge : a case study

248) Managing change through information technology in hospitality

249) Internet growth in India and its future in hospitality

250) Interfacing hotel business functions : an application

251) Computerised food production and some control : a case study

252) Computerisation and its influence on organisation re-structuring

253) Critical success factors for computerization and its applications : a case study

254) Information technology and its role in new service product development

255) Automation and use of robots in Indian hotel company : a case study

256) Information technology application in an a hotel : a case study

257) Technical skills : Major problems faced in using it

258) Using information technology products and services

289) Performance of a hotel after information technology implementation : a case study

260) Common problems leaders of information technology face in system applications : a case study

261) Intranets and their role in managing multi location hotel

262) Use of computers in controlling time and cost in service industry

263) Teleconferencing : trends and Indian scenario 2020

264) Quantitative status of application of information technology in hotels

265) Hotel corporate policy frame work and role of information technology strategies

266) Analysis of the marketing strategies of hospitality and tourism manufacturers

267) Value through distribution and brand equity : a case study

268) Computerised management control system in hotel industry : a perspective

269) An industry analysis of information technology

3

Synopsis Preparation and Submission

Once the work of selection of the topic for study is completed, the next and first essential requirement is the submission of the synopsis to the concerned authority for approval. The detailed study can not be undertaken unless the synopsis is approved and permission is granted for 'Go ahead'. For preparing the synopsis the typical flow chart is given in Figure 3.1.

Synopsis Proposal

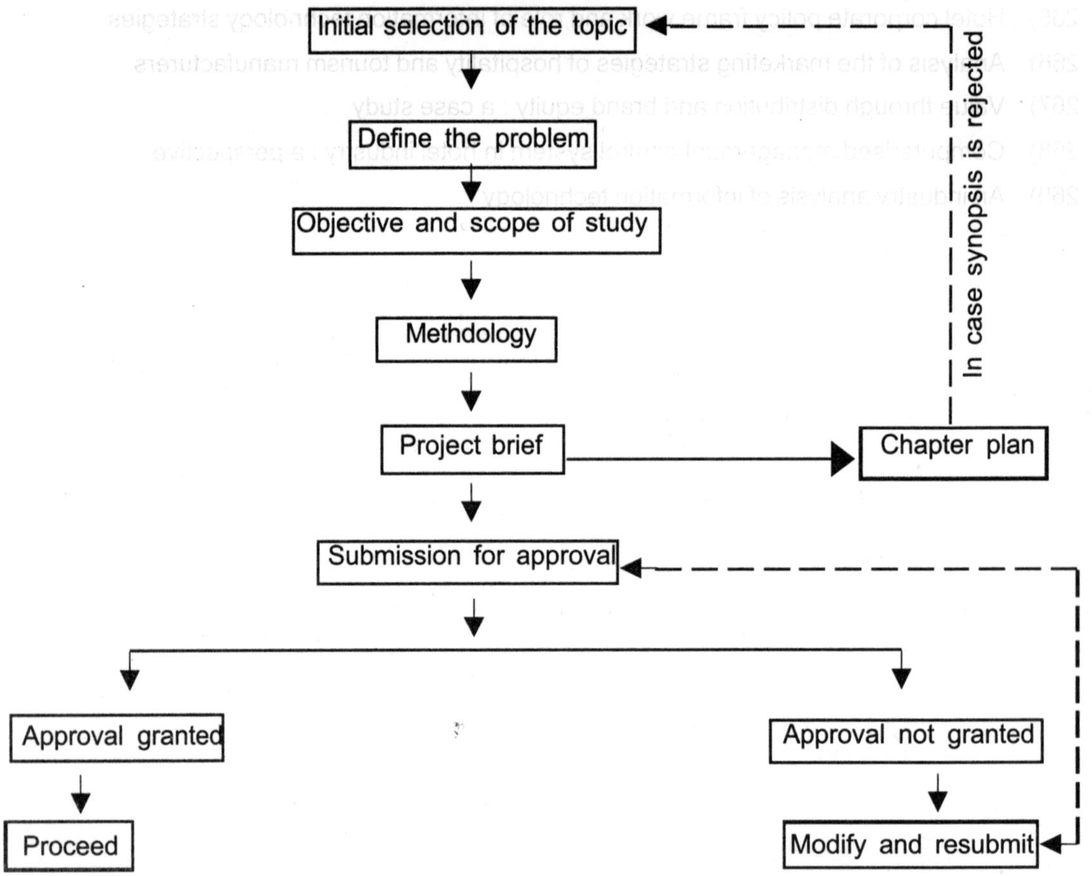

Fig. 3.1: Typical Flowchart for Synopsis Proposal

Synopsis Proposal

Name and Address of the Institute Department/University ....

Synopsis Proposal : ....

Project Title : ....

Name (in block letters) : ....

Registration No. : ....

Permanent Address : ....

Address of Communications : ....

: ....

Telephone : ....

Mobile : ....

e.mail : ....

Name of the project guide : ....

Designation and address : ....

....

....

Signature of the Student   Signature of the Guide

For office use only

Project proposal No ....

Status: Accepted/Rejected

....

Signature of Evaluator

Fig. 3.2 : Specimen for Approval of Project Synopsis Proposal

TABLE OF CONTENTS

Executive Summary

I) Introduction

II) Literature Reviews

III) Research Study

- (A) Research objectives
- (B) Research methodology
- (C) Research methodology adopted

(IV) Indian Hospitality & Tourism Industry

- (A) Overview of Indian hospitality industry
- (B) History of Indian hospitality industry
- (C) Recent achievements & milestones
- (D) Statistical profile (2000-2010)
- (E) Present scenario of Indian hospitality industry
- (F) Landmarks in Indian hospitality industry
- (G) Indian hospitality industry development
- (H) Overview of ITC and Maurya Sheraton
- (I) Briefing of the other hotel companies
- (J) Top 25 hotels in the world.

V) Data analysis and interpretations

VI) Conclusions

VII) Recommendations

VIII) Limitations

IX) Appendix

- (A) Questionnaires used in research study
- (B) Indian hospitality industry: accommodation (rooms food and beverages and other illustrations

X) Bibliography

Fig. 3.3 Specimen Layout: Chapter Plan

TABLE OF CONTENTS

Fig. 3.4 Specimen Layout: Chapter Plan

Indian School of Hospitality

New Delhi

Proforma for Approval of a Project Proposal

Registration No....................

Year of registration............

Name of address of the student : ....

Project title : ....

Subject area : ....

Name and address of the : ....

Project guide : ....

Is the guide from academic/industry : ....

Signature of student :

Date: ....

(Please do not forget to enclose the synopsis of the project and the bio-data duly signed by the guide.)

For Office Use Only

Synopsis	Guide
Approved	Approved
Not Approved	Not Approved

....

Signature of Director/Coordinator (Project)

Date : ....

Comments/Suggestions for reformulating the project ....

Fig. 3.5 Proforma for Approval of Project Proposal

General Guidelines for Synoposis

The synopsis for the preparation of the report has to be prepared as per guidelines given in the flow chart (Ref. Fig. 3.1) and submitted along with a proforma (See Figs. 3.1 and 3.2) duly signed by the guide for approval. It is desirable to enclose the biodata of the guide along with the synopsis. Some institutes have set guidelines for selecting the project guide. A typical requirement is as given in Table 3.1:

TABLE 3.1: Typical : Requirements laid down for selection of research guide

1) Senior Faculty
2) Academic counsellors of hotel and tourism management programmes having relevant experience.
3) Professionals holding PhD/Master's degree in hotel and tourism management or allied disciplines and having a minimum of five years in the relevant area. In exceptional cases, a supervisor with bachelor degree.

Re-submission and Modification of Synopsis

Sometimes synopsis may not be approved. The researcher is informed accordingly. These could be two reasons for re-submission/modifications of the topic:

1) The guide is not approved by the institute or the student want to change the guide.
2) The topic selected is not approved by the school/institute.
3) He or she is required to modify or submit a fresh proposal.

In case, the guide is not approved by the school, student should change the guide before the synopsis is considered for approval. It is quite likely that the new guide may not approve your topic or may need modification or may suggest altogether a new topic.

In such cases the student will have to submit the fresh synopsis, and the synopsis proforma shall be signed by the new guide.

When a student wants to change the guide for any reason, a fresh proposal need to be submitted.

When the institute suggests certain modification in the synopsis proposal, the student shall resubmit the modified synopsis for approval.

The new synopsis should be submitted along with the rejected proposal, and synopsis proforma bearing comments of evaluator along with proposal number.

Consider the following points for submission of synopsis of project proposal:-

1) to ensure the synopsis submitted is complete. Incomplete synopsis is likely to be rejected.
2) to follow the typical flow chart for preparing synopsis.
3) to ensure the synopsis proforma is filled and signed by the student as well as guide.

4) to the project proposal number allotted should be initial stage itself.
5) to select guide as per norms of the institute at the initial stage itself.
6) to ensure that guide is able to provide you sometime to solve your problems.
7) to ensure following documents are submitted:
   (a) Proforma for synopsis
   (b) Bio-data of supervisor
   (c) Project brief as per chapter plans
   (d) Questionnaire, in case primary data collection is required.
8. If approval is not granted or modification suggested ensure re-submission with following documents:—
   (a) New proposal/modified proposal
   (b) New proforma for synopsis duly signed
   (c) Copy of the rejected proposal
   (d) Project proposal number allotted to the project
   (e) Bio-data of guide (In case the earlier guide has not been accepted)

Specimen of a Project Synopsis

This part includes typical sample synopsis for projects relating to various hospitality and tourism management streams. These can be used as guidelines to prepare the project synopsis for approval.

You should ensure that synopsis is submitted as per guidelines of the university/institute. Use the checklist given in Chapter 2.

Proforma for Approval of Project Proposal

Enrolment No.....................................

Study Centre....................................

Regional Centre.....................................

Name and Address of Student : ....

....

....

Specimen Project Synopsis

Title of the Project : Consumer Behaviour and Brand Preference for deluxe Category Hotels

Subject area : Hospitality - Tourism Marketing

Name and address of the supervisor : ....

Is the supervisor an academic : Yes ☐ No ☐

Counsellor of management programme of your university : ....

If 'Yes' name and code of study centre and the courses he/she is counselling for and since when : ....

Number of Student currently working under the supervisor for MS-100 : ....

(Please refer to point No. 4 in the guidelines)

Signature of student... Signature of supervisor...

Date :

Please do not forget to enclose the synopsis of the project and the Bio-data duly signed by the guide

For Office Use Only

Synopsis	Guide
Approved	Approved
Not Approved	Not Approved

Signature of...

Director/Coordinator (Projects)

Date: ....

Comments/suggestions for reforming the Project...

....

....

Fig. 3.6: Proforma for Approval of Project Proposal

Synopsis Preparation

Objectives :	1) The objective of the project is to know the guest perception and brand preference. 2) The study will analyse the influencing tourism product which determines the brand preference.
Methodology :	The market research exercise will be a systematic enquiry of the various attributes and will be planned in an orderly investigation process. The general process used in this study will involve: 1) Defining the problem 2) Statement of research objectives 3) Planning the research design 4) Planning the sample 5) Collection of data 6) Analysing the data 7) Formulation of conclusion 8) Preparation of the report.
Planning Research Design :	The objectives of the problem will be the main focus of the research design and to ensure that data collected is relevant to the objectives. The right source of data collection, sampling and data timing will be pivotal to the research. The design shall be descriptive in nature.
Sampling :	a) Sampling involves procedures that use a small number of parts of population to make conclusion regarding the whole population. b) Sampling method: c) Non-probability sampling (Convenient sampling) d) Sample size : 100 e) Sample unit : costomers who own work in hotels
Sample Design :	Convenient sampling is based on the convenience of researcher who selects the sample. Respondents in the sample are included in it merely on account of their availability and owning hopitality business. This method has been selected as whole process would be dependent on availability of the respondents.

Sources of Data :	The data shall be collected through the structured non-disguised questionnaire which will focus on: a) Knowing respondent's perceptions b) Decision making attributes c) Respondents profile.
Limitations :	a) The sampling procedure used being the convenient sampling, the analysis and findings would lack accuracy. b) The sample size is not very large owing to time constraint. This may cause inaccuracy. c) There is a chance of respondent being biased in terms of product characteristics.
Report:	After the data collection and analysis the report shall be presented in the following general chapter plan: Part I : Prefatory inclusions Part II : Main Report Chapter 1 : Executive Summary Chapter 2 : Introduction Chapter 3 : Research Methodology Chapter 4 : Data Collections Chapter 5 : Data Analysis and Interpretation Chapter 6 : Conclusions Chapter 7 : Recommendations Chapter 8 : Limitations Chapter 9 : Bibliography Bibliography

References:

1) Marketing and Sales Techniques in Tourism and Travel Industry : Dr. Jagmohan Negi
2) Marketing Management : Philip Kolter
3) Market Research : Boyd and Westfall
4) Magazines
5) Special newspaper features

Fig. 3.7 Specimen Synopsis

CURRICULUM VITAE

Personal Data:

Name : ....

....

Date of Birth : Day/Month/Year

☐ ☐ ☐

Education:

	Marks	Year	University
B.Com.(H)	....	....	....
CA	....	....	....
MBA (Global Leadership Corporate Program) (Full-Time)	....	....	....
Ph.D.	....	....	....

Permanent Address ....

....

E. mail ....

Phone ....**Mobile** ....

Employment Details

Head of Department/Director

Professor (International Hospitality and Tourism Development)

Area of Specialisation

- Financial management
- Human resource management
- International business
- Aquisition and amalgamation

- Investment analysis
- Foreign direct investment

Co-ordinator for Following Activities

- Training programs
- Seminars
- Summer placement
- Final placement
- Study tours
- Hospitality and tourism
- AICTE follow up
- P.G.D.B.M. admissions

Visiting Faculty

1) Indian School of Hospitality, Indian University
2) Delhi University,
3) Y.M.C.A.,
4) I.G.N.O.U.,
5) I.M.T., and
6) Delhi College of Engineering.

Major Achievements

1) Visited Cornell University (USA) and presented country paper on International Financing in Indian Hospitality Industry in an International Seminar organised by GE.
2) Certificate of Accredited Management Teacher in area of Marketing Management by IMA & CCI & FICCI
3) Hon. Secretary of Himalayan Tourism and Recreation in Mountains, New Delhi.
4) Associate Member of International Culinany Foundation (FCI), New Delhi.
5) Fellow member of Himalayan Tourism and Recreation in Mountains (HTRM), New Delhi.

Fig. 3.8: Specimen Curriculum Vitae

QUESTIONNAIRE

Questionnaire : Consumer Behaviour and Brand Preferences

Dear Respondent,

I am a student of Indian School of Hospitality. As a part of my project, I am conducting a survey and would be grateful if you could spare some of your precious time to fill this questionnaire for the same.

Respondents name:..

Age .... Sex .... Male/female ....

Martial status .... Married/unmarreid..............................

Address..

---

1) Monthly income Rs. 60000-80000 ☐ Rs. 80001-100000 ☐

Rs.100001-150000 ☐ Rs.150001-200000 ☐

Rs.200000+ ☐

2) Is this your first laptop? Yes ☐ No ☐

If no, which brand you had earlier?

3) Since when you are using this brand?

4) Where did your get confirmation about this brand?

Family ☐, Friend ☐, Mechanic ☐, Showroom ☐,

Newspaper ☐, TV ☐, Hoarding ☐, Others ☐.

5. When you think of a laptop what all brands come to your mind, please specify (in order of recall): ☐ ☐ ☐ ☐ ☐

6. Which brand of laptop do you have?

7. What motivated you to buy this particular brand of Laptop (Please indicate your choice on the following scale).

	Highest Motivator					Lowest Motivator	
(a) More popular	1	2	3	4	5	6	7
(b) Power efficiency	1	2	3	4	5	6	7
(c) Speed	1	2	3	4	5	6	7
(d) Power	1	2	3	4	5	6	7
(e) Price	1	2	3	4	5	6	7
(f) Less maintenance	1	2	3	4	5	6	7
(g) Service network	1	2	3	4	5	6	7
(h) Model offered	1	2	3	4	5	6	7
(i) Fits with your personality	1	2	3	4	5	6	7
(j) Advertising	1	2	3	4	5	6	7
(k) Dealer push	1	2	3	4	5	6	7

4) Are you satisfied with the brand you own ? Yes ☐ No ☐

5) Would you buy the same brand when you buy next time ? Yes ☐ No ☐

6) If answer to Q 5 is 'No' of which of the following brands you will buy:

   i) .... ii) ....

   iii) .... iv) ....

7) Rank the reasons of purchase decision (rate them on 1 to 9 scale. 1 being most important and 9 least important).

   (a) Innovations (models offered) ....

   (b) Indianisation of the brand ....

   (c) Advertising ....

   (d) Style/looks ....

   (e) Service network ....

   (f) Dealer network ....

   (g) Better technology ....

(h) Power efficiency ....

(i) Less maintenance ______________________

(j) Fits with your status ______________________

8) Do you remember buy Tag line of Laptop ? Yes ☐ No ☐

9) If yes, then which one ? ....

10) Can you identify yourself with the ad of a Laptop

.... Yes ☐ No ☐

11) What kind of person comes to your mind when you see ....?

12) What kind of person comes to your mind when you see ....?

13) What kind of person comes to your mind when you see ....?

14) What kind of person comes to your mind when you see ....?

Thank you.

Fig. 3.9 Specimen Questionnaire

4

The Structure and Organisation of the Report

No one format is best for all occasions. The nature of the audience and the topic of the report combine to determine the most desirable format. However, a general format is suggested that can be altered to meet the requirements of most situations.

Table 4.1: Generalized Format for a Research Report

I. Title page
II. Table of contents
III. Executive summary
IV. Introduction
V. Methodology
VI. Findings
VII. Limitations
VIII. Conclusions and recommendations
IX. Appendixes

The project reports could be arranged in different groups. These groups may be expressed as

(A) Prefatory Group
(B) Main Report Group
(C) Appended Part Group

The contents/parts of these groups should be decided by the researcher in consultation with the project guide. The following are typical part details for each group of the report;

Group	*Part of the Group*
A) **Preparatory group**	1) Title Fly
	2) Title Page

	3) Letter of Authorization
	4) Letter of Transmittal
	5) Preface or Foreword
	6) Table of Contents
	7) Table of Illustrations
	8) Glossary of Terms/Abbreviations
	9) Executive Summary
B) **Main Body Report**	1) Introduction
	2) Objectives
	3) Methodology
	4) Findings
	5) Limitation
	6) Conclusions and Recommendations
C) **Appended Part**	1) Bibliography
	2) Appendices
	3) Index.

Title Fly

The build up of the title is a around five Ws : Who?, What?, Where?, When? & Why?. Some researcher sometimes may also add another dimensions to this *i.e.* How?. In case of some problems, it is not essential to use all the Ws. The following example given is typical case of how to build a title.

Who:?	ITC Hotel
What:?	Analysis of Food and Beverages
Where:?	India
When:?	2008
Why:?	(Implied).

The Title may read like:

"Analysis of the ITC Hotels 2010 – food and beverage sales performance in India."

The title must be carefully worded. It should ensure completeness of the coverage.

The title fly page of the report only contains the title of the report. For the typical title fly page construction refer to Figure 9.5 Now-a-days, the practice of using title fly is fading out and use of title page is gaining prominence. The title fly only contains the title of the report. This is the first page of the report and therefore must be impressive. The title is centered and placed relatively high on the page. This is usually printed in capital letters. The spacing of the lines can be selected depending upon the length of the title. As most of the researchers want their name to appear on the first page, the practice of attaching a title fly is fading out.

Abstract

1) The abstract page is Page 2.
2) Center the word Abstract on this page, then begin typing on the very next double-spaced (i.e., do not insert any extra blank lines here).
3) Type this section as a single (double spaced) paragraph in block format (i.e., do not use identification).
4) The purpose of this section is to provide a brief (100-120 words), comprehensive summary of the study. It is very important because one which many people will read.
5) It should include brief description of the problem being investigated, the methods used, the results, and their implications.
6) It is good idea to write this section last (after all of the other sections are written). You might try taking the lead sentences or two from the introduction, method, results, and discussion sections and integrates them to form the abstract.
7) Avoid citing references in the abstract.

Title Page

The title page should identify the date of the report, the researcher(s), the topic, and for whom the report is prepared. If the report is for limited distribution, this fact should also be noted on the title page. The title of the report should indicate the nature of the research project as precisely and as distinct as possible

This is the front cover of the report. In order to give a business like appearance, the report should be bound. In doing so students use an illustrated cover to make it attractive. The title page should display following information:

1) Title of the Report
2) Identification of researcher
3) Identification of authorizer/recipient of report
4) Date of writing the report.

Letter of Authorization

School/institutes may authorise the student either orally or in writing. As an usual practice the acceptance of synopsis is communicated orally or in writing and this authorises the researcher to proceed on the study. Many universities/academic institutes have made it mandatory to attach the authorisation with the final submission.

In case the authorisation is oral, the author may review it in the letter of transmittal.

Letter of Transmittal

A research report is not simply dropped on a manager's desk. Instead, it is delivered with a transmittal letter (or memo if it is an internal research department). The transmittal letter:

1) Identifies the research report,
2) Restates the authorization for the study,
3) Indicate who is receiving copies of the report, and
4) It may also focus the manager's attention on key aspects of the report.

Finally, it is the appropriate place to initiate follow-up research – "I'll call you after you've had a change to read this to discuss some follow-up suggestion".

This letter transmittal reports to the authorities. It helps in establishing the completion of task and token of submission to the concerned authorities. A letter should be carefully drafted. Warm note of appreciation and use pronounce to create a friendly environment.

Introduction

1) The introduction begins on Page 3.
2) Start this page by retyping your title (centered), then begin typing the section (on the next double spaced line) using normal (5 space indented) paragraphs. Do not type the word 'Introduction'.
3) The main purpose of this section is to tell the readers why you performed the study. In other words, you have to inform the reader of the research questions and indicate why it is important, and how it is unique when compared to previous studies.
4) It starts out broad and becomes more and more specific. For example, you might begin by defining any relevant terms. Then go on to review the relevant literature. Avoid an exhaustive and historical review. Then go on to make clear the connection between previous research and the present work.
5) You might include any hypotheses and the rationale for them.
6) The final paragraph usually contains a statement which clearly and explicitly states why the study was performed, such as:

   "The purpose of this study is to....."

   or

   "The present study is designed to investigate the ....."

   Be especially careful not to use a sentence of this type earlier in your introduction.
7) Thus, this section should contain an absolute minimum of four paragraphs:
   (a) The general introduction,
   (b) The literature review,
   (c) The connection of the present study to the literature, and
   (d) The explicit statement of purpose.

Foreword/Preface

Both Foreword and Preface perform the function of transmittal. Foreword and Preface are usually long and include helpful comments about the report. It also expresses indebtedness to those who helped in the research work.

Acknowledgements

Acknowledge all those who assisted you in the completion of this task. It may be diplomatic to mention certain individuals at work, in order to avoid causing offence, but generally speaking it is usual to make special acknowledgements only to those people who you have asserted beyond the normal call of duty. The acknowledgements can be included in any one of the following ways:

1) If the number of people who assisted you in preparation of the report is large, you may construct a special section titled 'Acknowledgements'.
2) If the number of people who assisted you in the preparation of the report is small you may include them:
    (a) In the letter of transmittal, or
    b) in the last paragraph of the chapter titled 'Introduction'.

Table of Contents

Unless the report is exceptionally brief, it should contain a table of contents, including the page numbers of major sections and sub-divisions within the sections, and a list of all appendixes. If numerous tables or charts are used, they should also be listed on a separate page immediately following the table of contents.

The table of contents is a valuable part of the report. Preferably it should be:

1) Properly headed by a caption *i.e.,* Contents or Table of contents
2) Proper page layout should be used for this
3) Set up columns below the heading
4) The last digits of the page numbers should be aligned.

This is a guide map describing the structure of the report. This is a valuable document. It greatly assists the reader in finding particular section. Make sure that contents are listed in the same order as they appear in the report and with the same wording. Figure 4.1 gives a typical table of contents.

List of Tables/Charts/Illustrations

There is a separate one section of table of charts and illustration. If number of charts and illustrations is large you may construct separate table of charts and illustration. The table shall consist of descriptive title below which two columns could be constructed. Column one contains headings and column two contains page numbers. Align the last character of the page number. Use proper numbering system to show the contents of the table. Figures show the typical table of charts and contents.

The report may have number of charts. Illustrations and tables, the author may include list of illustrations as part of the report. Figure 4.1 gives the typical table of contents and illustrations.

Table of Contents

List of Charts, Figures and Tables

Charts

Number	Title	Page
....	....	....
....	....	....
....	....	....

Figures

Number	Title	Page
....	....	....
....	....	....
....	....	....

Tables

Number	Title	Page
....	....	....
....	....	....
....	....	....

Fig. 4.1 : A Typical Table of Contents and Illustrations

Glossary of Terms

There may be several technical terms or expressions used in the report. It is necessary to include glossary of terms. It will consist of the list of words and their meaning in the layman's language.

If only one or two terms are used in the whole report, their explanation can be given in the text when they are used for the first time.

Abbreviations

Abbreviations are generally used in writing the report. It is necessary to include exclusive section on abbreviations. It will consist of the list of abbreviations and their full form to facilitate the reader.

Executive Summary

The executive summary is the most important part of the research report. It must clearly and concisely present the heart of the report. The objectives, findings, conclusions, and recommendations must be presented forcefully and briefly.

Many executives will read only this part of the report. In fact, the executive summary may be all that is provided to some managers. Others will use the executive summary to determine if, and what, they should read in the main report.

It presents the report in miniature. This part of the report summaries all the salient points from the body of the document such as the introduction, findings and conclusions. It is the most important section of the report, taking pride of place at the front where it will be read by everyone. Although it is positioned at the front of the report, but it is the last section to be written.

Summaries may be written in words but depending on the objectives and findings. Tables, charts or diagrams can be effective in adding the impact.

Some busy executives do not have time to go through the whole report. For them the executive summary serves as a brief documents giving the concentrate.

The executive summary should be about one fifth in length of the total report and everything significant should be covered in the summary. It should be written in the present tense. It describes the structure, purposes, methods and overall significance of the work. It should enable the evaluator to asses if the project report contains material that is relevant to the context. The summary may be broken down into about 20 key points with as many paragraphs, each containing just a few sentences.

Executive summaries are also usually the first things and analyzed by potential readers, so it's a very important part of your project.

Your executive summary should be no more than a page or two and it should summarize all the other sections of your research. It should include key financial numbers from your research, as well as brief summaries of other important sections.

It should be the last thing you write in your research, even though it's usually the first thing to read by others. A concise length summary format will enable the reader to quickly understand what you plan to do with your business.

Banks and venture capitalists are busy people and if their interest is not piqued at the start they will not continue to read your plan. VCs receive thousand of plans, many of them of the size of a book. They will only read a plan if the first few pages indicate that it is worthy of further exploration, that is why your executive summary is so important.

For more information on executive summaries, see our sample executive summaries or use Business Plan Pro, which helps you write an executive summary as well as containing over 400 executive summary examples.

Main Report Parts/Group

The opening of the main report gives the back ground information. The reader creates in his/her mind a picture of your work environment. The purpose of introduction is to orient the reader/evaluator/assessor to know the problem at hand. In writing introduction, following general topics may be considered:—

1) Origin of the report : General background
2) Purpose of the report : Reasons for and the aim of this particular study
3) Scope of the report : Concise description of scope and contents
4) Main findings : Main finding and claims.

While writing this section consider the following points:-

1) Create background picture of your organisation and work situation as a help to reader.
2) Describe the method of study and its purpose.
3) Explain briefly the difficulties encountered in the preparation of the report.
4) Make sure it leads the reader smoothly to the next section.

Introduction

The introduction should provide

(a) Background material.
(b) A clear statement of the research objectives, and
(c) An overview of the organization of the report.

The first section of the introduction should contain a detailed description of the management problem and the factors that influence it. The researcher cannot assume that everyone who will read the report is familiar with the underlying problem.

The next section of the introduction should be concise statement of the objectives, which will involve the management problem and its translation into a research problem. The objectives arise out of the background data but are so critical that they should be stated explicitly. The introduction should conclude with a brief overview of the organization of the report.

This may include a short account of the project study and problem faced by the project study and the problem faced by the project sponsor/organisation *e.g.*

"The Global Hospital Corporate is considering to enter into the Indian market for deluxe hotels survey. They require an investment of Rs. 90 Crore. . . . In order to evaluate the viability of the project, GHC requires a full understanding of Indian market for hotels, has commissioned this study to understand the market against objectives agreed in the proposal dated March 2008."

Objectives

This section may also be termed as objectives, problem, aim, goal, mission, assignment, project etc.

The statement of the overall aims of study and areas of information which will be covered. The background of the main issue can be given which will set the scene.

The objection may be studied in the following context:-

1) Broad objectives
2) Sub-objectives.

Broad-objectives

A short statement of the aims expressed in just one or two sentences *e.g.*

"To *analyse the market for international tourist, to assess the opportunities* for GHC, the limitations which could prevent these *opportunities and make recommendations on if* and how the company can *enter* the market."

Sub-objectives

In addition to the main objectives, there may be some sub-objectives which also form the part of the project and the study of the these objectives may lead to the overall aim of the project study being fulfilled *e.g.*

(a) To asses the size of the market and segmentation for the last five years.

(b) To product market size for the future three years.

(c) To assess market shares and profile and competitors.

(d) To know what motivates specify tourist generating area in their choice.

(e) To identify barriers preventing GHC hospital company's entry into India market.

(f) To recommend a suitable product range.

Methodology

This section summarizes the methodology used to meet the objectives of the research project. Technical details should be minimized. Where necessary, such details should be placed in appendixes. The researcher must remember that, although he or she is deeply interested in research design, managers are not. This should not be the major section of the report.

Thus, this chapter explains the methodology by which the information was obtained. It includes

1) Research planning and design
2) Data collection method
3) Sampling
4) Field work
5) Analysis.

Research Design

The researcher must clarify the following points:-

1) Whether the study is exploratory or conclusive in nature ?
2) Whether it is a case study ?
3) Whether it is statistical or experimental in design ?

Data Collection Method

The researcher must clarify the following points:-

1) Whether the data is collected from primary sources ?
2) Whether the data is collected from secondary sources ?
3) Whether the data is combination of primary and secondary sources ?
4) Whether data is collected by observation or survey ?
5) Why a particular method has been adopted ?

Copy of form or questionnaire for recording observational data should be included here. If the form is too lengthy it should be including in the appendix.

Sampling

1) Describe sampling procedure.
2) Indicate the nature of universe studied.
3) Specify exact sampling units and describe size of the sample.
4) Describe reasons for selecting the sample size.
5) Point out any differences between the sample unit refused and actual interviewed to avoid possible errors.
6) Explain geographical location of samples (preferably map them)

Field Work

Describe the method used to carry field studies.

Analysis

1) Describe the statistical method and techniques used.
2) Present the relevant facts and opinions collected.
3) Don't mix analysis with the conclusion.

Delimitations

The researcher should not overlook or hide any problem in the research. Furthermore, care should be taken to point out limitations, that are apparent to skilled researchers but that a manager might overlook. For example, the danger in generalizing to the national market from local studies or the potential problems of non-response errors are often overlooked by executives. The limitations section should, without unduly degrading the overall quality of the work, indicate the nature of any potential limitations.

Every project has certain limitations. A good researcher should always include the limitations for the attention of project sponsor/evaluator. The limitations of the project work helps the sponsor evaluator to make accurate interpretations. While writing limitations the following issues should be kept in mind:—

1) Explain the degree to which the limitations could affect the results.
2) Don't over emphasise the limitations. This may loosen the confidence of the researcher and may also discharge the project sponsor.
3) Limitations must be put in right perspective.

Findings

The major portion of the report should be devoted to the findings, which should be organized around the objectives of the study. The findings should not consist of an endless series of statistical tables. Instead they should describe, in meaningful terms, what the research found. Summary tables and visual aids (charts, graphs, and the like) should be used to clarify the discussion.

In this section of the report you describe the results of the project work. The idea is not just to present certain colourful charts, graphics or statistical tables but an organised presentation of the results of the project work, strictly in line with the objectives of the study. The information included in findings must match the objectives of the study.Therefore, the findings include:—

1) The tabulated data which has huge details should be appended.
2) Include all tables, graphics, charts which directly relate to objectives of the study.
3) Use colour graphic for impact.
4) Make liberal use of summary tables and histro graphics.
5) The placement of tables graphics should be logical (preferably in the sequence of questionnaire).
6) Avoid generality.
7) Be specific.

Conclusions and Recommendations

The researchers should draw conclusions from the findings in the light of the objectives of the study. A good way to organize this section is to state each objective and then present the specific conclusions relevant to that objective.

Recommendations should be made where appropriate. Having the researcher recommended specific courses of action can have three beneficial effects. First, it forces the researcher to "lay it on the line". Second, it keeps the researcher closely attuned to the management process. Both of these effects should ultimately lead to better, more usable research. Even more important, however, is the fact that the researcher's recommendations may help solve the problem. This section is also the appropriate place to suggest additional research if such research is justified.

You should write conclusions keeping the specific objectives in mind *i.e.*, there should be a direct references between conclusion drawn and objectives of the study. Sometimes the data collected is such that it is difficult to draw conclusions in line with objectives. Highlight this fact in your report. This will facilitate proper evaluation.

In writing conclusion and recommendations, you can make use of standard models for structure. SWOT is tried and tested paradigm for arriving at the conclusion. Considerations of the strengths and weaknesses of the hotel (client organisation) balanced against opportunities and threats can be studied using SWOT as detailed below for a hospitality market study:-

Typical Use of SWOT

Hospitality Market Study

Strengths	:	What is the hotel good at in terms of its management structure which supports products?
	:	The range of products and search
	:	The quality of products and search
	:	The guest base and distribution
	:	The prices, promotion and service
Weaknesses	:	What the hotel is weak at In terms of same issues *i.e.* its management infrastructure, product, customer base and price?
Opportunities	:	How fast the tourism market is growing?
		What is happening to competition?
		Is there a favourable exchange rate?

Threats : Political and social climate
: Economic consideration
: Demographic
: Legislative and legal issues.

Suppose the hotel requires to redesign the product marketing mix and you have been assigned to investigate into issues related to 4P's. You should look into the following questions before making conclusions:—

Product
1) How could the design, range of products and quality of products be changed to bring them in line with market needs ?
2) What service issue should be associated with the products (delivery period, technical services, speed of service) ?

Price
1) What improvements should be made in pricing structure, (rebates, discounts etc. ?
2) What price changes should be effected to maximise return on investment ?

Place:
1) How to increase customer/guest base ?
2) What improvements could be made in the distribution network ?

Promotion:
1) How to build awareness ?
2) How to create drive ?
3) What message ?
4) What media ?
5) Other issues.

Appendices and Enclosures

Appendices and enclosures of information which are used as supporting evidence there need to be referred to a number of times by the reader. These are better put in this section rather than included in the text.

Items that will appeal to only a few readers or that may be needed only for occasional reference should be confined to an appendix. Details of the sampling plan, detailed statistical tables, interview verification procedure, copies of questionnaires and interviewer instruction and similar items generally belong in an appendix.

The information contained in the main body of the report is supported by an appendix. It is a way of providing adequate detail for readers who require it without breaking the thread of the mainbody.

How do you know what the information to put in appendices ?

What to include in the main body ?

What to exclude from the report altogether ?

Figure 4.2 explains an algorithm that will help you to decide the answer.

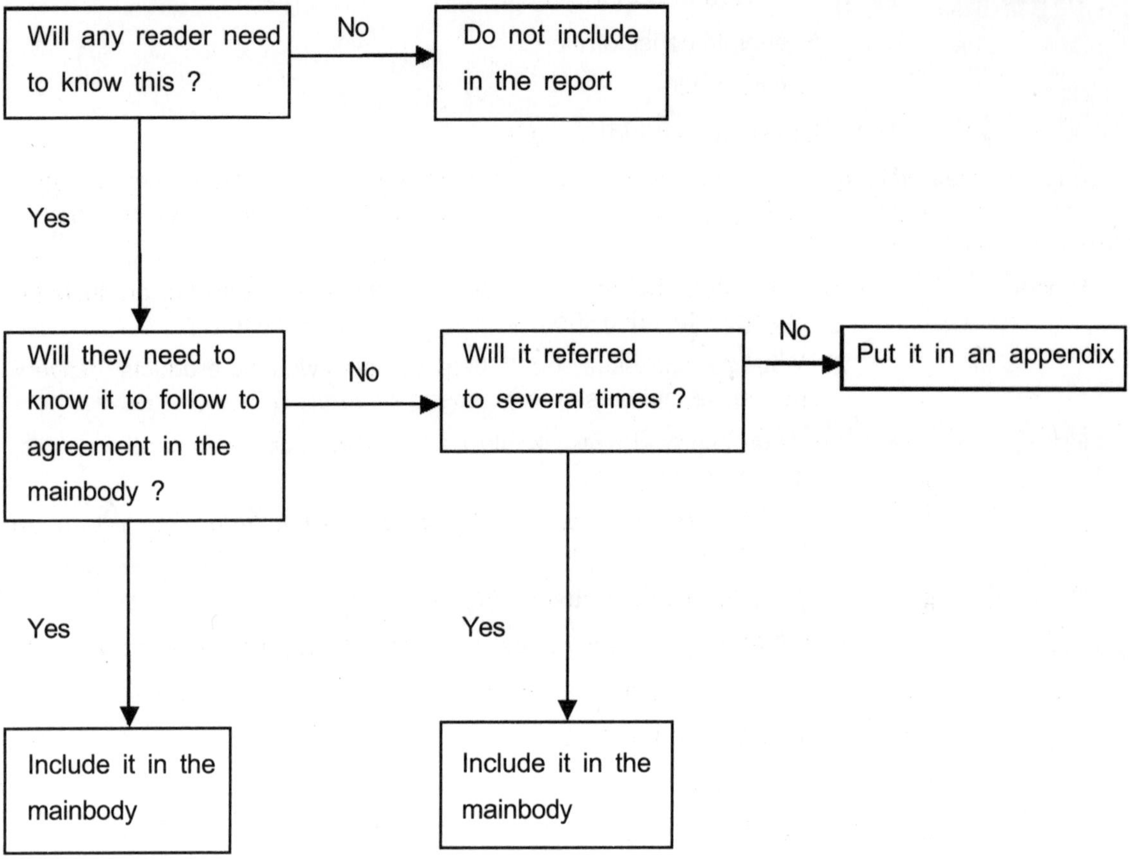

Fig. 4.2: Algorithms for Appendix

Consider the following points while deciding about appendix:—

1) to include supporting evidence like diagrams, graphics, charts, tables, illustrations, brochures, questionnaire and so on in the appendices.
2) to arrange the documents in the logical sequence.
3) to caption them properly and support by legend where necessary.
4) to give nomenclature to each appendix.
5) to don't clutter up the report with irrelevant appendices.
6) If an appendix is larger than A4 size paper make sure it is folded in a manner which makes it easy to handle and read.

Bibliography

List of books, publications, reports with names of authors, year of publication and name of publication company.

5

Research Methodology or Survey Techniques

Most of the surveys, are generally into management, finance, commerce, economic, sociological or political problems. These are conducted quite often in real life and research is done concerning various phenomena. Conducting an experiment or organising a survey and doing research has become the part of life in modern times. In *an experiment* you as an investigator measure the effects of an experiment which you conduct intentionally. *In a survey,* an investigator examines those phenomena which exist in the universe independent of your own action. For doing all this you has to be familiar with the survey techniques of research methodology.

The research in common parlance refers to a search for knowledge. But a statistical survey or research means the search for knowledge through statistical methods. Research may be defined as the objective and systematic method of finding solution to a problem i. e., systematic collection, recording, analysis, interpretation and reporting of information about various facets of a phenomenon under study. In other words, research refers to the systematic method consisting of enunciating the problem, collecting facts or data, analysing the facts critically and reaching conclusions based on them. For instance, if you are interested in doing market research, then you should do research concerning with existing or potential markets, marketing strategies and tactics, and the interaction between markets, marketing methods and current or potential products or services. Research plays a major role in applying a truly analytical approach to decision making. Besides, it also assists in the evaluation of the effect of decisions which have been taken. According to the social scientists the ultimate aim of research must be the social benefit i.e., they opine the problem faced by the society that must be solved by the research workers.

Research methodology refers to the various sequential steps adopted by a researcher in studying a problem with certain object/objects in view. Research projects are not susceptible to any one complete and inflexible sequence of steps. The type of problem to be studied will determine the particular steps to be taken and their order too. However, the following steps provide a useful procedural guideline for a research methodology:

Step 1. Tentative selection of the research topic/problem

Step 2. Initial survey of literature

Step 3. Defining or selecting the research problem

Step 4. Extensive literature survey

Step 5. Specification of the information required

Step 6. Design of the research project

Step 7. Sample design

Step 8. Collection of data : construction of questionnaires

Step 9. Execution of the project

Step 10. Analysis of the data

Step 11. Testing of hypotheses

Step 12. Arriving of generalization

Step 13. Preparation of the report.

A detailed explanation of all these above stated points have been presented:

1) Tentative Selection of the Problem

At the very outset you as a researcher must single out the problem you wants to study. In an academic institution you can seek the help from a guide (who is more experienced and who has several study problems in his mind) in this task. In a government department the problem is earmarked by the administrative agencies. Selecting the appropriate problem is the secret of success in research.

2) Selecting Survey of Literature

Two types of literature may be reviewed- the conceptual literature concerning the concepts and theories; the research literature consisting of studies made earlier which are similar to the one proposed. The basic outcome of this initial survey of literature is what is known as a 'Frame of Reference' for the research. If this frame of reference is successfully developed then you are able to select your own research problem in meaningful context.

3) Selecting the Research Problem

The initial survey of literature and the discussions with the research guide should enable you as a researcher scholar to pick up a topic which you may undertake. It should not be too broad nor very narrow. Hence this step (of defining the research problem) is of the greatest importance in research methodology. The problem to be investigated must be defined unambiguously for that will help in discriminating relevant data from irrelevant ones. Care must, however, be taken to verify the objectivity and validity of the background facts concerning the problem before defining it. Prof. W. A. Neiswanger correctly states that "statement of the objective is of basic importance because it determines the data which are to be collected, the characteristics of the data which are relevant, relations which are to be explored, the choice of technique to be used in these explorations and the form of the final report". Once the problem is selected, a brief summary of it should be written down. It is compulsorily required from a research worker writing a thesis for Ph.D. degree to write a synopsis of the topic and submit it to the committee or the research board for obtaining the latter's approval.

4) Extensive Literature Survey

Once the problem is clear and you as a research scholar has written it down, you should then undertake extensive literature survey connected with the problem. For this purpose, the abstracting and indexing journals and published or unpublished bibliographies are the first place to go to academic journals, conference proceedings, government reports, books etc. i.e., every type of source must be tapped depending on the nature of the problem. In this process, it should be remembered, that one source will lead to another. The earlier studies, which are similar to the study in hand, should be carefully gone through. A good library will be a great help to the researcher at this stage.

5) Specification of the Information Required: Formulating the Hypothesis

After extensive literature survey, you as a researcher should give attention to the specification of the information required i.e., you should specifically mention the information that you are going to collect in order to study the problem under consideration and also the sources of collecting this information. Data is generally classified as either primary or secondary. *Primary data* refers to the information which has originated directly as a result of the particular problem under investigation. *Secondary data* are those data which already exist and may be used for investigation. It is usually cheaper to use secondary data than to set up special investigations. Care must be taken to ensure that the data is relevant, can be adjusted to the problem, and is reliable. The sources of secondary data are many. There is a wealth of published information available from government departments, trade associations, banks, professional bodies, research organizations, the press, and various other agencies. The unpublished information with various bodies and organisations along with the researcher himself can as well be used.

The researcher should accurately and unmistakably define the statistical unit. A good statistical unit is an unit which is appropriate to the object of the enquiry, self-explanatory, definite, specific, and uniform. Standard of accuracy for each item and every endeavour should be made to bring each recorded instance upto this standard. The standard should be laid down keeping in view the object of the Investigation.

Before embarking upon the research further, the researcher at this juncture should state the working hypothesis or hypotheses. Hypothesis is a "tentative assumption made in order to draw out and test in most types of research. Hypothesis should be very specific and limited to the piece of research in hand because it has to be tested. For example usually we talk about the Null hypothesis. If we are to compare method 'A' with method 'B' about its superiority and if we assume that both methods are equally good, then we are using the null hypothesis. Similarly if we presume that sample result does not differ significantly from expectations then also we are stating the null hypothesis or what is termed as statistical hypothesis. The role of hypothesis is to guide the researcher by delimiting the area of research and to keep him on the right track. It sharpens his thinking and focuses attention on the more important facets of the problem. It also indicates the type of data required and the type of methods of data analysis to be used.

6) Design of the Research Project

You as researcher will then be required to prepare a design of the research project. The research design refers to the conceptual structure within which the research is conducted. A research design is the arrangement of conditions for collection and analysis of data in a manner that aims to combine relevance to the research purpose with economy in procedure. (Ref. Claire

Settinz and others, 'Resarch Methods in Social Sciences,' rev., 1962, p.50). The preparation of the design involves the consideration of the following:—

a) The means of obtaining the information;

b) The availability and skills of the research staff and/or agencies;

c) Methodology i.e., a detailed explanation of the way in which selected means of obtaining information (for instance, observation studies, questionnaires etc.) will be organised and the reasoning leading to the selection.

7) Sample Design and the Size of Sample

All the items under consideration in any field of inquiry constitute a 'Universe' or 'Population'. A complete enumeration of all the items in the 'population' is known as a census inquiry. It can be presumed that such an inquiry will get larger and larger as the number of observations increases. Moreover, there is no way of checking the element of bias or its extent except through a survey or use of sample checks. Besides, this type of inquiry involves a great deal of time, money and energy. Therefore, when the field of inquiry is large, this method becomes difficult to adopt in view of the resources involved. At times, this method is practically beyond the reach of ordinary researchers. Perhaps, government is the only institution which can get complete enumeration carried out. Even the government adopts this in very rare cases such as population census conducted once in a decade. Further, many a times it is not possible to examine every item in the population and sometimes it is possible to obtain sufficiently accurate results by studying only a part of the total population. In such cases then there is no utility of census surveys. But one should remember that when the universe is a small one, it is no use resorting to a sample survey. Hence, when field studies are undertaken in practical life, considerations of time and cost almost invariably lead to contact being made with a selection of respondents i.e., selection of only a few items. The respondents selected should be as representative as possible of the total population in order to produce a miniature cross-section. The selected respondents constitute what is technically called a sample and the selection process is called sampling technique and the survey so conducted is known as the sample survey. Algebraically, let the population size be *'N'* and if a part of size *'n'* (which is <*'N'*) of this population is selected according to some rule for studying some characteristics of the population, the group consisting of these *'n'* units is called the 'sample'.

Primary Considerations in Sampling

1)	Population	: Determine who could provide information
2)	Sample frame	: Develop a list of population members
3)	Sampling unit	: Determine the bases for drawing the sample (individual, independent hotels, hotel chains etc)
4)	Sampling method	: Determine how the sample will be selected
5)	Probability (chance)	
6)	Non-probability (some means)	
7)	Sample size	: Determine how many population members are to be included in the sample

8) Sample plan : Develop a method for selecting and contacting the sample members

9) Execution : To carry out the sample plan.

Minimum Sample Sizes

Table 5.1 helps for determining the minimum sample size required to generalize results to apply to a entire population. Level of confidence is 95 percent that the sample proportion will be within plus or minus .05 of the population proportion. Sample size refers to questionnaires returned, not those sent out. Assuming a 50 percent return rate, send out at least twice the minimum sample size.

Table 5.1: Approximate Minimum Sample Sizes

Sl. No.	Population Size	Sample Size
1.	10	10
2.	50	44
3.	100	80
4.	200	132
5.	300	169
6.	400	196
7.	500	217
8.	600	234
9.	700	248
10.	800	260
11.	900	269
12.	1,000	278
13.	2,000	322
14.	3,000	341
15.	4,000	351
16.	5,000	357
17.	6,000	361
18.	7,000	364
19.	8,000	367
20.	9,000	368
21.	10,000	370
22.	20,000	377
23.	30,000	379
24.	40,000	380
25.	50,000	381
26.	100,000	384

Type of Sample

There are two types of samples:

(*a*) Probability or random samples are those samples which are so constructed that every element from the total population has an equal probability of selection and the limits of probable error in relating results to the whole population are known mathematically in advance.

(*b*) Non-probability or purposive samples are those samples which are based on the choice of the researcher.

The researcher must prepare a *'sample design'* i.e., he must plan how a sample should be selected. In other words, the sample design specifies the procedures to be used in collecting the sample. In this context he must give due weightage to the following points:

1*) The type of universe*

The first step of any sample design is clearly to define that set of objects (technically called the Universe) to be studied. What is the nature of the universe from which sample is to be constituted ? The universe can be finite or infinite. In finite universe the number of items is certain. The population of a city, number of workers in a hotel and the like are examples of finite universes. In infinite universe the number of items is infinite i.e., we cannot have any idea about the total number of items. The number of stars in a sky, listeners of a specific radio program, the viewers of a TV channels, throwing of a die are a few examples of infinite universes.

2*) A Sampling unit*

A decision has to be taken concerning a sampling unit before selecting a sample. Sampling units are usually of the following types:

(*a*) *Geographical units* such as state, district, town etc.

(*b*) *Construction units* such as house, flat etc.

(*c*) *Social units* such as family, club, school etc.

(*d*) *Individuals.*

The researcher must decide as to which one of such units he has to select for his purpose.

3*) The Source list*

The next step in any sample design is to develop the source list. Source list (also known as 'Sampling Frame') contains the names of all the items of a universe (only in case of finite universe). Items for the sample are selected from this source list. In case source list is not available, the researcher has to prepare it. Such a list should be comprehensive, correct, reliable and appropriate. It is extremely important for the sapling frame or the source list to be as representative of the population as possible.

4*) This Size of sample*

This means how many items be selected from the universe to constitute a sample. This is a major problem before a researcher. The size of the sample should not be excessively big nor too small but should be optimum. Though nothing definite can be said in this context but for general guidance it can be mentioned that an optimum sample is one which fulfils the requirements of efficiency, representativeness, reliability and flexibility. It should, however, be remembered that mere size of the sample does not assure representativeness in a sample. A small random sample is apt to be much superior to a larger but badly selected sample. Hence, the sampling selection technique plays an important part in determining the size of the sample. The following points deserve mention in this context:

(*a*) *Homogeneity or Heterogeneity of the universe:* If the items of the universe are homogeneous, a small can serve the purpose but if the items are heterogeneous, then a larger sample will be needed.

(*b*) *Number of classes proposed:* If many class-groups are to be formed then a larger sample will be required because a small sample might not be able to give a reasonable number of items in each class-group.

(*c*) *Nature of study:* If items are to be intensively and continuously studied then the sample should be small. For a general survey the size of the sample should be large but a small sample is considered appropriate in technical surveys.

(*d*) *Other considerations.* Type of sampling, nature of units, size of the questionnaire, standard of accuracy etc. are other factors which affect the decision concerning the size of the sample. A researcher must pay attention to all the factors as well. Besides, the availability of finance, trained investigators and the time and the availability of finance and trained investigators and the time at the disposal of the researcher, are a few other important practical considerations affecting the size of the sample.

However, two approaches are generally talked about with regard to the determination of the size of the sample. The first approach is "to specify the precision of estimation desired and then to determine the sample size necessary to insure it" and the second approach uses Bayesian statistics "to weigh the cost of additional information against the expected value of the additional information." (*Rodney D. Johnson and Bernard R. Sukin, Quantitative Techniques for Bussiness Decision*, pp., 374.75). In practice the first approach is most common.

We now explain and illustrate the determination of the size of the sample using the first approach in finite as well as in infinite universes.

Sample size (when estimating a percentage)

Suppose a simple random sample is to be drawn from a finite Universe of size *'N'* in order to estimate the percentage *'p'* in the population, we may state on the basis of our experience that we want the estimate of *'p'* to be basis of our experience that we want the estimate of *'p'* to be within δ of the true value of *'p'* with probability α [i.e,. $p(|P - P| < \delta) \leq \alpha$ where *'p'* is the estimator of 'p'], then the sample size *'n'* is given by the following formula :

$$n = \frac{Z^2 \alpha N p(1-p)}{(N-1)d^2 + Z^2 \alpha p(1-p)}$$

where *Z* represents that value such that the probability of a standard normal variable exceeding it is $(1 - \alpha)/2$. The value for a chosen level can be obtained directly from the table giving *Z* value for the standard normal distribution. (Refer the statistical table giving Z value for the standard normal distribution.) But what value to be assigned to *'p'* in the above formula is a formidable problem, for *'p'* is the unknown value we are actually trying to estimate. One method may be to take the value of *'p'* = 0.5 conservatively in which case *'n'* will be maximum and the sample will yield at least the desired precision. The other method may be to make an initial estimate of *'p'* which may either be based on personal judgement or may be the result of a Pilot Study. (It has been observed by many that a Pilot Study of 225 or more items may result in a reasonable approximation of *'p'* value for the purpose.) In case of infinite universe the above formula concerning the sample size is reduced to–

$$n = \frac{Z^2 \alpha p(1-p)}{d^2}$$

Example 1.

What should be the size of the sample if a simple random sample from a population of 2,000 items is to be drawn to estimate the per cent defective within 2% of the true value with 95% probability ? What would be the size if sample if the population happens to be infinite in the given case ?

Solution

In this question we have been given:—

$N = 2{,}000$

$\delta = 2\%$ or 0.02

$\alpha = 95\%$ (corresponding to which Zx value for the table of standard normal variate is 1.96)

Let the value of *'p'* = 20% *i.e.*, 0.02

(This may be on the basis of experience or on the basis of Pilot Study)

The sample size for a population of 2,000 items in the given case would then be worked out as follows:

$$n = \frac{(1.96)^2.(2000).(.02).(1-.02)}{(2000-1)(.02)^2 + (1.96)^2(.02)(1-.02)}$$

$$= \frac{(3.8416)(2000)(.02)(.98)}{(1999)(.0004) + (3.8416)(.02)(.98)}$$

$$= \frac{(3.8416)(39.2)}{(.7996) + (.0753)} = \frac{150.59}{0.8749}$$

$$= 172 \text{approx.}$$

But if the population happens to be infinite then sample size would be as follows:

$$n = \frac{(1.96)^2(.02)(.98)}{(.02)^2}$$

$$= \frac{(3.8416)(.02)(.98)}{(.0004)} = \frac{(.0753)}{(.0004)}$$

$$= 188 \text{ approx.}$$

Sample size (when estimating an average)

Suppose a simple random sample is to be drawn from an infinite universe of size *'N'* in order to estimate an average concerning the population, we may state on the basis of our experience and the purpose of the enquiry that we desire the estimate of μ the average parameter value to be within δ of μ with probability α [i.e., $?(|\bar{x}-\mu|< d) \le a$] then the sample size *'n'* is given by the following formula:

$$n = \frac{Z^2 \alpha N s^2}{(N-1)d^2 + Z^2 \alpha s^2}$$

This formula requires knowledge of the variance (viz. σ^2) of the population which is never really known and for working purpose it is necessary to substitute for σ^2 an approximation based either on experience and personal judgment or on the basis of the results of a Pilot Study. If the population happens to be infinite the formula for determining the size of the sample is reduced to:

$$n = \frac{Z\alpha^2 s^2}{d^2}$$

This result can alternatively be obtained as per sampling theory as under:

The limits of the proportion assuming normal distribution are: proportion = *Z* (SE prop.) at a given level of significance.

The value of *Z* at 95% confidence is 1.96 from *Z* table.

Z (SE.prop.) = 0.2;

$$\therefore 1.96\sqrt{\frac{.02 \times .98}{n}} = .02$$

Hence, $n = 188$ approx.

Example 2

Determine the size of the simple random sample for estimating the true weight of the cereal containers for the universe with $N = 5{,}000$ on the basis of the following information:

(*i*) The variance of weight = 4 ounces on the basis of the past records;

(*ii*) Estimate should be within 0.4 ounces of the true average weight with 99% probability.

What would be the size of the sample if infinite universe is assumed in the given case ?

Solution

The information given is:

$N = 5000$

$s^2 = 4$ ounces

$\delta = 0.4$ ounces of the true average

α = 99% (corresponding to which $Z\alpha$ value from the table is 2.57)

Hence the size of the sample will be worked out as follows:

$$n = \frac{(2.57)^2(5{,}000)(4)}{(5{,}000-1)(0.4)^2+(2.57)^2(4)}$$

$$= \frac{(6.6049)(20{,}000)}{(4{,}999)(.16) = (6.6049)(4)}$$

$$= \frac{1{,}32{,}098}{(799.84) = (23.4196)} = 160 \text{ approx.}$$

But if the population happens to be infinite, then the sample size would be as follows:

$$n = \frac{(2.57)^2(4)}{(0.4)^2} = \frac{(6.6049)(4)}{(0.16)}$$

$$= \frac{26.4196}{0.16} = 165 \text{ approx}$$

We can as well get this result per sampling theory as under:

The limits of the mean assuming normal distribution are $\bar{x} \pm Z\,(\text{S.E.}_{\bar{x}})$ at a given level of significance. The value of Z at 99% confidence is 2.57 from the Z table

$\because\ Z\,(\text{S.E.}_{\bar{x}}) = 0.4$

$\therefore\ 2.57\,\frac{2}{\sqrt{n}} = 0.4$

Hence n, = 165 approx.

It may be noted that in order to double the accuracy *i.e.,* taking half of the given 'd' level for a fixed probability level, it becomes necessary to increase the sample size four-fold. But in real life situation the size of sample, to a great extent, depends on the amount of money available for the purpose of sampling. One should not forget that increasing the reliability of the estimates also increases the cost of obtaining the estimates and may, at times, not be justified. The ultimate object of the enquiry must always be kept in view to determine what level of precision is justifiable.

Bayesian Approach Concerning Sample Size

Under the Bayesian approach concerning the sample size one has to work out the Expected Value of Sample Information (EVSI) and also the Expected Net Gain (ENG) for any given sample size. The cost of taking a sample of a given size can as well be reasonably approximated. This is done for samples of various sizes. From all this the Optimal sample size is determined. The optimal sample size is one which maximizes the difference between the EVSI and the cost of the sample. In other words it is that size for which the ENG is the maximum possible. The usual procedure for finding the optimal value of *'n'* is to compute the EVSI for every possible *'n'* and compare it to the respective cost. This normally is a very ticklish job and is feasible only with computer help. Hence in practice this approach is rarely used.

The Sampling Techniques

Researcher after determining the size of the sample should also decide the technique he will use in selecting items for the sample. Mainly there are two sampling techniques viz., random sampling and purposive sampling. Normally one should resort to random sampling because under it the bias is generally eliminated and the sampling error can be estimated. But when the enquiry is confined to a small universe and the sample also is to be kept small, then purposive sampling can serve the purpose well. Purposive sampling can also be adopted when a known characteristic of the universe is to be studied intensively. In all other cases random sampling is considered superior. There are various designs of random sampling and one or more of these can be adopted by the researcher depending upon the nature of inquiry and other related considerations.

8) Construction of Questionnaires and/or Preparation of Briefs for Field Interviews

Data (Primary data) can be collected either through observation or through direct communication with respondents whether by mail, telephone or personal interviews. The main features along with points of merits and demerits of each of the important methods are as follows:

Observation method

The observation method is most commonly used specially in studies relating to guests/tourists (consumers) behaviour. Under this method the information is sought by way of investigator's own observation without asking from the respondent. For instance, instead of asking the brand of wine used by the respondent, an investigator may himself look at the wine.

The main advantage of this method is that subjective basis is eliminated if observation is done accurately. Secondly, the information obtained under this method relates to what is currently happening, it is not complicated by either the past behaviour or future intentions or attitudes.

The main draw backs of this method are:

i) it is an expensive method, and

ii) the information provided by this method is very limited.

Mailing of questionnaires

The method of collecting data by mailing the questionnaires to the respondents with a request to return after completing it, is most extensively employed in various economic and business surveys. The merits claimed in favour of this method are as follows:

1) Low cost even when the universe is large and spread widely geographically.

2) Free from the bias of the interviewer;

3) Respondents have more time to give well thought answers;

4) Respondents who are not easily approachable can also be reached conveniently;

5) Large samples can be made use of and thus the results be made more dependable and reliable.

The main demerits usually listed are:

1) Low rate of return of the duly filled in questionnaires;
2) Can be used only when respondents are educated and cooperating;
3) Inbuilt inflexibility because there is always the difficulty of amending the approach once questionnaires have been dispatched;
4) Possibility of ambiguous replies or omission of replies altogether to certain questions;
5) Difficulty of knowing whether willing respondents are truly representative;
6) The problem of constantly updating the mailing lists.

Before using this method it is always advisable to conduct *Pilot Survey* for testing the questionnaires. In a big inquiry the significance of Pilot survey is felt very much. Pilot survey is in fact the replica and rehearsal of the main survey. Such a survey being conducted by the experts brings to light the weaknesses (if any) of the questionnaires and also of the survey techniques. From the experience gained in this way, the improvement can be affected.

Essentials of a good questionnaire

To be successful, questionnaire should be comparatively short and simple i.e., the size of the questionnaire should be kept to a minimum. Questions should proceed in logical sequence moving from easy to more difficult questions. Personal and intimate questions should be left to the end. Technical terms, vague expressions capable of different interpretations should be avoided in a questionnaire. Questions may be dichotomous ('yes' or 'no' answers), multiple choice (alternative answers listed) or openended. The latter type of questions are often difficult to analyses and hence be avoided in a questionnaire to the extent possible. There should be some *'control questions'* in the questionnaire which indicate the reliability of the respondent. For instance a question designed to determine consumption of particular materials may be asked first in terms of financial expenditure and later in terms of weight. The control questions thus introduce a cross-check to see whether the information collected is correct or not. Questions affecting the sentiments of the respondents be avoided. Adequate space for answers should be provided in the questionnaire for ease of editing and tabulating. There should always be provision for indications of uncertainty e.g. "do not know", "no preference", and so on. Finally, brief directions with regard to filling up the questionnaire should invariably be given in the questionnaire itself.

Personal interviews

This method of collecting the information is usually carried out in a structured way. In other words, under this method, the investigator (or the interviewer) follows a rigid procedure laid down asking questions in a form and order prescribed. The chief merits of this system are:

1) More information and that too in greater depth can be obtained;
2) Interviewer by his own skill can overcome the resistance, if any, of the respondents;
3) There is greater flexibility under this method as the opportunity to restructure questions is always there;
4) Observation method can as well be applied in addition to recording verbal answers to various questions;
5) Personal information can as well be obtained easily under this method;

6) Samples can be controlled more effectively as there remains no difficulty of the missing returns.

But certain weakness of this method have also been experienced. Important weaknesses are given below:

1) Very expensive specially when large and widely spread geographical samples are taken;
2) There remains the possibility of the bias of the interviewer and also that of the respondent;
3) Certain types of respondents such as important officials or executives or people in high-income groups may not be easily approachable under this method and to that extent the data may prove inadequate;
4) This method is relatively more time consuming specially when the sample is large and recalls upon the respondents are necessary.

For successful implementation of this method, interviewers should be carefully selected, trained and briefed. They should be honest, sincere, hardworking, impartial, and must possess the technical competence and necessary practical experience. Occasional field checks should be made to ensure that interviewers are neither cheating nor deviating from instructions given to them for performing their job efficiently. In addition to this, some provision should also be made in advance so that appropriate action may be taken if some of the selected respondents refuse to co-operate or are not available when an interviewer calls upon them.

Telephone Interviews

This method of collecting the information consists in contacting the respondents on telephone itself. This is not a very widely used method but plays important part in tourists/ industrial surveys in developed regions particularly.

The chief merits of such a system are:

1) More flexible in comparison to mailing method;
2) Faster than other methods;
3) Cheapre than personal interviewing method;
4) Ease of recall;
5) Higher rate of response than what we have in mailing method;
6) Replies can be recorded without embarrassment to respondent;
7) Interviewer can explain requirements more easily, and
8) Access can at times be gained to respondents who otherwise cannot be contacted for one reason or the other.

The demerits of this system of collecting information are:

1) Possibility of the bias of the interviewer;
2) Little time is given to respondent for considered answers;
3) Surveys restricted to respondents having telephone facilities;
4) Extensive geographical coverage may be restricted by cost considerations; and

5) Not suitable for intensive surveys where comprehensive answers are required to various questions.

The researcher should decide one of these methods of collecting the information or the data taking into consideration the nature of investigation, object and scope of the inquiry, financial resources, available time and above all the desired degree of accuracy. Though he should pay attention to all these points while taking a decision concerning the method (of data collection) to be adopted but much depends upon the ability and experience of the researcher. Dr. A. L. Bowley's remark in this context is very appropriated when the says, "In collection of statistical data commonsense is the chief requisite and experience the chief teacher."

Other Methods of Data Collection

Some of the other methods of data collection used by big business houses are as under:

1) *Warranty cards* are usually postal sized stamped cards which are used by dealers of consumer durables to collect information regarding their products. The information sought is printed in the form of questions on the 'warranty cards' which is placed inside the package along with the product with a request that the consumer may fill in the card and post it back to the dealer.
2) *Distributor audits* are performed by distributors as well as manufacturers through their salesmen at regular interval of time. Distributors get the retail stores audited through salesmen and use such information to estimate market size, market share, seasonal purchasing pattern, etc.
3) *Pantry audit technique* is used to estimate consumption of the basket of goods at consumer level. In this type of audit the investigator collects an inventory of types, quantities and prices of commodities consumed. An extensions of this idea on a regular basis is known as *Consumer Panels* where a set of consumers are arranged to come to an understanding to maintain detailed daily records of their consumption and the same is made available to investigator on demands.
4) *Indirect interviewing techniques* have also been developed by psychologists to use projections of respondents for inferring about underlying motives, urges or intentions which are such that the respondent either resists to reveal them or is unable to figure out himself.
5) *Use of mechanical devices* has been widely made to collect information by way of indirect means. Eye Camera, Pupilometric Camera, Psychogalvanometer, Motion Picture Camera, and Audiometer are the principal devices so far developed and commonly used by modern big business houses for the purpose of collecting the required information.
    (a) *Eye cameras* are designed to record the focus of eyes of a respondent on a specific portion of a sketch or diagram or written material. Such an information is useful in designing advertising material;
    (b) *Pupilometric cameras* record dilation of the pupil as a result of a visual stimulus. The extent of dilation shows the degree of interest aroused by the stimulus;
    (c) *Psychogalvanometer* is used for measuring the extent of body excitement as a result of the visual stimulus;

(d) *Motion picture cameras* can be used to record movement of body of a buyer while deciding to buy a consumer good in a shop or big store. Influence of packaging or the information given on the label would stimulate a buyer to perform certain physical movements which can easily be recorded by a hidden motion picture camera in the shop's four walls;

(e) *Audiometers* are used by some television concerns to find out the type of programs as well as stations preferred by people. A device is fitted in the television instrument itself to record these changes. Such data may be used to find out market share of competing television stations.

9) Execution of the Project

Execution of the project is a very important step in the methodology of research. If the execution of the project proceeds on correct lines, the data to be collected would be adequate and at the same time dependable. The researcher should see that the project is executed in a systematic manner and in time. If the survey is to be conducted by means of structured questionnaires, data can be readily machine processed. In such a situation, questions as well as the possible answers may be coded. The questionnaire should be framed keeping in view the essentials of a good questionnaire as stated earlier. If the data are to be collected through interviewers then arrangements be made for proper selection and training of such interviewers. The training may be given with the help of instruction manuals which explain clearly the job of the interviewers at each step. Occasional field checks should be made to ensure that the interviewers are doing their assigned job sincerely and efficiently. A careful watch should as well be kept for unanticipated factors of importance in order to keep the survey as much realistic as possible. This in other words means that steps should be taken to ensure that the survey is under statistical control so that the collected information is in accordance with the pre-defined standard of accuracy. If some of the respondents do not cooperate, a suitable machinery for dealing with such respondents should be set up. One method of dealing with the non-response problem is to make a list of the non-respondents and take a small sub-sample of them and then with the help of experts vigorous efforts can be made for securing response.

10) Analysis of Data

After the data have been collected by any one or more of the methods outlined above, the same should be properly edited and then organised in the form of tables or charts or graphs. The unwieldy data should necessarily be condensed into a few manageable tables for further analysis. This would help the researcher in finding out the salient features of the data. As a result, comparison in also facilitated. When the data have been tabulated the researcher must start the work of analysing them. The mechanical devices can be made use of at this juncture. A great deal of survey work in modern times, specially in large inquiries, is tabulated by computers. Computers not only save time but also make it possible to study large number of variables affecting a problem simultaneously.

The analysis work is generally based on the computation of various percentages, derivatives, coefficients etc. by applying various well defined statistical formulae. In the process of analysis, relationships or differences supporting or conflicting with original or new hypotheses should be subjected to statistical tests of significance to determine with what validity data can be said to indicate any conclusions. For instance, if there are two samples of weekly wages, each simple being drawn from factories in different parts of the same city, giving two different mean values, then our problem may be whether the two mean values are significantly different or the difference is just a matter of chance. Through the use of statistical tests we can establish whether such a difference is a real one or is the result of random fluctuations. If the diference happens to be real, the inference will be that the two samples come from different universes but if the difference is due to chance, the conclusion would be that the two samples belong to the same universe. Similarly, the technique of analysis of variance can help us in analysing whether three or more varieties of seeds grown on certain fields yield significantly different results or not. In brief, the researcher can analyse the collected data with the help of various statistical measures.

(11) Testing the Hypothesis

Once the researcher has analysed the data he is in a position to test the hypothesis he had formulated earlier. Do the facts support the hypothesis or go contrary? This is the usual question which should be answered while testing the hypothesis. Statisticians have developed several tests for hypothesis testing specially in context of sampling theory which may be used by the researcher. Amongst the several significance tests the important ones are the Chi-Square test, Student's *'t'* text, *'z'* test and *'F'* test. The hypotheses may be tested through the use of one or more of these significance tests depending upon the nature and object of the enquiry. The general procedure for testing the hypothesis can be depicted in the form of a flow diagram given in Fig. 5.1.

HYPOTHESIS TESTING

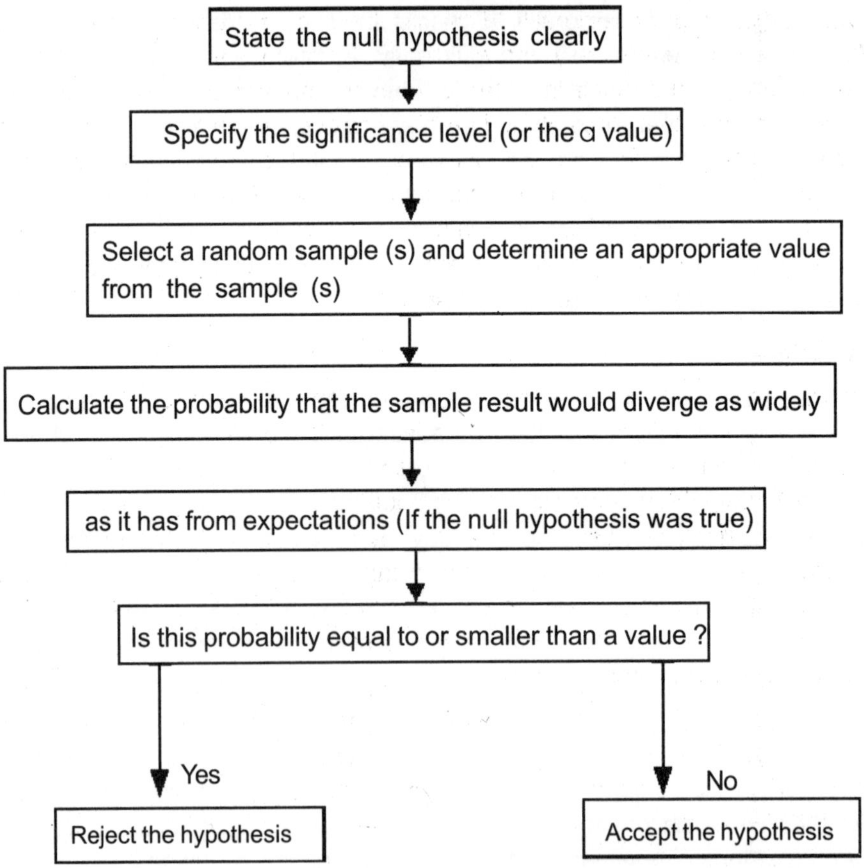

Fig. 5.1: Flow Diagram for Hypothesis Testing

12) Arriving at Generalisations

If a hypothesis is tested and upheld several times, then it may be possible for the researcher to arrive at generalisations i.e., to build a theory. As a matter of fact, the real value of research lies in its ability to arrive at certain generalisation.

13) Preparation of the Report (or the Thesis)

The last step in research methodology is to prepare the report or to write down what has been done. The writing of the report though last but happens to be a very important step which must be completed with great care. The following points provide the guideline with regard to the contents and layout of the report:

1) The layout of the report should be as follows:
   (*a*) Preliminary pages;
   (*b*) Main text; and
   (*c*) End matter.

   In its preliminary pages the report should carry a *title and date* followed by Acknowledgments (in the form of Preface) and Foreword. Then there should be a *table of contents* so that the decision maker (or anybody interested in reading the report) can locate the required information in the report without difficulty. Followed by this there should also be a *list of tables* and *list of groups and diagrams* (if any) given in the report.

   Then comes the main text of the report. The main text of the report should have the following sections:

   a) *Introduction.* The purpose of introduction is to introduce the research project to the readers. It should contain a clear statement of the objective of the research and an explanation of the methodology adopted in conducting the survey. The scope of the study should be clearly stated and the boundary lines demarcated. The various limitations may as well be narrated under which the research project was completed.
   b) *Summary of findings.* After introduction there would appear a statement of findings and recommendations in non-technical language. If the findings are extensive, they should be summarised.
   c) *Main report.* The main body of the report should be presented in logical sequence and broken down into readily identifiable sections.
   d) *Conclusions and implications.* Towards the end of the main text the researcher should again put down the results of his research clearly and precisely. In fact, it is the final summing up.

   At the end of the report, *appendices should be enlisted in respect of all technical data* such as questionnaires, sample information, and the like ones. *Bibliography* should as well be given in the end. *Index* should also be invariably given specially in a published research report or thesis.
2) Report should be written in a concise and objective style in simple language avoiding vague expressions such as 'it seems', 'there may be,' and the like ones.
3) Charts and illustrations in the main report should be used only if they present the information more clearly and more forcibly.
4) Calculated 'confidence limits' must be mentioned and the various constraints experienced in conducting the survey may as well be stated.

6

Conducting Primary and Secondary Research

Once you have identified and formulated a research problem and determined the objectives of research, now you have to face the problem of data collection. The information collected should be both accurate and relevant, as per the requirements of the researcher, who has to work out a suitable data collection method. Some important methods of data collection are:

1) Survey research: systematic collection directly from respondents
   (a) Telephone interviews
   (b) Mail interviews
   (c) Personal interviews
   (d) Home interviews
   (e) Central location interviews.
2) Secondary research: utilizing data that are developed for some other problems.
   (a) Internal secondary data
   (b) External secondary data.
3) Experimental research:
   (a) Laboratory experiments
      (i) Basic designs
      (ii) Statistical designs
   (b) Field experiments
      (i) Basic designs
      (ii) Statistical designs.

Data collection methods can be broadly classified into:-

(i) Primary methods, and

(ii) Secondary methods.

Primary Methods of Collection

The population for research enquiries is the target audience: the group of people that you will ask to respond to your questionnaire. The population that you elect to sample needs to be reasonable in number. However, if you start narrowing the population base, you start limiting the potential importance of study. If, for example, the question regarding front desk managers is narrowed, the result would not apply to front desk managers to the other parts of the world

Data directly collected by a researcher scholar is known as primary data. The methods used for collecting primary data may be:

(a) Survey technique

(b) Observation techniques.

Cox has distinguished between the two forms of collecting primary data with respect to five criteria. as given in Table 6.1:

Table 6.1: Character of Survey and Observation Method

Characteristics	Data Collection Method	
	Survey	**Observation**
1) Type of information	I Awareness/Attitude	a) Current behaviour sought and results
2) Control over data gathering	III Relatively high	b) Relatively low
3) Data accuracy	IV Relatively low	c) Relatively high
4) Time factor	V Relatively high	d) Relatively low
5) Personnel skills required	VI Relatively high	e) Relatively low

(*Source: Cox. William E., Industrial Marketing Research* 1979 p. 83.)

Sources of Primary Data

The following sources are generally used in collection of primary data for marketing research project.

Primary Measurement Techniques

(A) Questionnaire : A formalized instrument for asking information directly from a respondent.

I) Attitude Scales

II) Rating scale

III) Composite scale

IV) Multi-dimensional scale

V) Conjoint analysis.

(B) Observation : Direct observation of behaviour or the results of behaviour

(C) Projective Techniques and depth interviews: Designed to gather information that respondents are either unable or unwilling to provide in response to direct questionnaire–

I) **Projective techniques** – Allow respondents to project or express their own feeling

II) **Depth interviews** – Allow individuals to express themselves without any fear of disapproval, dispute or adirex.

Primary measurement technique may also be classified as under:—

1) Interview Methods
   (a) Depth Interviews
   (b) Mail Interviews
   (c) Telephone Interviews
2) Delphi Technique
3) Projective Techniques
4) Focus Group Interviews
5) Questionnaire Methods
   (a) Structured
   (b) Semi-structured
   (c) Unstructured.

Interview Method

In this method a respondent and a researcher come into direct contact with each other in some form or the other. The researcher may go from door-to-door for interviews or may contact the respondents at some central place. The technique of interviews provides the researcher with an opportunity to ask the respondents any additional relevant questions. Modern techniques of recording may also be used to ensure accuracy, verification, etc. Many marketing researchers use this technique because it is useful to have accurate information for a research project (Ref. Fig. 6.1).

The advantages of interview method are:

1) Accurate information/data
2) Additional informations, needed
3) Flexibility in information collection
4) Ease in communication
5) Ease in obtaining personal information.

The disadvantage of interview method are:

1) Cost factor: Interviews are more expensive than the other techniques.
2) Difficulty in sampling control: No respondent can be forced to give an interview. Non-response can vitiate the character of a sample.
3) The interview technique are highly time-consuming, forcing the researcher to limit the size of his sample.

4) Possibility of getting fictitious information.

Depth Interview

A researcher continues asking probing questions to secure as much information as possible. His probe, of course, is conditioned by the response of the respondent.

DECISION ON TYPES OF INTERVIEWS

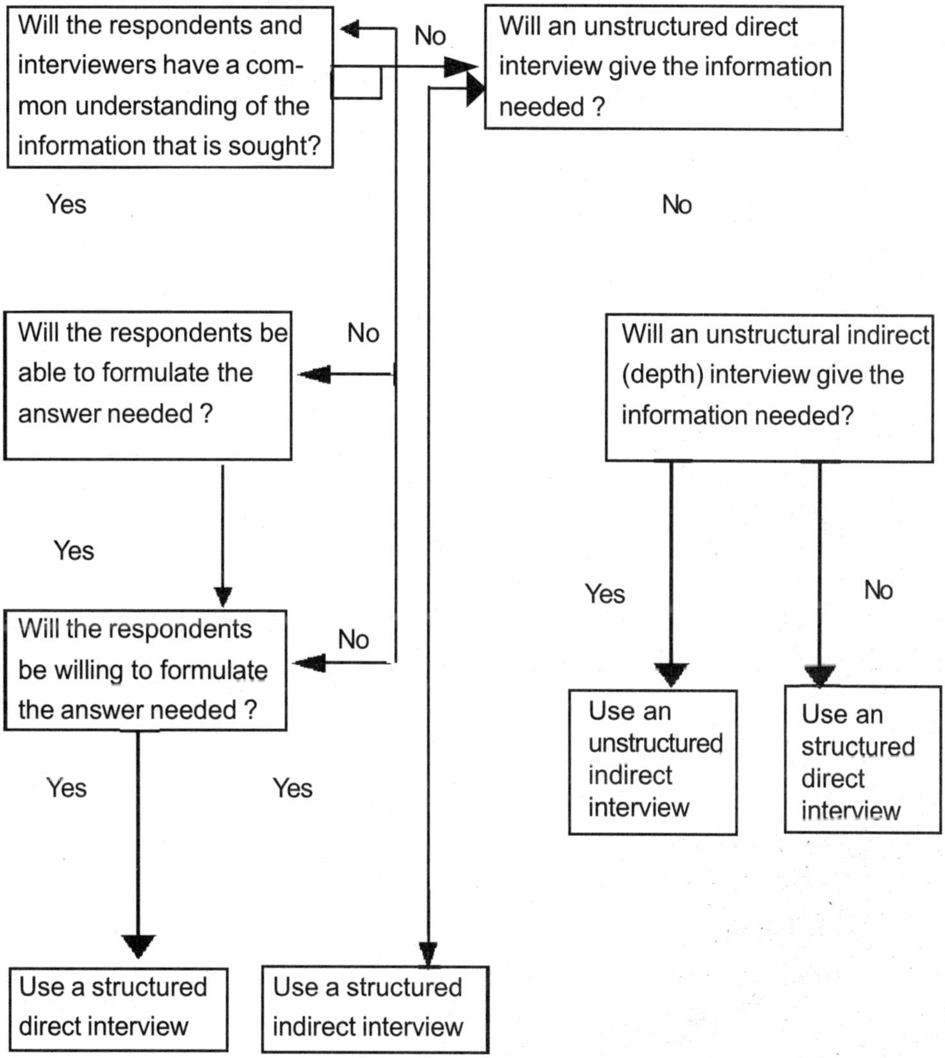

Fig. 6.1: Flow Chart for decision on type of interview to use

Example

1) What brand of hotel did you prefer ?
2) Which star category did you prefer to stay ?
3) Did you compare different hotel before making reservation in our hotel ?

4) What has been your experience with it ?
5) Is it comfortable ?
6) Is it reliable ?
7) Are you satisfied wit its performance ?

Thus, the researcher will continue asking questions till he is satisfied with the information he requires.

The advantages of depth interviews are:

1) Hidden information: The researcher will, in all likelihood, access the information that he might not have otherwise got.
2) Flexibility: It offers flexibility to an interviewer because it is like an informal discussion between him and the interview on the latter's experiences.

The disadvantages of depth interwiews are:

1) Lack of proper structure and system: There is a lack of systematically defined way of analysing the information obtained. In the Indian hospitality marketing research context depth interviews lack popularity because of non-availability of professional personnel.
2) Time-consuming: This method requires considerable amount of time in interviewing which might not be available.
3) Difficulty in tabulating and analysising the data: Since this method lacks a proper structure and system the researcher faces a host of problems in tabulating and analysing the data.

Mail Interviews

This is a method where a researcher take interviews by mailing the questionnaire to respondents.

The advantages of mail interviews are:

1) The only method able to reach respondent
2) Sampling frame easily developed when mailing lists are available
3) Not subject to interviewer bias
4) Respondent work at his own pace
5) Assures anonymity of respondents
6) Wide distribution possible.

The disadvantages of mail interviews are:

1) Very little control in securing response from specific individual
2) Cannot secure responses from illiterates
3) Cannot control speed of response long response time
4) Researcher cannot explain ambiguous questions
5) Does not allow probing with open-ended question
6) Difficult to change sequence of questions.

Telephone Interviews

In this method where a researcher ask the questions to respondent on telephone.

The advantages of telephone interviews are:—

1) Relatively low cost
2) Wide distribution possible
3) Interviewer supervision
4) Relatively strong response rate
5) One of the quickest methods of data collection.

The disadvantages of telephone interviews are:—

1) Difficult to establish representative sampling frame due to unlisted numbers.
2) Cannot use visual aids.
3) More difficult to establish rapport over the telephone.
4) Does not handle long interviews well in most cases.
5) Subject to some degree of interviewer bias.

Delphi Technique

It is a technique whereby a researcher elicits information by means of discussions with various experts in the field. Each expert is asked to comment on the different aspects of a problem. Clearly, the success of this technique depends on a proper selection of experts.

Projective Techniques

These techniques play an important role in marketing research. This group of techniques is based on indirect interviews in collecting data and is useful where data cannot be collected directly. These techniques are helpful in exploring the 'why' of market and consumer behaviour. In projective techniques, respondents are requested to interpret the behaviour of 'others'.

The following are some of the projective techniques:

1) Thematic Apperception Test (TAT)
2) Role Playing
3) Cartoon Completion
4) Word Association
5) Sentence Completion.

(a) TAT: A popular technique in marketing research. The researcher shows a set of pictures to the respondents and then asks them to describe what they think the pictures represent.

(b) Role Playing: In this technique the respondents report their realistic behaviour in imaginary situations. They assume their roles in these situations as actors playing their parts on a stage or in a movie. Most role-playing situations involve interaction in a real business situation.

(c) Cartoon Completion: In this respondents are shown a cartoon with one or more persons in a particular situation. They are then asked to come up with ideas about these characters.

(d) **Word Association:** It consists of presenting a series of words to respondents and recording their opinions for a detailed study.

Focus Group Interviews

It is the best known and most of people jointly participate in an unstructured indirect interview conducted by a moderator. Here, attempts are made to focus the discussion on the problem areas in a relaxed, non-directed manner. Focus group interviews can be used for a number of different purposes.

The advantages of focus group interviews are:

1) Provides complex and varied data, because the discussion covers different group members
2) Saves time as well as cost.

The disadvantages of this method are:

1) Difficulties in sample selection
2) Samples are very small
3) Responses may be influenced by what others have to say
4) Difficulty in analysing the results.

7

Questionnaire Construction and Design

One of the basic tools of research is a questionnaire. A researcher is visual, someone armed with a set of questions, asking them and writing the answers down. Therefore, a questionnaire serves as a useful guide for the communication process and may be used with survey research in any form-whether the questions are in written or verbal form. Without a questionnaire the interview has no structure. Questionnaires help to recognise the tastes, preferences and perceptions of various people so that the marketer may be able to formulate his future people, and future strategies regarding new product launch, sales promotions, etc.

Questionnaire Construction

Following points should be considered while constructing a questionnaire:—

1) Primary decisions :
   (a) Exactly what information is required
   (b) Exactly who are the target respondents
   (c) What method of communication will be used to reach these respondents
2) Decision about question content :
   (a) Is this question really needed ?
   (b) It this question sufficient to generate the needed information ?
   (c) Can the respondent answer the question correctly ?
   (d) Will the respondent answer the question correctly ?
   (e) Are there any external events that might bias to response the questions ?

To ensure a sincere response it is necessary to adhere to three basic conditions:

1) Respondents must be able to understand the questions,
2) They must be able to provide the information requested, and
3) They must be willing to provide the information.

So, you should keep in mind your requirements, in which the questionnaire should be based, these may be:

1) How many interviews will there be?

2) Who will be interviewed ?
3) How will interviews be carried out ?
4) Who will be administering the interviews ?

Recognition of these broader issues will help in designing questionnaires for researchers.

Decision Concerning Question Phrasing

1) Do the words used have but one meaning to all the respondents ?
2) Are any words or phrases loaded or leading any way ?
3) Are there any implied alternative in the question ?
4) Are there any unstated assumptions related to the question ?
5) Will the respondents approach the question from the frame of reference desired by the researcher ?

Decisions about the response format

Can this question best be asked as an open-ended, or multiple-choice question?

1) Decision concerning the question sequence:

   Are the question organized in a logical manner that avoids introducing errors.?

2) Decision on the layout of the question :

   Is the questionnaire designed in a manner to avoid confusion and minimize recording errors ?

3) Pretest and revise :

   Has the final questionnaire been subjected to a through pretest, using respondents similar to those who will be included in the final survey ?

Questionnaire Design

Suppose we are curious about some aspect of another individual. Our curiosity could involve behaviour, knowledge, personal characteristics, or attitudes. How would we satisfy this curiosity? For any one of a fairly wide range of topics, we would simply ask the individual to tell us. Most of us, at one time or another, have asked strangers for "the time", Most people consider this an entirely proper question and respond to it as freely and as accurately as possible.

There are other questions that we would hesitate to ask a foreign tourists, or even a friend. Few of us would ask a stranger, "How much money do you have with you"? Even if we obtain an answer, we may suspect some distortion.

The point is that questioning is a common, every day approach to obtaining information. There are, however, some types of information for which questioning is appropriate and other types for which it is less appropriate.

A questionnaire is simply a formalized set of questions for elicting information. As such, its function is measurement and it represents the most common form of measurement in marketing research. Although the questionnaire generally is associated with survey research, it is also frequently the measurement instrument in experimental designs as well. When a questionnaire is administered by means of the telephone or by a personal interviewer, it often is termed an interview schedule, or simply schedule. However, the term questionnaire is used throughout this text to refer to a list of questions, regardless of the means of administration.

A questionnaire can be used to measure:-

1) Behaviour - past, present, or intended;
2) Demographic characteristics - age, sex, income, occupation;
3) Level of knowledge; and
4) Attitudes and opinions.

All four areas are frequently measured by questionnaire and often on the same questionnaire.

Do your best to make the research questions workable and reasonable in terms of both breadth and depth. Consider the target (populations) and write with precision and clarity. You should review the list of research questions randombly selected from dessertation abrastracts. Try retesting these questions. You may test your research question on friends, relatives and follow students. If several people interpret it in a way different from you expected them to consider changing the wording.

The analysis of the context of each question results in construction of a questionnaire. Why is it being included, types of questions, their sequence and wording, the final layout of questions and the final output in the form of a questionnaire. Figure 7.1 may help in understanding the form of a questionnaire:

Contents of Individual Questions

Use only those questions seeking the required information. So, if we require specific information regarding profession, or if you are targeting an American tourists you should ask relevant questions pertaining to them be. Questions may be used keeping in mind the targeted respondents. The respondents should at least know the type and level of questions expected. Questions seeking specific details about data and time of events should be avoided. Care must be taken in designing the questions seeking information on personal facts such as, sex life, bad habits or status symbol. A single question may also be split into multiple questions for better response from the respondents.

Types of Questions

The decision on which form of questions to use must be based on the objective set for the particular question. There are three main types of questions which are commonly used in hospitality and tourism market surveys:

1) Open-ended questions
2) Multiple choice questions
3) Dichotomous questions.

Open-Ended Questions

These questions, call for a response of more than a few words. Respondents are free to express their views/ideas in their own words. The degree of openness varies from question to question.

For example, the question, "What do you think about deluxe hotel accommodation?"

Allows respondents almost total freedom to express their views to particular brands, advertising slogans, convenience and other issues.

Construction of a Questionnaire

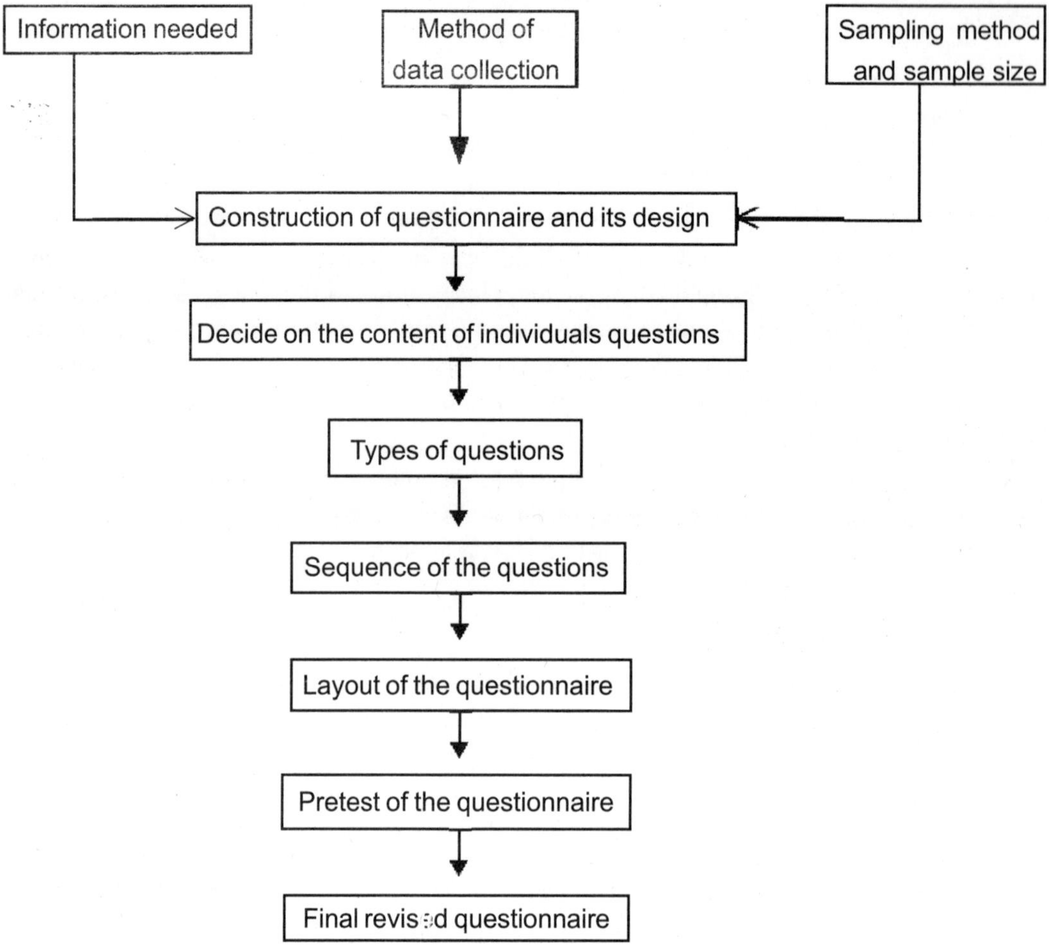

Fig. 7.1 : Basic Steps in Construction of a Questionnaire

The advantages of these questions are:

1) These questions avoid persuading the respondent with a pre-stated set of response categories.
2) These are helpful for exploratory and problem-identification research.
3) These questions provide the basis for the researcher to judge the actual values and views of the respondents.

The disadvantages of these questions are:

1) These are more time consuming.
2) Interviews will vary in their ability to record the respondents' answers, in terms of probing the objectivity.

3) The responses obtained may be so varied that it may be impossible to arrive at any conclusion.
4) Coding or categorising the respondent's answers in open-ended questions is a very costly and a labourious act.

Multiple Choice Questions

Questions for which there are number of choices as answers are termed as multiple-choice questions. There may be a fixed number of choices or in case the number of alternatives or choices is more, the respondents have to rank the alternatives according to their choices.

The advantages of such questions are:

1) These are easier for both the interviewer and respondents.
2) These questions tend to reduce interviewer bias and bias caused by varying levels of respondent's articulation.
3) The tabulation and analysis in multiple-choice questions is much simpler.

The disadvantages of these questions are:

1) To develop a sound set of multiple choice questions requires considerable effort.
2) The list of potential answers can cause several types of distortions in the resulting data.
3) Too many questions and choices make the questionnaire monotonous.

Dichotomous Questions

This is an extreme form of the multiple choice questions, which allows only two responses, such as:—

1) 'Yes' or 'No',
2) 'Agree' or 'Disagree',
3) 'Male or Female', and
4) 'Did' or 'Did not'.

Often these two categories are supplemented by a neutral category such as:

1) 'Don't know',
2) 'No opinion',
3) 'Both' or 'Neither'.

The advantages of their questions are:

Most of the advantages are similar to those of the multiple choice questions. These questions are well suited to clean-cut issues on which respondents are likely to hold very clear and concise views.

The main disadvantage of these questions is:

The choice between just two alternatives might be too restricting for respondents. For example, the question "Do you plan to travel within the next three months?" May result in "Yes" from one individual and "No" from another. If both the individuals have the travelling capacity then appropriate alternatives would be (a) May be (b) Probably (c) Yes (d) No.

The Language and Wording of the Questions

Avoid questions for which the answer is very obvious or which indicate the researcher's own point of view. The questions should be either subjective or objective on the type of information required. Questions stating or focusing directly on personal information such as income, expenditure level and bad habits, are usually not asked outright. Instead, a series of questions leading up to the relevant issue should be asked. A combination of negative and positive statements should be used to avoid any bias towards certain attitudes. For example:

1) Do you think the quality standard of the low priced hotel is not as good as that of the expensive one - negative attitude.
2) Frequently advertised brands of hotels are of a higher quality—positive attitude.

Sequence of Questions

The specific order in which the respondents receive the questions is a potential source of error. Use the following general guidelines in avoiding errors:

1) The opening question should be simple, objective and interesting, thus arousing the curiosity of the respondent towards the subject matter of the questionnaire.
2) The overall pattern of the questionnaire should be in a logical manner moving from one topic to another. Difficult questions should be placed towards the end of the questionnaire.
3) Initial questions should avoid providing a biased frame of reference or suggesting answers to following questions.

Design and Layout of a Questionnaire

In mail surveys, the physical appearance of the questionnaire is very important as the data collection instrument is self-administered. So, the questionnaire should encourage the respondents' cooperation. It should not appear to be a long one and especially, questions should be short and simple.

Reproduction of the questionnaire should be neatly done on quality grade paper. In general, a self-administered questionnaire should be printed on quality paper using an open format and type that is easy to read. The questions should be in sequence so that there is an ease of administration.

Finally, the response should be tabulated and subjected to computer analysis. Every response must be coded so that it facilitates in the final tabulation and analysis.

Pretest of Questionnaire

On a small selected sub-sample of the population, which the researcher is interested in, it is very useful to administer the questionnaire. This can result in valuable insight that might otherwise be expensive and difficult to obtain. A number of factors may be apparent at this stage, such as:

1) Whether the subject needs additional information regarding a question
2) The time consumed during the entire questionnaire
3) Whether the initial question has generated interest
4) Whether the questions are interpreted correctly
5) To narrow the alternatives, some options might have to be dropped

6) Do the answers require a premeditated thought ?
7) Are there any unnecessary questions ?

Pretesting a questionnaire has many benefits. It gives an interesting opportunity to experiment with various approaches to a given question or topic, examination of the effect of different question sequences, and potential insight into the existence of position bias in the location of either the questions of their possible answers. Such experimentation may be carried out by using alternative forms of the questionnaire and then comparing the responses obtained through each approach.

Final Draft of the Questionnaire

Once the pretesting process is over, some questions may be eliminated from the questionnaire, some close-ended questions may be changed to multiple choice questions or the sequence may be changed. Wording may also be changed and extra questions may be added to ensure a good questionnaire.

Thus, the final structure given to the questionnaire may serve the researcher's purpose.

Types of Questionnaires

A questionnaire can take any form, but they are generally categorised according to the structure and directness. Structure refers to the degree to which the questions and possible responses are formed and standardised. Questionnaires could be classified into two different categories:-

1) Structured

A structured questionnaire consistently and repeatedly follows the same pattern and leaves little scope for a respondent to say beyond the structured format. Structured questionnaires and interviews are very handy in large quantitative surveys.

2) Semi-structured

These types of questionnaires use a mixture of questions those with pre-decided answers as well as those where the respondents are free to express their own view.

3) Unstructured

Unstructured questionnaires usually consist of general questions directed at the research topic and allows the interviewer a great deal of freedom in formulating specific questions and probing for additional information as per requirements.

The type of questionnaire to be used by will depend on:

1) The nature of information your project requires
2) The number of people whom you would like to interview
3) The survey research mode you have selected
4) The nature of the respondents who are expected to provide the information required
5) The type of interviewers who will be administering the question.

Specimen Questionnaires

Here an attempt is made to provide the researchers a helpline to design their own survey instruments. Typical questionnaires related to consumer need determination, customer satisfaction survey, brand analysis, service quality and several others are included in Figs. 7.2 to 7.13.

QUESTIONNAIRE DESIGN I

Confidential Survey of Readers of Hospitality and Tourism Today

1) Did you read or look through any part of the current issue of Hospitality and Tourism Today?

   Yes ☐ No ☐ Haven't receive it yet ☐

   If "Yest" please continue.

   If "No" skip to question 3:

   If "Haven't received if yet," skip to question 5.

2) Have you read or do you plan to read any of the following articles and features which appear in the current issue of Hospitality and Tourism Today ? (Please check 1 box for each line.)

	Have read	Have not read: Plan to read	Have not read: Do not Plan to read
(a) What to do after a serious accident by .... (p. 15)	☐	☐	☐
(b) Travel and Leisure by ....(p. 26)	☐	☐	☐
(c) The Endless Drama of America by .... (p. 27)	☐	☐	☐
(d) Home by ....(p. 35)	☐	☐	☐
(e) EL Boom on Costa Del Sol by William A Krauss (p. 37)	☐	☐	☐
(f) The Gentle Thaw of the Four Seasons by .... (p. 41)	☐	☐	☐
(g) The Strange Rhapsody of Flight by .... (p. 43)	☐	☐	☐
(h) Dial-A-King by .... (p. 46)	☐	☐	☐
(i) Victoria, B.C. by .... (p. 51)	☐	☐	☐
(j) The Small Hotels of India by .... (p. 54)	☐	☐	☐

3) (a) Has your spouse read this issue.? Yes ☐ No ☐

   (b) In addition to yourself and your spouse, how many other adult (over 18) members of your household read or looked at your copy of the above issue of Hospitality and Tourism Today ?

   How many adults from outside your household?

	Number of men readers	Number of Women readers
	....	....
In your household (other than you or your spouse)	....	....
Outside your household	....	....

(Contd.)

4) After you have finished reading this issue of Hospitality and Tourism Today what will you do with it ?

(a) Keep it ☐

(b) It goes into a waiting room ☐

(c) Give it to a friend or relative ☐

(d) Discard it ☐

(e) Give it to a hospital or school ☐

(f) Other ☐

5) How many of the last three issues of Hospitality and Tourism Today have you read or looked through ?

One ☐ Two ☐ Three ☐ None ☐

6) Please indicate how much of an average issues you usually read.

Less than 1/3 ☐ 1/3 to 1/2 ☐ Over 1/2 ☐

7) How do you obtain your copies of Hospitality and Tourism Today ?

Paid Subscription ☐ Buy at newsstand ☐

Other (please specify) ☐

8) We would like to know if anything you read or saw in Hospitality and Tourism Today during the past year or two interested you sufficiently to induce you to talk about it or to take any of the sections below. You may check one or more boxes.

(a) Discussed articles with other ☐

(b) Visited a country or area ☐

(c) Decided on or modified a travel plan ☐

(d) Stayed at a hotel, motel etc. ☐

(e) Asked for more information on a product or service ☐

(f) Bought or ordered a product ☐

(g) What else? ....

If you gave any answer from "b" through "g", please jot down a short "case history" of the last time this happened.

....

....

(Contd.)

....

....

About you and your family (confidential information, for the statistical analysis of previous data).

1) Are you male or female ? Male ☐ Female ☐

2) What is your age ? Under 30 ☐ 45-49 ☐ 30-34 ☐ 50-54 ☐ 35-39 ☐ 54-64 ☐ 40-44 ☐ 45 or over ☐

3) Please indicate the highest level of schooling you reached. (check one)

Basic school ☐
Attended high school ☐
Graduated from high school ☐
Attended college ☐
Graduated from college ☐
Postgraduate study ☐

4) What is your title or position?

Manager ☐ Propietor ☐
Professional ☐ Sales/Clerical ☐
Other (Pl specify) ☐

5) What was your total household income before taxes in 20...... (Please include income from all household members and from all sources, such as wages, profits dividends, rentals. etc.)

Under

Rs. 3,00,000 ☐ Rs.1,50,000-8,00,000 ☐ Rs. 1,00,000-12,00,000 ☐
Rs. 3,00,000-5,00,000 ☐ Rs. 8,00,000- 9,00,000 ☐ Rs. 12,00,000-14,00,000 ☐
Rs. 5,90,000- 7,50,000 ☐ Rs. 9,60,000-1,00,000 ☐ Rs. 14,00,000-15,00,000 ☐

Thanks for your help.

Fig. 7.2: Specimen Questionnaire I: Confidential Survey of Readers of 'Hospitality and Tourism Today'

Analysis of a Bread Market

AKC Bakeries, a small, independent bakery, recently completed a series of focus groups designed primarily to help management "keep in touch with the market". Prior to conducting the focus group interviews, 95 open-ended telephone interviews are conducted. The purpose of the telephone interviews is to guide the development of the topic outline for the focus groups and to determine the appropriate compositions of the focus groups. A plus-one sample technique is used. The questionnaire is shown to in the focus group. Proposal that resulted from an analysis of the questionnaire results as follows:—

1) Is this a sound approach ?
2) Evaluate the questionnaire
3) Evaluate the topical outline for the focus group.
   (a) Focus Group Proposal
   (b) Composition and Scheduling.

Four group sessions of 6-12 bread consumers are conducted on four consecutive evenings, Jan 30, 31 Feb. 1 and 2, at 7-9 P.M. Individuals are recruited on the preceeding week from the individuals in the preliminary phone survey who indicated a willingness to participated in such groups. Additional calls asking a five or six qualifying questions and soliciting focus group cooperation, will allow us to "over recruit" for each group to ensure adequate attendance. Each group member is rewarded (Rs. 500) for his or her cooperation and will receive a reminder letter and phone call to again ensure maximum attendance.

The group sessions are conducted at Indian University Campus, Noida. Their facilities include a one-way corridor and small viewing room. Thus, all were welcome to attend one or more sessions if one so desires.

One major goal achieved in the premilinary phone interviews, as well as through the literature search, is to compose four reasonable segments of consumers, containing enough homogeneity to reduce conflicts (thus reducing inhibitions and increasing social interaction) and yet, maintaining enough heterogeneity to maintain interested and spirited discussions.

In terms of consumption patterns, the following categories has emerged:

Bread Consumed	Number of Consumption Units
(a) White Only	23
(b) White plus others	22
(c) Wheat only	16
(d) Whole wheat/whole grain only	30
(e) Entirely homemade	3
(f) No bread consumed	95

It was clear that there was some confusion in consumers minds between wheat, whole wheat, and whole grain. Therefore, those categories are not totally distinctive. However, the break-down by consumption patterns corresponds nicely with reasons why that consumption occurred, particularly in noting the extreme concern about nutrition/health/ fiber among whole wheat/whole grain users and the total lack of nutritional concern among white bread only users. The mixed and wheat groups seemed to be in the middle range on health and taste concerns. Therefore, it appears reasonable to make the first break on consumption patterns-

1) White only,
2) White plus,
3) Wheat only, and
3) Wheat/whole wheat/whole grains.

Groups 3 and 4 need an additional split because the distinctions in many consumers minds is less than clear. However, primarily blue collar families are purchasers of wheat bread, whereas managerial/professionals are purchasers of whole wheats and whole grains. Althoutgh both groups seemed about equally divided on taste and health reasons, the wheat purchasers are more concerned with "buying the cheapest". Also, an examination of their responses to brands indicated a lack of awareness of brands purchasesd e.g. possibly store wheat brands. Thus, there appears to be a strong relationship between occupation and bread consumption patterns. The third and fourth groups are, therefore, be segmented on occupational class: Group (3) = Wheat/WW/WG purchasers, either blue-collar families or white-collar (with no college), Group (4) = Wheat/WW/WG purchasers, either managerial/professionals or white-collar (with some college).

Further, there is an effort made to control for other variables in each group, including a good dispersion of young, middle-households; and a small percentage of males sprinkled among the predominantly female gatherings.

The proposed focus group topical outline given in Fig. 7.3:

Focus Group Topical Outline

QUESTIONNAIRE DESIGN II

Analysis of a Bread Market

1) Introduction:

   Study of bread consumption, being recorded; will tell them name of the baker. At the end of the session administer short questionnaire to first get some individual perspectives and for later analysis of reponses.

2) Bread Purchase :

   (a) Who purchases it ? (Who in the family decides on type of brand?)

   (b) Purchased how often?

   (c) When ?

   (d) Where ?

   (e) Why ?

   (f) Sales ?

   (g) Store brands purchased often ?

   (h) What is the different between store brands and other brands ?

3) Bread Consumption :

   (a) When do you eat it ?

   (b) Eating situations–toast, snack, sandwiches, major part of meal ?

   (c) How about other bread products- eaten when ?

   (d) Other family members- do they have different eating patterns ?

   (e) Different bread preferences ?

4) Bread Attitudes:

   (a) Why eat one type of bread rather than another ?

   (Do you eat what you prefer consumption vs. preference?)

   (b) Degree of weight concern ?

   (c) Texture ?

   (d) How much are you influenced by habbits ? (e.g. "what you were raised on ?")

   (e) Has your bread type changed in past five years ?

   (f) From what to what ?

   (g) Why ?

   (h) Has the amount of bread you eat changed ?

(Contd.)

(i) Why ?

(j) Other eating habits that might have caused you to switch ?

(k) Other activity habits that might have caused you to switch ?

5) Bread knowledge:

(a) What are the different types of bread ? (establish categories)

(b) What differentiates these types ? (list attributes)

(c) How do you know about breads ? (read labels, listen to ads, read articles)

(d) What about other bread products - rolls, muffins, French bread ?

6) Bread/Bakery Perceptions :

(a) What are the various brands on the market in Delhi ?

(b) What are your perceptions/feelings towards these brands/bakeries

(c) Why ?

(d) Where are these bakeries located ?

(e) What are the problems with the various alternatives on the market ? (high prices; nutrition/ fiber level; calories/ variety, firmer white breads)

(f) Show box of different loaves of bread; pick a loaf; sell us on it- how would you convince me to buy it or eat it ?

Have the other members discuss sales pitch? Repeat with a second loaf.

(g) Discuss (1) whole white (2) all natural loaf (or loaves) separately-

(I) what do you think of this ?

(II) Tried it ?

(III) Like it Why ?

(IV) Why not ?

(h) What suggestions would you like to give to a bakery for improvement on bread or bread alternatives ?

(i) Tell them the name of the sponsor: Obtain their reactions to this.

(j) Thank them. Give them some bread and say “Good Night”.

Fig. 7.3: Specimen Questionnaire II: Analysis of a Bread Market

QUESTIONNAIRE DESIGN III

Bread Consumption

Hello, my name is Ramesh and I'am taking a survey on people's bread consumption for a commercial bakery. May I speak to the main grocery shopper in the household ?

(Repeat it now. Persons comes on phone) (if unavailable, ask when it would be convenient to call again)

We are interested in your opinions about, the consumption of bread. This is strictly a survey. You will not be able to buy anything because of this. I would like to ask you eight brief questions about bread, if I may.

1) Think about the average consumption of bread on normal week at your house. About how many loaves of bread are consumed

   Large ☐ Regular ☐

   (if none, or nearly none, skip to question 7)

2) (a) What types or kinds of bread are consumed ?

   ....White................................

   ....Wheat................................

   ....Wholewheat................................

   ....Wholegrain................................

   ....Rye................................

   ....Souroddough................................

   ....Homemade................................

2) (b) Do you recall the brand names of any of these ?

   No ☐ Yes ☐

   (Interviewer : Rate confidence of respondent in brand awareness)

   High .... Moderate ....

   Low .... None ....

   (If more than one kind of bread is reported, ask question 2C)

2) (c). Are the different types eaten by different household members ?

   No ☐ Yes ☐?

(Contd.)

Who eats which type ?

Adult male ☐

Adult female ☐

Children ☐

3) (a) Are there particular meals or situations that influence the type of bread your household eats ?

No ....

Yes ....

(b) Would you describe them ?

Breakfast ....

Toast ....

Lunch ....

Sandwiches ....

Dinner ....

4) Where do you purchase most of your bread ?..................................

Why ?..................................

5) Why does your household eat the types of bread it does ? (Probe to record impressions)

....

....

6) Why does your household eat the amount of bread it does ? (Probe – why don't you eat either more or less bread ?)

....

....

7) What are the particular reasons that your household does not consume bread ?

....

....

8) Is there any advice you would like to give a bread bakery ?

....

....

Thanks, now I'd like to ask six questions about yourself so we can see if different groups of people think differently about bread.

Male .... Female ....

1) How many people are in your household ?

(a) ☐ (b) ☐ (c) ☐ (d) ☐

(e) ☐ (f) ☐ (g) ☐

(Contd.)

2) How many of these people are under 18 ?

   (a) ☐ (b) ☐ (c) ☐ (d) ☐

   (e) ☐ (f) ☐ (g) ☐

3) What is the age of the youngest member of your household ? ☐

4) Age of the oldest ? ☐

5) What is your occupation ?

   (a) Blue C ☐ (b) White C ☐ (c) Mgmt/ Prof ☐

6) What are the occupations of the other adults in your household ?

   (a) Blue C ☐ (b) White C ☐ (c) Mgmt/ Prof ☐

7) Number of other adults ☐

8) How far have you gone in school ?

   (a) GS ☐ (b) HS ☐ (c) SC ☐

   (d) CE ☐ (e) GD ☐

9) How far have the other adults in your household gone in school ?

   (a) GS ☐ (b) HS ☐ (c) SC ☐

   (d) CE ☐ (e) GD ☐

Thanks very much for your help. In a few weeks we are going to get four or five small groups of consumers together to discuss bread consumption. Of course, the group members will be paid for their time. Could we call you back and invite you to one of these sessions ?

No...............Yes...................

Name....................................

Phone ....

Time ....

Date..............................

Thanks again for all your help

Fig. 7.4: Specimen Questonnaire III: Analysis of Bread Consumption

(Contd.)

QUESTIONNAIRE DESIGN IV

For Restaurant Review

We request you to spare a few minutes of your precious time to review our restaurant. And tell us how we measure up on the following areas. Once you have completed this form, please place it in the suggestion box. Thanks for helping us to serve you better.

	Excellent	Good	Ok	Bad
Service:				
Courtesy	☺	☺	😐	☹
Speed	☺	☺	😐	☹
Food:				
Appearance	☺	☺	😐	☹
Taste	☺	☺	😐	☹
Cleanliness:				
Outside	☺	☺	😐	☹
Dining Areas	☺	☺	😐	☹
Toilets	☺	☺	😐	☹
Value for Money	☺	☺	😐	☹
Overall Experience	☺	☺	😐	☹

Date of Visit .... Time of Visit..............................

Outlet Visited..............................

Please Tick

Male ☐

Female ☐

Name.......................................

Date of Birth..............................

Date of Anniversary...................

Address....................................

....

....

....

Telephone..........................

(Contd.)

How often do you visit our Restaurant (s)/?

		Age Group	
Daily	☐	1-7	☐
Weekly	☐	8-12	☐
Monthly	☐	12-15	☐
		16-24	☐
Occasionally	☐	25-34	☐
		35-44	☐
		44+	☐

N.B.: Please contact the duty manager with any questions, complaints or suggestions to allow us to deal with them now, if possible.

Fig. 7.5: Specimen Questionnaire IV: For Restaurant Review

(Contd.)

QUESTIONNAIRE DESIGN V

For Launching of a New Product for a Hotel

Dear Respondent

I am a student of Indian School of Hospitality. As a part of my curriculum, I am conducting a survey and would be grateful if you could spare some of your precious time to fill this questionnaire. Please tick (✓) or circle ⊗ where appropriate.

1) Do you have a water plant in your hotel ?

   Yes ☐ No ☐

   If 'yes' go to Question 2 if 'No' go to Question 14

2) Which type/brand of the water plant is this ?
   - (a) Water Cooler ☐ Brand ☐
   - (b) Water Cooler and Water Purifier ☐ Brand ☐
   - (c) Mineral Water Cooler/Dispenser ☐ Brand ☐

3) Number of coolers and their brands installed in your premises
   - (a) Water Cooler ☐ Brand ☐
   - (b) Water Cooler and Water Purifier ☐ Brand ☐
   - (c) Mineral Water Cooler/Dispenser ☐ Brand ☐

4) Are you satisfied with it ? Yes ☐ No ☐

5) If not satisfied, list three reasons of your dissatisfaction.
   - (a) ....
   - (b) ....
   - (c) ....

6) Which water do you serve to your customers ?
   - (a) Mineral Water ....
   - (b) Tap Water ....
   - (c) Filtered Tap Water ....
   - (d) Any other (please specify) ....

7) In case you have a Mineral Water Dispenser, are you satisfied with its performance ?

   Yes ☐ No ☐

8) What is the kind of Mineral Water Dispenser that you use ?

   Plain & Cold ☐ Hot & Cold ☐ Any other ☐

(Contd.)

9) In case you use Hot and Cold model does it serve you real hot water for your tea/coffee ?

Yes ☐ No ☐

10) How is its performance ?

Excellent ☐ V. Good ☐ Good ☐ Fair ☐ Poor ☐

11) You bought your Mineral Water Dispenser from:

Showroom ☐ Salesman ☐ Any other ☐

12) You came to know about this product from:

(a)	Direct Mailer	☐	(e)	Existing User	☐
(b)	Press Advertisement	☐	(f)	Co. Salesman	☐
(c)	Dealer	☐	(g)	Interior Designer	☐
(d)	Direct Observation	☐	(h)	Any Other Source	☐

13) Why did you buy the above model ?

Price ☐ Brand ☐ Performance ☐ Any other ☐

14) Are you aware of any other brand for Mineral Water Dispenser ?

Yes ☐ No ☐

If yes (please name) ....

15) In case you do not have a Water Cooler/Mineral Dispenser, are you planning to buy one/or will consider buying one ?

Yes ☐ No ☐

16) Please rank any three of the following in order of preference for mineral Water Dispenser

(a) Sleek Looks and Finish ....

(b) Dependable Co./Brand ....

(c) Safety Features ....

(d) Performance ....

(e) After Sales Support ....

(d) Any other ....

17) Do you prefer Water Cooler over Mineral Water Dispenser ?

Yes ☐ No ☐

(Please 'tick' (✓) wherever applicable)

If 'yes' why ? : ....

(a) Recurring cost of mineral water : ....

(b) Less dependable product : ....

(c) Ordinary Water Cooler with filter is just as good : ....

(d) No good brand is available : ....

(e) Poor After Sales Service of the Company : ....

(Contd.)

If 'no' why ?

(a) Mineral water projects that you have more concern for your customers

(b) Mineral water is better than filtererd water

(c) Mineral water dispenser are sleeker than ordinary Water Coolers and fits with interiors

(d) Ordinary water coolers have planning problems

(e) Non availability of water

18) You would prefer

Hot & cold version ☐ Plain & cold version ☐

19) Mineral water is safer than filtered (purified) water

Yes ☐ No ☐ Equally Safe ☐

20) How do you measure following parameters of Mineral Water Dispenser using 5 point scale.

	Excellent	Very Good	Good	Fair	Poor
(a) Performance	☐	☐	☐	☐	☐
(b) After Sales Support	☐	☐	☐	☐	☐
(c) Appearance	☐	☐	☐	☐	☐
(d) Cooling Capacity	☐	☐	☐	☐	☐
(e) Dependable Company	☐	☐	☐	☐	☐

21) Kindly rate the following on 5-point scale

(SA = Strongly Agree, A = Agree, N = Neutral, D = Disagree, SD = Strongly Disagree)

	SA	A	N	D	SD
(a) It is important to serve hygienically clean water to your customers/staff	—	—	—	—	—
(b) Mineral Water is just for image projection, water Filter is equally effective and less costly.	—	—	—	—	—
(c) Serving Mineral Water is critical for your business.	—	—	—	—	—
(d) Cost of replacing mineral water jars is more than the benefit of serving mineral water	—	—	—	—	—
(e) Buying dispenser from a mineral water company ties you to buy Mineral Water from the same company	—	—	—	—	—
(f) The product should be from a dependable national	—	—	—	—	—
(g) The model should be available in various sizes company and cooling capacities	—	—	—	—	—
(h) The product should have efficient after sales support	—	—	—	—	—

(Contd.)

(i)	I would prefer to buy a dispenser and mineral water from the same company	—	—	—	—	—
(j)	Mineral water dispenser from all companies are almost similar in quality & technology	—	—	—	—	—

Please see the photograph of the product from Blue Star

22) If Blue Star offers you this product how would you rate (1 as highest and 7 as lowest)

	1	2	3	4	5	6	7	Brand owned by You	Blue Star	Your Preference
(a) Quality	☐	☐	☐	☐	☐	☐	☐	☐	☐	☐
(b) Looks	☐	☐	☐	☐	☐	☐	☐	☐	☐	☐
(c) Reliability	☐	☐	☐	☐	☐	☐	☐	☐	☐	☐
(d) Cost	☐	☐	☐	☐	☐	☐	☐	☐	☐	☐

23) Please rank the features in order of preference

(a) Sleek looks ☐

(b) Bimetal sensors to protect overheading ☐

(c) Less space ☐

(d) Static condenser for no noise ☐

(e) Spill proof bottle holder for no mess ☐

24) Anything you like about the product? ....

25) Anything you do not like about the product ? ....

26) How much would you like to pay for this product ? ....

27) How would you like to buy the product?

(a) From a showroom ☐

(b) Company salesman ☐

(c) Any other (pl. specify) ☐

28) Number of employees in your organisation. ....

29) Average number of visitors/customers who visit your establishment every day. ....

30) Average number of glasses (or water) consumed every day.

Summers ☐

Winters ☐

(Contd.)

31) What newspaper do you read ?

(a) Hindustan Times ☐ (d) Times of India ☐ (g) Pioneer ☐

(b) Economic Times ☐ (e) Business Standard ☐ (h) Financial Express ☐

(c) Nev Bharat Times ☐ (f) Punjab Kesari ☐ (i) Any other ☐

32) What magazines do you read ?

(a) India Today ☐ (c) Business Today ☐ (e) Business World ☐

(b) Business India ☐ (d) Architecture & Design ☐ (f) Any other ☐

33) Do you listen to FM Radio ?

Yes ☐ No ☐

If yes, at what time during the day (you may mention more than one timing)

....

....

....

....

Please tell us something about yourself

Name ....

Designation ....

Company/Organisation ....

Address ....

....

Telephone Number .... Mobile.........................

Fax No ....

We thank you for your co-operation

For the Surveyor

(Please tick the segment)

(a) Office ....

(b) Showroom (which product showroom) ....

(c) Restaurant/Hotel ....

Name of surveyor: ....

Date: ....

Fig. 7.6: Specimen Questionnaire V : For Launching of a New Product for a Hotel

QUESTIONNAIRE DESIGN VI

Soft Drinks: Study of Coka and Pepsi Brand

Dear Respondent,

I am a student of Hospitality and Tourism. As a part of my curriculum, I am conducting a survey and would be grateful if you could spare some of your precious time to fill this questionnaire. Please tick (√) your responses at the appropriate space provided in the question.

1) When you talk of soft drink which all brands comes to your mind, please specify (In order of recall):

   ....

   ....

   ....

2) Which brand of soft drink do you generally consume ?

   ....

3) If you don't get the drink of your choice, then do you change your brand ?

   (a) Yes ☐ (b) No ☐

4) In Cola drinks which do you prefer

   (a) Coca-Cola ☐ (b) Pepsi ☐

5) Please rate the following parameters on the 7 point scale for the two brands (score 1 being highest 7 the lowest)

	1	2	3	4	5	6	7	Cocacola	Pepsi
(a) Popular ability	—	—	—	—	—	—	—	☐	☐
(b) Packing attractive	—	—	—	—	—	—	—	☐	☐
(c) Fizz	—	—	—	—	—	—	—	☐	☐
(d) Availability	—	—	—	—	—	—	—	☐	☐
(f) Taste	—	—	—	—	—	—	—	☐	☐
(f) Fits your life-style	—	—	—	—	—	—	—	☐	☐

6) Do you like the bottle of Coca Cola and Pepsi

   Coca-Cola Yes ☐ No ☐

   Pepsi Yes ☐ No ☐

7) What according to you are the most attractive attributes associated with Pepsi that makes it (a better brand than Coca-Cola in India ?

   (Rate on a scale of 1-5, 1 is max. and 7 5 is min.):

   (a) Availability ....

   (b) Indianisation of the brand ....

(Contd.)

(c) Advertising ....

(d) Promotional activities ....

(e) Fountain Pepsi ....

8) "Always the Real Thing" is the Tag line of:

Pepsi	☐	Coca-Cola	☐
Campa-Cola	☐	Fanta	☐
Mirinda	☐	Thums-Up	☐

9) Do you remember any Tag Line of Pepsi ?

Yes ☐ No ☐

10) If yes, then which one ? Please state

....

....

11. If you are told about Pepsi, what kind of person comes to your mind ?

....

....

12. If you are told about Coca-Cola, what kind of person comes to your mind ?

....

....

Respondent's Particulars

Name : ....

Age : ....

Occupation : ....

Family monthly Income : Rs. 5,000-10,000 ☐ Rs. 10,001-15,000 ☐

Rs. 15001-20,000 ☐ Rs. 20,001 & above ☐

Thank you for your value and co-operation.

Fig. 7.7: Specimen Questionnaire VI : Soft Drinks: Study of Coca and Pepsi Brand

QUESTIONNAIRE DESIGN VII

Coke and Pepsi Vendors/Retailers

Dear Respondent,

I am a student of Hospitality and Tourism. As part of my curriculum, I am conducting a survey and would be grateful if you could spare come of your precious time to fill this questionnaire for the same. Please (√) where appropriate.

1) Which brand of Cola does the consumer generally asks for ?
   Rank them in descending order of preference (4 as max. and 1 as min.)

   (a) Coca-Cola ☐

   (b) Pepsi ☐

   (c) Thums-Up ☐

   (d) Campa-Cola ☐

2) Why do you think that consumer asks for a particular brand of Cola ?

   (Rate the following attributes on a 5 point scale 5 is max. & 1 is min).

	5	4	3	2	1
(a) More popular	☐	☐	☐	☐	☐
(b) Taste	☐	☐	☐	☐	☐
(c) Influence	☐	☐	☐	☐	☐
(d) Fits with his personality	☐	☐	☐	☐	☐
(e) Availability	☐	☐	☐	☐	☐
(f) Promotional activities	☐	☐	☐	☐	☐
(g) He likes the bottle	☐	☐	☐	☐	☐
(h) Fizz	☐	☐	☐	☐	☐

3) What are the attributes that influence you to decide which brand of cola to stock ?

   (Rank them on a 5 point scale of 5 max. 7 as min.)

(a) Company support	☐	☐	☐	☐	☐
(b) Brand name	☐	☐	☐	☐	☐
(c) Customer pull	☐	☐	☐	☐	☐
(d) Promotional schemes	☐	☐	☐	☐	☐

(Contd.)

4) Indicate your satisfaction level with Pepsi, regarding the following parameters.
(Rate these on 5 point scale where 5 is highly satisfied and 1 is highly dissatisfied):

	5	4	3	2	1
(a) Credit	☐	☐	☐	☐	☐
(b) Timely delivery	☐	☐	☐	☐	☐
(c) Replacement	☐	☐	☐	☐	☐
(d) Promotional activities	☐	☐	☐	☐	☐
(e) POP material	☐	☐	☐	☐	☐
(f) Commissions	☐	☐	☐	☐	☐
(g) Complaint handling	☐	☐	☐	☐	☐
(h) Company support	☐	☐	☐	☐	☐
(i) Advertising	☐	☐	☐	☐	☐

5) Indicate with Coca-Cola on the following parameters
(Rate these on the 5 point scale where 5 is highly satisfied and is highly dissatisfied):

	5	4	3	2	1
(a) Credit	☐	☐	☐	☐	☐
(b) Timely delivery	☐	☐	☐	☐	☐
(c) Replacement	☐	☐	☐	☐	☐
(d) Promotional activities	☐	☐	☐	☐	☐
(e) POP material	☐	☐	☐	☐	☐
(f) Commissions	☐	☐	☐	☐	☐
(g) Complaint handling	☐	☐	☐	☐	☐
(h) Company support	☐	☐	☐	☐	☐
(i) Advertising	☐	☐	☐	☐	☐

6) Does the promotional schemes of a company have any effect on the sale of the rival brand ?

Yes ☐ No ☐

Thank you for your co-operation:

Dealer Details

Name of the dealer ....

Address ....

....

....

Phone Number ....

Fig. 7.8: Specimen Questionnaire Design VII: Coce and Pepsi Vendors/Retailers

QUESTIONNAIRE DESIGN VIII

Study of Attributes of Hospitality Employees

Name of the hospitality employee : ....

Age : ....

Address : ....

Qualification : ....

Place of Work : ....

Speciality : ....

1) How many guest visit your hotel in a week ? ....

2) Which corporate guest have visited you in the last week ? ....

3) Does any of these corporate guest visited your hotel ? ....

(Please mention three companies)

Air India	☐	Reliance	☐
Sahara	☐	AIR France	☐
TATA	☐	WTO	☐
Rainbuxy	☐	UNDP	☐

4) What are the attributes which makes you attentive during the visit by a guest ? (Please mention at least three).

....

....

....

5) Rate the following attributes for the three corporate house you like most in the box provided below.

('1' being maximum and '10' being minimum)

		Name of the corporate house 1	2	3
(a) Attributes				
(b) Courtesy	1.....2.....3.....4.....5.....6.....7.....8.....9.....10	☐	☐	☐
(c) Well dressed	1.....2.....3.....4.....5.....6.....7.....8.....9.....10	☐	☐	☐
(d) Soft spoken	1.....2.....3.....4.....5.....6.....7.....8.....9.....10	☐	☐	☐

(Contd.)

		Name of the corporate house		
(e) Good communication skill	1.....2.....3.....4.....5.....6.....7.....8.....9.....10	☐	☐	☐
(f) Good product knowledge	1.....2.....3.....4.....5.....6.....7.....8.....9.....10	☐	☐	☐
(g) Assertive	1.....2.....3.....4.....5.....6.....7.....8.....9.....10	☐	☐	☐
(h) Regularity	1.....2.....3.....4.....5.....6.....7.....8.....9.....10	☐	☐	☐
(i) Friendly	1.....2.....3.....4.....5.....6.....7.....8.....9.....10	☐	☐	☐
j) Overall satisfaction	1.....2.....3.....4.....5.....6.....7.....8.....9.....10	☐	☐	☐

6) Please rate on 'five' point scale the following parameters considered by you in the detailing process of Market Research (MR) ?

(1 as max and 5 as min)

(a) Opening	1	2	3	4	5
(b) Interesting	1	2	3	4	5
(c) Clarity	1	2	3	4	5
(d) Precise	1	2	3	4	5
(e) Product knowledge	1	2	3	4	5
(f) Objection handling	1	2	3	4	5
(g) Asking for business	1	2	3	4	5
(h) Aggressive	1	2	3	4	5
(i) Assertive	1	2	3	4	5
j) Rationality	1	2	3	4	5

7. Whether you prescribe regularly the products detailed by corporate guest you like most ? Name of the company: Corporate House:

Yes ☐ No ☐ Depends ☐ Can't say ☐

Thank you for your co-operation

Fig. 7.9: Specimen Questionnaire Design VIII: Study of Attributes of Hospitality Employees

QUESTIONNAIRE DESIGN IX

Guest/Consumer Behaviour Study

Dear Respondent,

I am the student of hospitality and tourism marketing. As part of curriculum I am conducting on consumer behaviour for colour TV. I shall be greatful if you kindly spare some of your valuable time to response to following questions. Kindly circle (✓) where appropriate.

1) How many Colour TV Sets do you have ?

One ☐ Two ☐ More than two ☐

2) Which brands of Colour TV Sets do you have ?

BPL ☐ Akai ☐ Onida ☐
Sony ☐ Videocon ☐ Any other (Pl. specify) ☐

3) What do you like best in your televisions ?

Aesthetic ☐ Brand Name ☐ Sound quality ☐
Picture quality ☐ Price ☐ Others (Specify) ☐

4) Any problem in functioning of present TV Set ?

Yes ☐ No ☐

If you face problems

please specify three problems 1) ....

2) ....

3) ....

5) Which three brands of CTV immediately comes to your mind.

1. ....
2. ....
3. ....

6) Which TV set you would own next time ?

BPL ☐ Videocon ☐ Akai ☐ Sony ☐
LG ☐ Samsung ☐ Other (Pl. specify) ☐

7) What all features you will look while changing or buying a new TV set ?

Sound quality ☐ Picture quality ☐ No. of brands ☐ Brand name ☐
Price ☐ Warranty ☐ After sales service ☐
Any other (Pl. specify) ☐

(Contd.)

8) How much budget will you make while changing or buying a new TV set ?

Below Rs. 13000	☐	Rs. 13,001-16,000	☐
Rs. 16,001-19,000	☐	Rs. Above 19,001	☐

9) How would you rate the below mentioned schemes and offers on a scale of 1 to 3. (3, very much, 1 not at all)

	3	2	1
(a) Discounts schemes	☐	☐	☐
(b) Exchange offer	☐	☐	☐
(c) Complementary gifts	☐	☐	☐
(d) Finance schemes	☐	☐	☐

10) Whom would you consult while making your decisions ?

Friends	☐	Family	☐	Advertisement	☐
Dealers	☐	Solely self	☐		

11) What according to you is the best time to buy ?

Occasions (marriage etc.)	☐	Festival seasons	☐
Special events (sports events etc.)	☐	Not Specific	☐

Something about you. ....

....

12) Please indicate your monthly household income

Below Rs. 50,000	☐	Rs. 50,000-1,00,000	☐
Rs. 1,00,000-1,50,000	☐	Rs. above 1,50,000	☐

13)

Age		**Occupation**		**Region**		**Education**	
Below 18	☐	Service	☐	North	☐	10+2	☐
18-25	☐	Self-employed	☐	East	☐	Graduate/Post-graduate	☐
25-40	☐	Business	☐	West	☐	Professional	☐
Above 40	☐	Student	☐	South	☐	Any other	☐
				Central	☐		

Respondent Name ....

Address ....

Phone: ....

Thank you for your kind co-operation and time.

Fig. 7.10: Specimen Questionnaire Design IX: Guest/Consumer Behaviour Study

QUESTIONNAIRE DESIGN X

Guest experieance is a restaurant

(Example of a Restaurant)

Part 1—Guest Satisfaction Survey

We would like your impresssion about how well this restaurant provides service relative to your expectations. Please think about the two levels of expectations defined below :

Minimum Service Level: the minimum level of service performance you consider adequate.

Desired Service Level: the level of service performance you desire.

For each of the following statements, please indicate:

(a) your *minimum service level* by circling one of the numbers in the first column;

(b) your *desired service level* by circling one of the numbers in the second column, and

(c) your *perception of service* by circling one of the numbers in the third column.

When it comes to..	**Minimum service level is:** Low High	**Deesired service level is:** Low High	**Perception of performance in the restaurant is:** Low High No Opinion
1) Prompt service to guests	1 2 3 4 5 6 7 8 9	1 2 3 4 5 6 7 8 9	1 2 3 4 5 6 7 8 9 N
2) Employees who are with guests in a caring fashion	1 2 3 4 5 6 7 8 9	1 2 3 4 5 6 7 8 9	1 2 3 4 5 6 7 8 9 N
3) Employees who deal with guest in a caring fashion	1 2 3 4 5 6 7 8 9	1 2 3 4 5 6 7 8 9	1 2 3 4 5 6 7 8 9 N
4) Providing services at the promised time	1 2 3 4 5 6 7 8 9	1 2 3 4 5 6 7 8 9	1 2 3 4 5 6 7 8 9 N
5) Employees who understand the needs of their guests	1 2 3 4 5 6 7 8 9	1 2 3 4 5 6 7 8 9	1 2 3 4 5 6 7 8 9 N
6) Visually appealing materials associated with the service (e.g., in-restaurant signs)	1 2 3 4 5 6 7 8 9	1 2 3 4 5 6 7 8 9	1 2 3 4 5 6 7 8 9 N
7) Having the guest' best interest at heart	1 2 3 4 5 6 7 8 9	1 2 3 4 5 6 7 8 9	1 2 3 4 5 6 7 8 9 N
8) Willingness to help guests	1 2 3 4 5 6 7 8 9	1 2 3 4 5 6 7 8 9	1 2 3 4 5 6 7 8 9 N
9) Maintaining error-free records	1 2 3 4 5 6 7 8 9	1 2 3 4 5 6 7 8 9	1 2 3 4 5 6 7 8 9 N
10) Keeping guests informed about when services will be performed	1 2 3 4 5 6 7 8 9	1 2 3 4 5 6 7 8 9	1 2 3 4 5 6 7 8 9 N
11) Providing services as promised	1 2 3 4 5 6 7 8 9	1 2 3 4 5 6 7 8 9	1 2 3 4 5 6 7 8 9 N
12) Employees who instill confidence in guest	1 2 3 4 5 6 7 8 9	1 2 3 4 5 6 7 8 9	1 2 3 4 5 6 7 8 9 N
13) Employees who have the knowledge to answer guests questions	1 2 3 4 5 6 7 8 9	1 2 3 4 5 6 7 8 9	1 2 3 4 5 6 7 8 9 N

(Contd.)

	When it comes to..	Minimum service level is: Low High	Deesired service level is: Low High	Perception of performance in the restaurant is: Low High No Opinion
14)	Dependability in handling guests service problems	1 2 3 4 5 6 7 8 9	1 2 3 4 5 6 7 8 9	1 2 3 4 5 6 7 8 9 N
15)	Readiness to respond to guests request	1 2 3 4 5 6 7 8 9	1 2 3 4 5 6 7 8 9	1 2 3 4 5 6 7 8 9 N
16)	Performing services right the first time	1 2 3 4 5 6 7 8 9	1 2 3 4 5 6 7 8 9	1 2 3 4 5 6 7 8 9 N
17)	Visually appealing restaurant	1 2 3 4 5 6 7 8 9	1 2 3 4 5 6 7 8 9	1 2 3 4 5 6 7 8 9 N
18)	Giving guest individual attention	1 2 3 4 5 6 7 8 9	1 2 3 4 5 6 7 8 9	1 2 3 4 5 6 7 8 9 N
19)	Employees who have a neat, professional appearance	1 2 3 4 5 6 7 8 9	1 2 3 4 5 6 7 8 9	1 2 3 4 5 6 7 8 9 N
20)	Convenient business hours	1 2 3 4 5 6 7 8 9	1 2 3 4 5 6 7 8 9	1 2 3 4 5 6 7 8 9 N
21)	Modern fixtures	1 2 3 4 5 6 7 8 9	1 2 3 4 5 6 7 8 9	1 2 3 4 5 6 7 8 9 N
22)	Making customers feel safe in their transactions.	1 2 3 4 5 6 7 8 9	1 2 3 4 5 6 7 8 9	1 2 3 4 5 6 7 8 9 N

Part II–Rating Quality, Value and Features

1) How would you rate the overall quality of service provided by the restaurant ? (Circle one number below):

Extremely Poor								Extremely Good
1	2	3	4	5	6	7	8	9

2) Thinking about service overall, please rate the value you feel you get for your money. (Circle one number below):

Extremely Poor								Extremely Good
1	2	3	4	5	6	7	8	9

3) Listed below are five general features pertaining to restaurant and the services they offer. We would like to know how important each of these features is to you when evaluate its quality of service.

Please allocate a total of 100 points among the five features according to how important each feature is to you–the more important a feature is to you, the more points you should give it.

(Contd.)

Please be sure the points you give add up to 100.

(a) The appearance of the restaurant's physical facilities, fixtures, personnel, and communications material ....Points

(b) The restaurant's ability to perform the promised services dependably and accurately ....Points

(c) The restaurant's willingness to help customers and provide prompt service ....Points

(d) The knowledge and courtesy of the restaurant's employees and their ability to convey trust and confidence ....Points

(e) The carying, individualized attention the restaurant provides its guest ....Points

Total Points Allocated **100 Points**

Part III–Rating Quality, Value and Features

Based on your overall experience with service in the restaurant, please indicate how likely you are to take the following actions. Circle the number that indicates your likelihood of taking each action.

How likely are you to...	Not at all likely						Extremely likely
1) Say positive things about to other people ?	1	2	3	4	5	6	7
2) Recommened to someone who seeks your advice ?	1	2	3	4	5	6	7
3) Encourage friends and relatives to do business with ?	1	2	3	4	5	6	7
4) Consider your first choice to buy the types of services that it provides ?	1	2	3	4	5	6	7'
5) Do more business within the next few years ?	1	2	3	4	5	6	7
6) Do less business within the next few years ?	1	2	3	4	5	6	7
7) Take some of your business to a competitor that offers more attractive precies	1	2	3	4	5	6	7
8) Continue to do business with if its prices increased somewhat ?	1	2	3	4	5	6	7
9) Pay a higher price than other restaurant charge for the benefits you currently receive from ?	1	2	3	4	5	6	7'

(Contd.)

How likely are you to...	Not at all likely						Extremely likely
10) Switch to another restaurant if you experience a problem with service ?	1	2	3	4	5	6	7
11) Complain to other consumers if you experience a problem with service ?	1	2	3	4	5	6	7
12) Complain to restaurant employees if you experience a problem with service ?	1	2	3	4	5	6	7
13) Complain to external agencies, if you experience a problem with service ?	1	2	3	4	5	6	7

Part IV–For Statistical Purposes Only

The following questions are for statistical purposes only. Your answers will be combined with others and will be kept strictly confidential.

For each question, please circle (o) one number.

1) How long have you been a guest in this hotel ?
   (a) Less than 1 year 1
   (b) 1 to less than 2 years.................................. 2
   (c) 2 to less than 5 years 3
   (d) 5 years or more.. 4

2. How frequently do you have face-to-face or telephone contact with employees ?
   (a) More than once a month.............................. 1
   (b) once a month... 2
   (c) About once every three months 3
   (d) About once every six months 4
   (e) About once a year 5
   (f) Less than one a year 6

3. Have you recently had a problem with any of the serves ?
   (a) Yes 1
   (b) No 2
   (If "No" skip to question 5)

4. If you did have a problem, was it resolved to your satisfaction ?
   (a) Yes 1
   (b) No 2

(Contd.)

5. Your sex is:
   - (a) Male 1
   - (b) Female 2
6. Your marital status is:
   - (a) Single 1
   - (b) Married 2
7. Your age is:
   - (a) Under 25 1
   - (b) 25-34 2
   - (c) 35-44 3
   - (d) 45-54.. 4
   - (e) 55-64 5
   - (f) 65 or over 6
8. Your total annual family income is:
   - (a) Under Rs. 199,990....................................... 1
   - (b) Rs. 200,000–Rs. 39,9990 2
   - (c) Rs. 400,000–Rs. 59,9990 3
   - (d) Rs.600,000–Rs. 79,9990 4
   - (e) Rs. 800,000–Rs. 99,9990 5
   - (f) Rs. 100,0000 or above 6
9. Highest level schooling you have completed is:
   - (a) High school or less 1
   - (b) Some college 2
   - (c) College graduate 3
   - (d) Any other qualification 4
     (please mention)
10. Your rationality
    - (a) British 1
    - (b) American 2
    - (c) German 3
    - (d) Italian 4
    - (e) Franch 5
    - (f) Swiss 6
    - (g) Chinese 7
    - (h) Other (Please specify) 8

Fig. 7.11: Specimen Questionnaire Design X: Guest Experieance is a Restaurant

QUESTIONNAIRE DESIGN XI

Hospitality Customer Survey

Instructions

Please tick (✓) the appropriate number or write your answer in the space provided.

All information will remain anonymous and completely confidential.

Thank you for responding to our survey. Your answers will help us improve our services and products.

1) Which hotel do you stay most often ?
   1) .... One star
   2) .... Two star
   3) .... Three star
   4) .... Four star
   5) .... Five star
   6) .... Five star
2) How many times do you visit that particular hotel during a month ?
   On average............. times (If you don't visit please write '0')
3) How long have you been a guest of this hotel ?............... years
4) Please indicate how satisfied you are with each of the following items:

Very Satisfied	(4)	VS
Somewhat Satisfied	(3)	SS
Somewhat Dissatisfied	(2)	SD
Very Dissatisfied	(1)	VD

	VS	SS	SD	VD
(a) Availability of the General Manager	4	3	2	1
(b) Overall speed of service you receive at the	4	3	2	1
(c) Speed of service you receive	4	3	2	1
(d) Friendliness of employees	4	3	2	1
(e) Employee knowledge of hotelieing	4	3	2	1
(f) Willingness of employees to solve your problems	4	3	2	1
(g) Employee familiarity with you	4	3	2	1
(h) Speed of service you receive from tellers	4	3	2	1
(i) Hours the hotel is open	4	3	2	1
(j) Courtesy of employees	4	3	2	1
(k) Accuracy with which your requests for service (such as guest bills, account transfers, paperwork preparation) are handed	4	3	2	1

(Contd.)

	VS	SS	SD	VD
(l) Availability of automated machines	4	3	2	1
(m) Availability of parking at the hotel	4	3	2	1
(n) Adequacy of drive-in facilities	4	3	2	1
(o) Ability of service representatives to present the product and services that would be most beneficial to you	4	3	2	1
(Answer "P" and "Q" only if you have applied for a loan at the bank)				
(p) Speed of response to your requirements	4	3	2	1
(q) Ease of the requirements process	4	3	2	1

5) Do you consider this hotel to be your primary or main property to stay ?

Yes ☐ No ☐

6) Please indicate which services you are currently using with hotel or other hotel. Circle (O) the number in the appropriate column for each service you have.

	This hotel	Other Hotel
Reception	1	2
Guest Rooms	1	2
Restaurants	1	2
Room Service	1	2
Lounge	1	2
Bar	1	2
Checkout	1	2

7) What are the names of the other hotels with which you have stayed ?

....

8) Have you reserved accommodation in any other hotel within the past year ?

Yes ☐ No ☐ (If no, please go to question 9)

(a) What kind of hotel was it ? ....

(b) Where did you reserved accommodation ? ....

(c) Why did you select that hotel ? ....

9) Have you stopped staying in any other hotel ?

Yes ☐ No ☐ (If no, please go to question 10)

(a) What type of hotel you stopped to stay ? ....

(b) What type was it with ? ....

(c) What was your reason for not reserving room in that hotel ? ....

(Contd.)

10) What is your age ?

11) What is the highest level of formal education you've completed ?

   1) .... Middle ☐
   2) .... 10+2 ☐
   3) .... Graduate ☐
   4) .... Post Graduate ☐
   5) .... Technical/Vocational ☐

12) Are you ... 1. single ☐ 2. married ☐ 3. divorced/widowed ☐?

13) What was your total household income last year, before taxes ?

   (a) .... Under Rs. 150,000
   (b) .... Rs. 150,000 to Rs. 1,90,999
   (c) .... Rs. 200,000 to Rs. 2,90,999
   (d) .... Rs. 300,000 to Rs. 4,90,999
   (e) .... Rs. 500,000 to Rs. 7,40,999
   (f) .... Rs. 7,50,000 or more

Thank you for your co-operation and your answers.

Fig. 7.12: Specimen Questionnaire Design XI: Hospitality Guest Customer Survey

QUESTIONNAIRE DESIGN XII

Hospitality Guest (Customer) Survey

Thank you for visiting the Indian Valley, Manesar. Our entire staff believes in service excellence. We trust your stay with us is most enjoyable.

We would welcome your comments regarding our services and facilities. Your impressions will help us in maintaining the high standards our esteemed guests expect. Please spare a moment to complete this card. You may leave it with the concierge or mail it at your convenience. All of us at the Indian Valley thank you.

I. Optional

Please provide the following information:

Arrival Date: ..../........../..........

Name...

Mailing Address...

City.............................State.............................Code.............................

Telephone/Fax________________________________

This Information is strictly confidential and for evaluation response only.

II. Guest Evaluation

	Excellent	Good	Fair	Poor
1. Reception				
(a) Greeting upon arrival	☐	☐	☐	☐
(b) Check-in experience	☐	☐	☐	☐
(c) Reservation information	☐	☐	☐	☐
(d) Luggage handling	☐	☐	☐	☐
(e) Parking facilities	☐	☐	☐	☐
(f) Message and wake up call services	☐	☐	☐	☐
2. Guest Rooms				
(a) Quality of guest room	☐	☐	☐	☐
(b) Quality of bathroom	☐	☐	☐	☐
3. The Restaurant				
(a) Service and ambiance	☐	☐	☐	☐
(b) Food selection and quality	☐	☐	☐	☐
(c) Overall restaurant	☐	☐	☐	☐

	Excellent	Good	Fair	Poor
4. Room Service				
(a) Friendly and knowledgeable order-taker	☐	☐	☐	☐
(b) Menu selection and food quality	☐	☐	☐	☐
(c) Delivery and clearing of order	☐	☐	☐	☐
5. Lounge				
(a) Service	☐	☐	☐	☐
(b) Atmosphere	☐	☐	☐	☐
6. Check-Out				
(a) Accuracy of bill	☐	☐	☐	☐
(b) Offer for Express check-out	☐	☐	☐	☐
(c) Overall check-out procedure	☐	☐	☐	☐
(d) Friendliness of Guest Service Agent	☐	☐	☐	☐
(e) How would you rate the hotel ?	☐	☐	☐	☐

(f) Would you return to the hotel on your next visit to the area ? Yes ☐ No ☐

(g) Is there anything in particular you liked or disliked about the hotel ?

....

(h) Are there any employee(s) who deserves special recognition for providing outstanding service ?..

(i) How did you hear about this hotel ?

Travel Agent ☐ Newspaper Ad ☐ Company ☐

Personal Referral ☐ Other (Specify) : ....

Fig. 7.13: Specimen Questionnaire Design XII: Hospitality Guest (Customer) Survey

8

Collection of Primary and Secondary Data

After deciding to use a questionnaire to complement your interviews and focus group training needs assessments, you carefully construct the questionnaire, involve everyone you can think of in the development phase, pilot test it, revise it, and send it out to your specified target group.

By using some important guidelines, you can dramatically improve the quantity and quality of information gathered by surveys, questionnaires, and other paper-and-pencil assessments.

Several major issues can make or break the relevance of information gathered through questionnaires. If your questionnaires don't go to a representative sample of your target audience, or if the sample that receives them won't complete them, then most of your important development and design effort has been wasted. Three questions are key:-

1) How can you ensure a representative sample when administering organizational questionnaires?
2) How can you determine what sample size is appropriate for your data gathering procedure?
3) How can you increase compliance to complete and return questionnaires?

Random and Representative

Once you have developed your questionnaire, you must define your target audience. That often involves an agonizing–and sometimes mysterious–process. The first critical decision is whether to send the survey to everyone in the target audience or to a representative sample.

In survey research, a general rule is "the more data, the merrier." Each time you administer a questionnaire to a sample group, you create a "soft" intervention. It may be worthwhile to include all in your target audience; that sends the message that everyone's feedback is important and will be considered in organizational change efforts.

It is not feasible or necessary to administer the questionnaire to all of your target audience, consider using a sample. A representative sample of a target audience allows you to generalize the results effectively to apply to the entire target audience. Sampling procedures can be more economical in terms of time and expense for such items as data analysis, key punching, and postage.

In making the decision to use a sample rather than the entire target audience, remember two important concepts – it must be random and it must be representative.

A random sample means that everyone in the target audience has an equal opportunity to be selected to complete your organizational questionnaire. If the employees you use are not sample selected from the target audience, the sample you select can strongly influence your results. That could make it hard to accurately generalize your questionnaire findings to apply to the entire organization.

Let's look at an example with a training needs-analysis questionnaire involving a hotel chain having three hotels of 500 employees each. You decide that it is not feasible to send out 1,500 questionnaires, so you will sample from the three hotels.

First, you hand-pick 50 sample employees whom you know personally; because you know you can count on them to complete the questionnaire. Next, you go to your organizational phone book and take the first 100 names. You send out 150 questionnaires and are happy to receive 100 back.

You quickly analyze the data and brief the division managers on your findings. But one of the hotel managers refuses to accept the results, because less than 10 percent of the sample from that hotel are included in the findings. He disregards all of your questionnaire findings and interpretations.

The problem is that not every one in the three hotel had an equal chance of being selected. The well meaning attempt to select 50 sample initially because you knew they would comply, is an example of random selection. In fact, those sample may be different because they know you. Their particular training needs may or may not be useful to generalize to the rest of the group in all three hotel. You thought that using the phone book would be a clever way to determine who should be included in the administration of the questionnaire, but it didn't work out that way.

Because the sample is not truly representative of the type and number of group in each of the three hotel the results of the survey are discounted.

1) How many is enough ?
2) If it is not necessary to send a questionnaire to everyone in the target population, how many should you send out ?
3) What is the minimum number of respondents needed for you to be confident that the sample size will reflect the sentiments of the entire target population?

The minimum number depends on several statistical factors:-

1) The expected response rate of the questionnaire (a 50 percent response rate is generally considered good);
2) The precision of the population estimate (for example, within plus or minus 5 percent);
3) The confidence level (for example, a 95 percent confidence level means that 95 out of 100 times a sample will provide the desired precision level).

You can calculate the minimum sample required using this formula:

Minimum sample size = (population size)/(.96) (.0025) (population size) + .96).

For example to make valid inferences from a population of 700 supervisors and managers, you would need to have at least 248 questionnaires returned to have a 95 percent confidence level that the results are within plus or minus .05 accuracy for the entire target population. The equation you would use to calculate that minimum sample size would be

{(700) (.96)} ÷ {(.0025) (700) + .96} = 248.

You anticipated a 50 percent return rate, you would need to distribute about 500 questionnaires in order to secure the minimum sample size required.

The accompanying figure summarizes the minimum sample sizes required for different sizes target populations, calculated from the formula. The minimum sample sizes given in the figure will provide a 95 percent confidence level that the sample is within plus or minus 5 percent of the actual population estimate. If your return rate is at least 50 percent, you can feel confident that your sample is providing you with information that is truly reflective of the target population.

Now, you have a statistical method for determining the minimum sample size required from your target population, you need to know how to guarantee that the sample is truly representative of the population. That will assist you in “selling” both the analysis and the interpretation of the information gathered. It may also help you to get managers to accept organization's interventions and training programs that may be recommended as a result of the questionnaire findings.

Getting Samples Group to Comply

Now that you have figure out how many questionnaires you have to get back to make worthwhile inferences about the target audience, go ahead and distribute them to a random, representative sample. Then, hope that sample will comply and return them to you. Low response rates raise important concerns.

For example, if significantly fewer than 50 percent of people in your sample return the questionnaires, the attitudes of the respondents may be very different from those of the non-respondents. Making inferences about sample group attitudes based on the information gathered may not be in the best interests of he organization. When response rates are low, interpret questionnaire results with caution, respondents may not be accurate barometers of the target audience.

It is not enough to design effective questionnaires, surveys, and other paper-and-pencil tools to assess sample group, observations, and opinions. The sampling procedure must be random, representative, and large enough to make valid inferences about the organizational population.

Getting sample group motivated to respond to your survey will ensure that all the hard work that went into questionnaire design, pilot testing, revision, and administration is well worth the effort. With the techniques outlined above, you are well on your way to successfully getting out your sample group questionnairs–and, more important, getting them back.

An Example

You have a target population of 1,500 that you want to sample for a training needs assessment study. The population is made up of he following:

1) 10 percent supervisors and managers;

2) 25 percent administrative and clerical staff;

3) 25 percent professional staff;

4) 30 percent technical personnel;
5) 10 percent manufacturing and production workers.

Questions

Q.1. How many questionnaires will you need to send out in order to meet the minimum sample size required to make reliable inferences about he questionnaire data, assuming a 50 percent return rate?

Q.2. How many questionnaires will you need to send out to receive a representative sample to professional staff of supervisors and managers?

Answers

Ans.1) Using the formula to find that the minimum sample size needed is 306 for a population of 1,500. Assuming a 50 percent response rate, you would need to send out at least 612 questionnaires.

Ans.2) To make sure that the sample was representative of the target audience, you would need to distribute about 153 questionnaires to the professional staff (25 × 612)/100. Again, assume that the response rate is 50 percent and the sample is randomly selected.

The example shows how to get a sample that is representative of the job classifications of the target population. You should try to ensure a representative sample with all demographic variables of interest to the project (such as job level, gender, ethnicity, geographic location, division, and product line). Of course, that assumes that you have thought about how you might want to analyze your questionnaire – before you distribute it. Remember, poor representation of your target audience will diminish the usefulness and acceptance of questionnaire findings.

Ways to Increase Response Rates

Following techniques may help to increase the compliance and response rates for questionnaires you use in your organization.

1) Make sure that participation is voluntary and either anonymous or confidential, who feel coerced into participating may comply, but may provide incomplete or biased answers.
2) Determine whether you need to identify sample (for example, you may require a post-intervention follow-up using a questionnaire). If so, inform of them of the rationale for identifying them and of what you will do to make sure that their results will be posted in the bathrooms or elevators), they may think twice about returning the questionnaire.
3) Provide a complete cover letter addressed personally to each employee. The cover letter should be signed by the highest-level executive you can find, and should include the following:
   a) Purpose of the questionnaire;
   b) Whether it is anonymous or confidential ?
   c) How the survey will be used ?
   d) How and to whom respondents should return the questionnaires ?
   e) When respondents should return the questionnaires ?

4) Make it easy for sample to return the questionnaires. Provide a postage-paid envelope (external mail) or pre-addressed mailer (company internal mail) to help employees.

5) Make the questionnaire look professional. With today's technology, including desktop publishing with laser printers and typeset-quality fonts, there is simply no excuse for producing a questionnaire whose appearance could minimize sample participation. You can greatly increase sample group compliance by spending a few more dollars to have a graphic artist or desktop-publishing specialist help with the layout, graphic design, typesetting, and reproduction.

   Remember, each questionnaire leaves an impression on the target sample who receives it. As in all organizational interventions, you want to create a professional, positive, and competent image with your internal customers.

6) In general, as the length of any questionnaire increases, its reliability increases and the compliance rate decreases. That rule creates a challenge in questionnaire design and administration within organizations. Make sure that your questionnaire is long enough to be reliable (or to have internal consistency or integrity) but not so long that is discourages employees from completing it.

   The "compliance/reliability" issue is often resolved by clarifying exactly what you wish to measure, eliminating redundancy, and using brevity as an absolute editor. Compliance can be increased with a longer questionnaire by ensuring that it is professional looking, with a pleasing graphic layout that is easy to read.

7) Include a separate demographics page with the questionnaire. It can come either at the beginning of the questionnaire or at the end; there is no agreement on which placement has a better effect on compliance. Limit the demographics to variables that you feel are relevant to the project and that you will analyze statistically. Remember, the more demographics you ask, the easier it is to identify individual employees. As demographic variables increase, the compliance rate will tend to decrease slightly.

   Controversial or potentially upsetting questions (such as those on substance abuse or discrimination complaints) should be placed towards the end of the questionnaire. Research has shown that compliance on controversial questions increases when they are placed in the middle or at the end of the questionnaire or survey.

8) Alert employees ahead of time that a questionnaire is being developed and will be sent out. Make special presentations to managers alerting them to the purpose of the questionnaire. Use organizational communication channels such as company newsletters or announcements to describe the importance of the questionnaire and the anticipated use of the results–before it is mailed out.

   Encourage supervisors and managers to make announcements encouraging sample group to fill out questionnaires and to return completed ones during staff and team meetings.

9) Provide incentives to reinforce sample compliance. Employees can be motivated to comply when some form of incentive is tied to the return of the questionnaire. Your organization may not be able to raffle off a new car, but it can provide some inexpensive incentives that most sample group will value. Some examples might include discount movie tickets, books, training programs, meals in the executive dining room, preferred parking spaces for a period of time,

discounts in the company store, and organizational paraphernalia such as office mugs, briefcases, and pen sets.

Such incentives can be used even when the questionnaires are completely anonymous. Randomly assigned "double raffle tickets" with numbers can be attached to each questionnaire sent to as sample. The group are instructed to keep one of the tickets and leave the other attached to the questionnaire when it is returned. One or more of the tickets is selected from the pool of returned questionnaires, and the winners can claim their prizes.

They may sound "too cute" for your organizational culture, but such incentives can dramatically increase employee participation. Remember, without an adequate response rate from your sample you may not be able to make valid inferences about the questionnaire results.

10) To increase the response rate, follow up with sample group after the questionnaire has been distributed. If the questionnaire is not anonymous, follow-up phone calls are effective for increasing compliance. When anonymity is preferred, follow up through a memo encouraging cooperation in completing the questionnaire. Post card size reminders and the use of organizational communications, such as a company newsletter, can also be used to encourage sample group to return the questionnaires by the target date.

    For a large organizational questionnaire, it may be valuable to conduct an evaluation of those who did not comply (assuming that the individuals can be identified). Such a study may provide important information about the organization's current climate, as well as delineating employees' reasons for not providing feedback.

    For example, one study revealed that sample group thought that the organizational questionnaire was too long, that questions were too personal, and that respondents could be easily identified despite assurances of confidentiality.

11) Provide sample with feedback about the questionnaire results. This is one of the most powerful ways to ensure participation in a survey sample, Number of sample group are curious; they want to know the major questionnaire findings. and, more important, what is going to be done about their concerns and recommendations.

    Organizations that break the "feedback rule" will pay later–the next time they ask sample to share their observations, attitudes, and feelings by using any data collection method. Employees who do not feel as if their opinions are heard and valued will simply stop providing them

    Feedback can occur in a variety of forms and can even be targeted to special audiences. Management and sample briefings, although time consuming, can be useful. They provide an opportunity to share questionnaire results and to discuss possible organization interventions. Written reports, executive summaries, and newsletter articles are also useful feedback tools to consider after your questionnaire has been analyzed.

Data Collection Procedure: An Exapmle

Indian World Hospitality and Tourism Research Development Centre is approached by the Grand Bakeries concerning a survey of purchase and consumption patterns of bread in its market area. Grand is a small, independents bakery that is like most independent brand breads of the food chains. The purpose of the survey is to obtain information about its market to help the bakery take action to reverse this declining trend in market share.

After some discussion it is agreed that you may conduct a survey as a part of an overall consulting project. The objectives of the survey is to determine whether there are viable market segments for bread based on

1) Characteristics of purchasing families and amounts of purchase
2) Communication media and appeals, and
3) Distribution outlets.

You as an analyst may began to prepare the questionnaire that would be used for the survey. Personal interviews are to be conducted and, to meet the objectives of the survey, information on amount of bread and where it is purchased, buyer's occupation, stage of life-cycle, level of education, exposure to print and electronic media, attitudes towards bread and its use, and income of the chief wage earner of he family would have to be obtained.

You may believe that the information that would be most difficult to obtain with the accuracy needed is on amounts of bread purchased. The information required is the average amount of bread purchased as measured by some standard unit, such as a pound, by type of bread, for some standard time period, such as a week. Two major problems are involved in obtaining this information, as you see it.

First, most people who buy bread, buy it by loaf rather than by weight. They would know the size of the loaf, they usually buy by sight but might not know how much it weighed. Second, many people buy bread on an "as needed" rather than on a regular basis. They may also buy different numbers of loaves as well as make irregular purchases. To obtain an accurate report on the average amount of bread purchased each week under such circumstances would be difficult.

You may considered two alternative ways of obtaining information on bread purchases. The way that would give the most accurage information, you may believe, is to have the housewife keep a diary of her bread purchases of ten weeks. She could be asked to look at the bread wrapper to obtain the weight of the loaf before recording it. The diary could be either picked up or mailed in at the end of the period.

Even though the information obtain in this way would be more accurate, you know that it would still have inaccuracies. People who keep a diary of purchases and then change their minds. Still others wait until and end of the recording period to record purchases and make mistakes in the amounts shown.

A panel of this sort would also be considerably more expensive than just asking the housewife questions about bread purchases. Some premium would have to be given to obtain cooperation from a large enough proportion of the sample to make it worthwhile. Callbacks would have to be made to check questionable entries if the diaries were mailed in, or a second call would be required if the diaries were collected by an inerviewer. In either case; added costs would be incurred.

The second alternative may be considered by you is that of obtaining the information soley by interview. To explore this possibility you draw up a tentative list of questions that could be used for obtaining the information and tried them on your wife. The questions appeared to serve the desired function with her. The questions for white bread that are the drawn up are as follows:

1) Do you usually do the shopping for food ?

Yes ☐ No ☐

2) (Do You) Does your family eat white bread ?

Yes ☐ No ☐

3) About how often would you say you buy white bread ?

- Three times a week ☐
- Twice a week ☐
- Once a week ☐
- Once a month ☐
- Twice every three months ☐
- Once every three months ☐

4) About how many loaves of white bread do you buy each time ?

- One loaf ☐
- Two loaves ☐
- Three loaves ☐
- Four loaves ☐
- More than four loaves (list number) ☐

5) Which size of loaves of white bread do you buy each time ?

- Extra large (approx.32 oz) ☐
- Large (approx. 15 oz) ☐
- Small (less than 5 oz) ☐

You are undecided as to which method to use.

1) Are there likely to be systematic errors in the method of measuring bread purchases ? If so, is the measurement likely to be high or low ?
2) Are there likely to be systematic errors in the questionnaire method of measuring bread purchases ? if so, is the measurement likely to be high or low ?
3) Evaluate the tentive list of questions that you have prepared. Could they be improved ? If so, how ?
4) Which method do you think you should use ?

   Why ?

An Example involving New Product Research

We present a very simplified example of a set of observations to illustrate the data reduction, estimation, variable association, and hypothesis test procedures. The example is simpler than most research studies. That is, it involves a smaller sample size, fewer variables, and "cleaner" data. However, this simplicity makes it easier to visualize and follow the procedures being described.

A regional soft drink firm is concerned about its ability to remain viable in the face of strong competition from national brands. The firm is currently evaluating a number of options including the introduction of a non-alcoholic carbonated apple cider. Preliminary research has been completed, and the company is now conducting a series of taste and preference tests among several potential market segments.

One market segment of interest is the college student market. As a means of examining the nature and extent of potential student demand for the product, the firm commissioned a small "pilot" (26,000 students). The experiment and the data collected in conjunction with it are designed to determine a number of different things, such as

1) The percentage of males, females and all students who consume a carbonated beverage at least one day a week.
2) The amount of carbonated beverages consumed per week by males, females, and all students.
3) The importance of price in general to students.
4) The importance to students of image or status for publicity used items.
5) The taste reaction of male and female students to the new product.
6) The relative preference for the product compared to five potential competitors by male and female students.
7) The likelihood of purchasing the product by males, females, and all students.
8) Which of two brand names is better for the product.
9) The differences in reactions between males and females to the product and the brand names.

It is decided that the study would involve a sample of 80 students. To provide a sampling frame, a list of all females and all males registered at the Indian University is generated. Sixty pėr cent of the students are male. Random samples of 40 males and 40 females are selected. The selected students completed a questionnaire dealing with their demographics, attitudes toward a variety of beverages, and beverage-consumption patterns. Then the selected students tested the new beverage.

Half of each group (20 males and 20, females) tested the beverage with the label Bravo while the other half tasted the identical beverage labeled Delight. The students then rated the taste of the product, ranked it overall appeal compared to four competitors, stated their likelihood of purchasing the product, and finally chose either a six-pack of the version they tasted or three as a payment for their participation in the study.

Table 8.1 contains some of the questions used in the study and Table 8.2 contains the responses to these questions.

Table 8.1: Selected Questions and Measurements for the Beverage Preference Study

1) Gender (a) Male ☐ (b) Female ☐

2) Age D ☐ M ☐ Y ☐

3) How many bottles, cans, and/or glasses of carbonated beverages do you drink in a typical week ?

4) How many days in a typical week do you drink at least one carbonated beverage ?

5) How important is price to you when you purchase beverages ?

☐ Extremely Important ☐ Very Important ☐ Somewhat Important ☐ Neither Important Nor Unimportant

☐ Somewhat Unimportant ☐ Very Unimportant ☐ Extremely Important

6. How important is the quality image of a brand to you when you purchase beverages ?

☐ Extremely Important ☐ Very Important ☐ Somewhat Important ☐ Neither Important Nor Unimportant

☐ Somewhat Unimportant ☐ Very Unimportant ☐ Extremely Important

7) Having tasted Bravo (Delight), indicate how much you like its taste by allocating 100 points such that 0 indicates extreme dislike, 50 indicates indifference (neither like nor dislike), and 100 indicates extreme liking. (Use any value between 0 and 100)

....

....

....

....

8) Please rank the following five brands in order of your overall preference. Let a "1" represent you most preferred brand and a "5" your least preferred brand. No ties, please (Note: the order of the brands is rated across the questionnaires).

		Rank
(a)	Perrier (or similar brands)	☐
(b)	Coke (or similar brands)	☐
(c)	7-1 P (or similar brands)	☐
(d)	Hi-c (or other fruit drinks)	☐
e)	Bravo (Delight)	☐

(Contd.)

9) Please indicate the likelihood or probability that you would purchase six or more bottles or Bravo (Delight) per month if it were available for 3.00 per six-pack. Indicate by allocating 100 points such that 0 indicates that there is no possibility that you would purchase the product, 50 indicates that you are equally likely to purchase or not purchase the product, and 100 indicates certainty that you would purchase the product. (Use any number between 0 and 100.

....

....

....

....

10) As an expression of our appreciation for your assistance, you may have either 3.00 or a six peck of Bravo (Delight). Which would you prefer ?

(a) 3.00 (b) 6.00 Bravo (Delight)

Completed by Editor

Respondent

Treatment: (a) ☐ (b) ☐ Bravo (Delight)

Data Reduction

The steps involved in the reduction of data are

(1) Field controls
(2) Editing
(3) Coding
(4) Transcribing
(5) Generating new variables, and
(6) Calculating summarizing statistics.

The first five or these steps are concerned with developing a basic data array that is as complete and as error-free as possible. The last step involves calculations made from the arrary.

The basic data array is a Table 8.1 comprised of the value of each variable for each sample unit. Table 8.2 is the basic data array for the beverage study described in the previous section. It consists of the values for 15 variables for 80 subjects, or a total of 1,200 measurements. This is a small data array compared to those encountered in most marketing studies.

Secondary-Data Collection

Once you have specified research objectives and information needs now, turn to the task of formulating research design and determining the appropriate sources of data. There are two types of data source available to the researcher—primary and secondary. Secondary data are already published data collected for purposes other than the specific research needs at hand.

Secondary Techniques

Data are not originally collected for use in the research project under consideration. Data for use by some other person or for some other project are termed as secondary data.

Table 8.2: Responses to Selected Questions and Measurements from a Beverage Preference Test

Respondent	Treatment	Gender	Age	Bottles comsumption	Day's consumption	Price importance	Image impor-	Taste reaction	Rank this Brand	Rank brand A	Rank brand B	Rank brand C	Rank brand D	Purchase	Choice
1	2	3	4	5	6	7	8	9	10	11	12	13	14	15	16
001	1	1	19	0	0	1	7	48	5	1	4	2	3	20	1
002	1	1	21	0	0	7	4	90	1	2	5	4	3	100	1
003	1	1	23	2	1	4	6	50	4	3	5	2	1	15	1
004	1	1	20	12	4	2	2	65	4	2	3	1	5	20	2
005	1	1	25	0	0	6	5	62	2	3	5	1	4	80	1
006	1	1	19	24	5	1	1	60	3	1	2	5	4	0	1
007	1	1	19	0	0	1	1	56	2	5	4	1	3	50	2
008	1	1	45	36	5	5	1	72	1	2	5	4	3	75	1
009	1	1	22	18	4	3	4	62	3	6	5	2	1	50	1
010	1	1	38	6	3	7	6	35	5	1	2	4	3	0	1
011	1	1	18	12	4	2	1	60	2	1	3	5	4	20	1
012	1	19	0	0	6	2	60	1	2	4	3	5	50	1	
013	1	1	27	24	5	7	1	64	2	3	5	1	4	80	1
014	1	21	10	3	1	6	70	2	1	5	3	4	90	2	
015	1	1	20	18	4	7	7	54	3	4	5	1	2	0	1
016	1	1	23	12	3	2	7	40	3	2	4	1	5	50	2
017	1	1	19	24	5	7	3	58	3	1	2	4	5	20	1
018	1	1	20	0	0	4	4	66	2	1	3	5	4	100	2
019	1	1	21	0	0	1	7	70	1	2	4	3	5	90	2
020	1	1	19	22	4	6	1	58	2	3	4	5	1	50	1
021	1	2	20	0	0	7	2	53	4	5	1	3	2	50	1
022	1	2	18	0	0	7	4	70	2	1	3	4	5	70	1
023	1	2	24	0	0	4	5	59	3	1	5	4	5	20	1
024	1	2	20	12	5	2	7	67	1	2	4	3	5	100	1
025	1	2	19	6	3	7	2	30	5	3	4	1	0	0	1
026	1	2	20	0	0	6	4	62	3	2	4	1	5	50	1
027	1	2	24	2	1	1	7	65	2	3	5	1	4	0	2
028	1	2	19	12	4	4	4	72	3	2	5	4	1	20	1
029	1	2	22	0	0	1	3	85	1	2	3	5	4	90	2
030	1	2	20	18	6	5	3	66	4	1	5	2	3	0	1

(Contd.)

Respondent	Treatment	Gender	Age	Bottles comsumption	Day's consumption	Price importance	Image importance	Taste reaction	Rank this Brand	Rank brand A	Rank brand B	Rank brand C	Rank brand D	Purchase	Choice
031	1	2	31	6	1	2	5	58	2	1	4	3	5	90	2
032	1	2	21	0	0	7	2	64	2	3	4	1	2	75	1
033	1	2	18	0	0	2	6	65	3	1	4	2	5	0	1
034	1	2	29	12	7	6	2	69	1	2	5	4	3	100	1
035	1	2	32	0	0	1	7	85	2	1	5	3	4	100	2
036	1	2	24	6	2	2	7	70	1	2	5	3	4	50	1
037	1	2	20	0	0	6	6	61	3	2	1	4	45	20	1
038	1	2	28	6	3	5	5	63	3	1	5	2	4	0	1
039	1	2	19	0	0	7	6	65	2	3	1	4	5	90	1
040	1	2	27	0	0	1	6	71	2	4	3	5	1	50	2
041	2	1	21	12	2	4	3	35	5	4	3	1	2	0	1
042	2	1	20	6	3	7	2	38	4	1	5	3	2	10	1
043	2	1	22	42	6	3	3	46	4	1	3	2	5	0	1
044	2	1	18	0	0	6	2	52	2	1	5	4	3	50	2
045	2	1	25	0	0	1	3	40	3	2	5	4	1	50	2
046	2	1	23	10	4	2	6	41	3	1	5	2	4	75	2
047	2	1	24	0	0	7	1	25	5	3	2	1	4	0	1
048	2	1	19	18	2	4	7	36	2	1	4	5	3	100	1
049	2	1	21	0	0	7	3	44	4	2	5	1	3	0	1
050	2	1	22	0	0	1	4	80	1	2	3	4	5	100	1
051	2	1	20	2	2	5	4	42	2	1	4	3	5	50	1
052	2	1	26	0	0	2	7	39	3	2	1	5	4	0	2
053	2	1	21	0	0	7	3	40	3	1	5	4	2	0	1
054	2	1	23	12	3	4	1	38	4	2	5	1	3	10	1
055	2	1	18	18	3	1	6	28	5	4	2	3	1	0	1
060	2	1	21	0	0	7	2	35	4	2	5	1	3	10	1
061	2	2	23	72	7	1	6	85	2	1	3	5	4	100	2
062	2	2	28	12	4	4	2	95	0	3	5	2	4	90	2
063	2	2	19	6	4	5	0	90	3	2	5	1	4	0	1
064	2	2	40	0	0	2	4	85	1	3	4	5	2	100	1
065	2	2	21	6	2	6	7	77	1	2	3	4	5	50	1
066	2	2	18	0	0	4	3	81	3	1	5	2	4	50	1
067	2	2	52	0	0	1	2	79	2	1	4	3	5	75	2
068	2	2	21	6	1	3	2	87	1	3	4	2	5	90	2
069	2	2	20	0	0	7	1	50	5	2	4	1	3	0	1
070	2	2	35	18	3	1	7	87	2	1	3	5	4	50	2

(Contd.)

Respondent	Treatment	Gender	Age	Bottles comsumption	Day's consumption	Price importance	Image importance	Taste reaction	Rank this Brand	Rank brand A	Rank brand B	Rank brand C	Rank brand D	Purchase	Choice
071	2	2	19	0	0	4	4	90	1	4	5	2	3	100	2
072	2	2	23	0	0	7	2	85	1	3	2	5	4	90	1
073	2	2	20	6	2	6	2	60	3	1	4	2	5	50	1
074	2	2	19	0	0	7	7	30	5	2	3	1	4	0	1
075	2	2	22	0	0	1	4	80	2	1	5	4	3	100	2
076	2	2	20	1	1	7	1	78	3	2	4	5	1	50	1
077	2	2	18	0	0	4	1	92	1	3	4	2	5	90	2
078	2	2	21	0	0	1	6	86	1	2	5	3	4	75	2
079	2	2	20	0	0	6	4	96	1	2	3	4	5	100	1
080	2	2	19	12	3	2	3	87	4	1	5	3	2	0	1

Types of Secondary Data

There are several ways to classify the secondary data. One of the most useful is by source i.e. internal and external source. Figure 8.1 provides an overview of these sources.

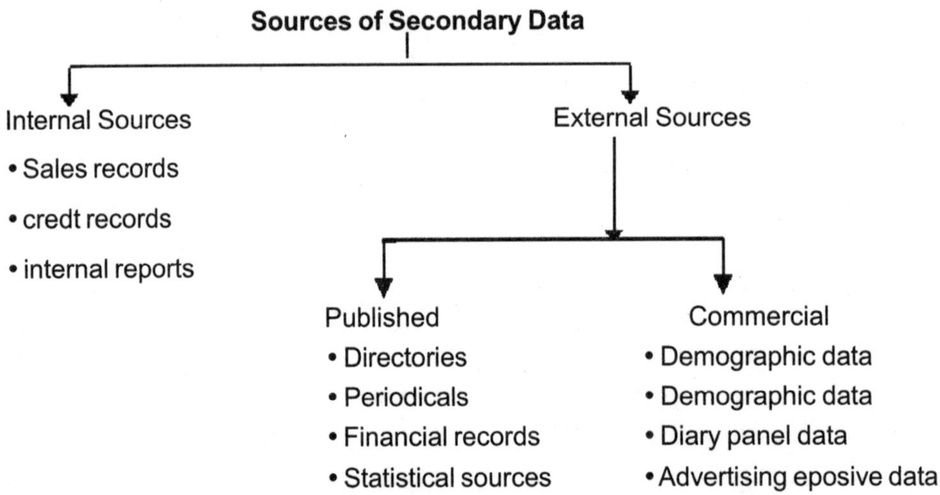

Fig. 8.1: Sources of Secondary Data

Robert W Joselyn suggests an approach for evaluation of secondary data (as given in Fig. 8.2):

The advantages of secondary data are:

1) The major advantage is economy in cost. As the data are already available, they can be obtained at a relatively low cost.
2) These data can be obtained quickly.

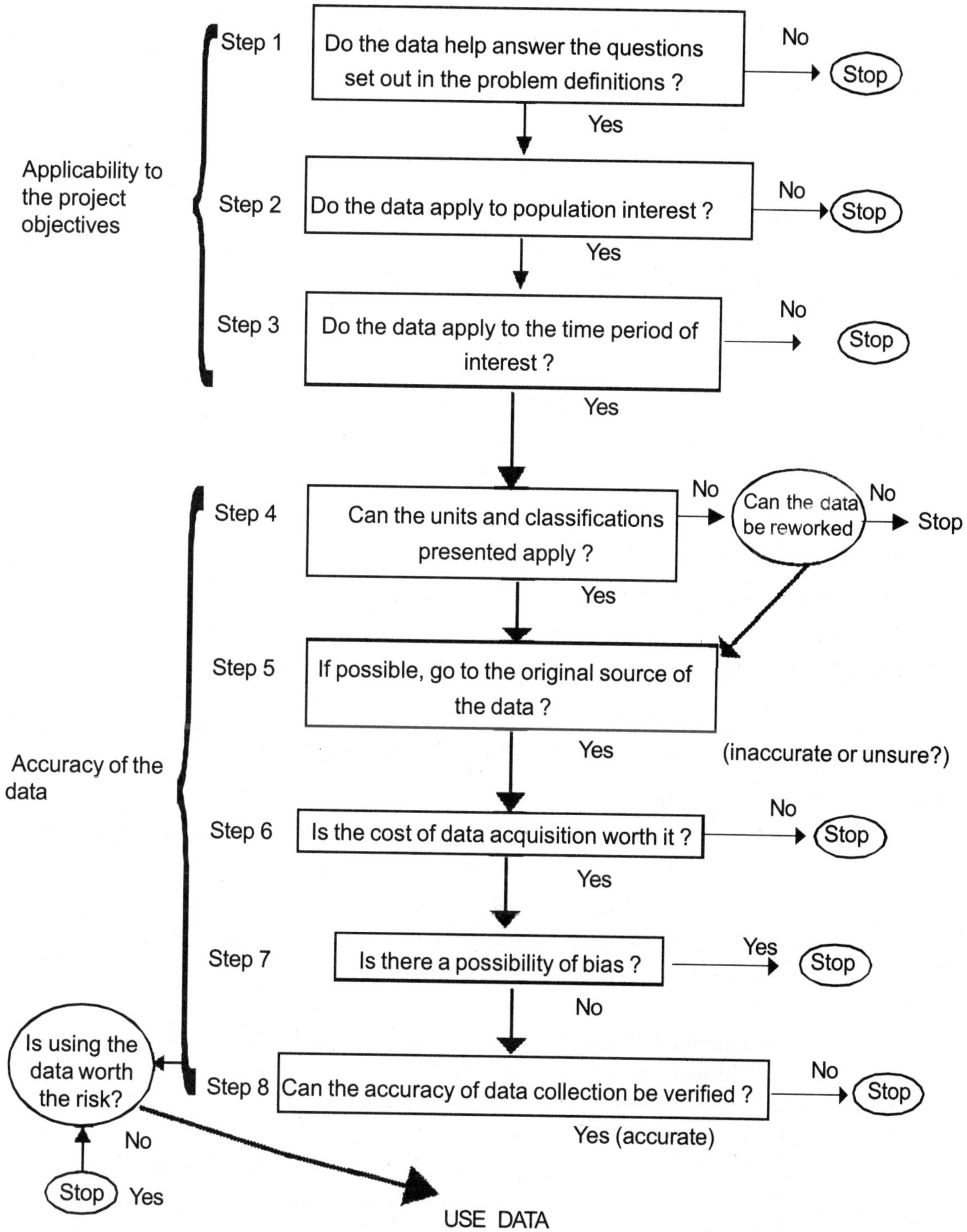

Fig. 8.2: Basic steps for Evaluation Procedure for Secondary Data

3) These data enables researchers to identify the deficiencies in the data and make primary data collection specific.
4) They are useful in the case of exploratory researches as they provide increased understanding of the problem.
5) These data act as basis for comparison after primary data are collected.
6) They provide for data which could not be obtained by the typical organisation like census reports.
7) Locating appropriate source and finally getting access to the data would be a time consuming exercise.
8) The data available might be too vast and a lot of time may be spent going through it.
9) It might not be up dated and not of much use in a dynamically changing environment.

The limitations of secondary data are:

1) The available data may not suit the current purpose of research, due to incompleteness, generalities and so on.
2) Information may be outdated or obsolete.
3) The methodology used in collecting the data such as the sample size and date of the research may be unknown.
4) All the findings of a research study may not be made public.
5) Conflicting data may exist.
6) It may be difficult to determine the accuracy of the secondary data.

Evaluation of Secondary Data

Before using any secondary data you need to satisfy himself as to their accuracy and reliability. You have to evaluate secondary data by observing following quidelines:

1) **Pertinency:** The units of measurement related to the secondary data must be the same as units of measurement intended to be used in the current research. It should also be applicable to the current time period. Further, the classes of data must also match the classes used in the current research.
2) **Source of the Secondary Data:** Examine the source in organisation who has collected the data and the purposes for which they have been collected and published. The authenticity, reliability and previous experience of the organisation may be a valuable consideration in examining the secondary data.
3) **Data Collection Methods:** Examine the data collection methods adopted by the source (who has collected the data) so as to determine the soundness of the methodology and accuracy of the data.
4) **General Evidences of Careful Work:** Look in for general evidences that may indicate the

care taken by the organisation collecting the data like presentation of the information in an organised manner, proper construction of tables, etc.

5) **Conflicting Data:** Compare the same data available from different sources so as to determine the most accurate data.

Sources of Secondary Data:

The main sources of secondary data are:

1) Census data
2) National sample survey
3) Sample registration system
4) Publications
5) Research institutes
6) Tourism departments
7) Hospital and tourism associations and other secondary sources.

1) Census Data

Since 1872, the census of India's population is being done once in a decade. The next census for which the machinery is already geared up will be done in 2010. Most of the demographic data are available through census. For example: household type, sex, race, age, martial status, etc.

2) National Sample Survey

This was started in 1950 and collects data about demographic, social and economic aspects of a households. Unlike a census which is done once in a decade, this is a continuous ongoing activity throughout the year.

3) Sample Registration System

This was started in 1964 and gives annual statistics on births and deaths.

4) Publications

Hospital and research organisations publish the data related to their field. This data can be used for research reference. The list of organisations and their publications are given in Table 8.3:

5) Research Institutes

Government and private research institutes publish their research data which can be referred. The list of some of these research institutes is given in Table 8.4.

6) Tourism-related Departments

Tourism departments at central and state level publish the data related to past performance, future projections and policy guidelines etc. from time to time. This data is very useful and can be used as research reference. The list of some of the government departments is given in Table 8.5.

Table 8.3: List of Trade Associations and Other Secondary Sources.

S.No.	Name	Publishers	Frequency
1)	*Automobiles:*	20, Noble Chambers, Parse	B-Monthly
	(a) Automobile Ancillaries and Accessories	Bazaar St., Mumbai-400001	
	(b) Automobile News Rd., Bombay-40003	Arun Chambers, J. Dadajee	Monthly
	(c) Automobile India	3495, Nivholdon Td. Delhi-110006	Monthly
	(d) Automobile Reporter	221, Kamala Market, New Delhi-110001	
2)	*Coffee:*		
	Coffee Statistics	Market Research and Statistical Bureau, Coffee Board, Vidhan Veedhi, Bangalore-560001	Annual
3)	*Hospitality, Tourism and Travel:*		
	Indian Hotelkeeper and Traveller	90/91 Maiden's Hotel, Post Box No. 1567 Delhi-110006	Monthly
4)	*Express Hospitality*	*Indian Express*	Monthly Hospitality Publication

Table 8.4: Research Institutes

Sl. No.	Name of Institute	Address
1)	Civil Aviation Department, Research & Development, Directorate Technical Centre, Civil Aviation Department,	Safdarjung, New Delhi-110003.
2)	Coffee Research Institute Central,	P.O. Coffee Research Station, Chikmagalur District, Karnataka State.
3)	Food Technological Research Institute,	Central Chaluvmba, Mension, Mysore-470013.
4)	Water Population, Central Board for Prevention and Control of Ex-AFO Mess,	Dr. R Prasad Rd., New Delhi-110001.
5)	Indian World Hospilality and Tourism Research Development Centre,	Indian School of Hospilality, Noida.
6)	Himalayan Tourism and Recreation in Mountins,	New Delhi.
7)	International Culinary Foundation	New Delhi.

Table 8.5: Government Departments

Sl. No.	Name of Government Department	Address
1)	All India Handicrafts Board,	Block 7 (West), R.K. Puram, New Delhi-110022.
2)	All-India Institute of Hygiene & Public Health,	110, Chittarajan Avenue, Kolkata-700012.
3)	Directorate-General of Employment and Training,	Sharam Shakti Bhavan, Rafi Mag, New Delhi-110011.
4)	Ministry of Tourism & Civil Aviation,	Sardar Patel Bhavan, Parliament St., New Delhi-110001.

7) Hospitality and Tourism Associations and Other Secondary Sources

Hospital and Tourism associations publish data as related to their trade in the journals. This data provide a reliable information that can be used as reference material. List of some of the trade associations and other secondary sources are given in Table 8.6 and Table 8.7.

Table 8.6: Trade Associations

Sl. No.	Name of Trade Associate	Address
1)	Biscuit Manufactureres of India Federation	17, Alipur Road, Delhi-110006.
2)	Dairy Association, Indian,	IDA House, Sector IV, R.K. Puram, New Delhi-110022.
3)	Hotel Association of India,	New Delhi
4)	Federation of Hotel and Restaurant Association of India,	New Delhi.

8) Other Secondary Sources

Table 8.7: List of Other Secondary Sources

Sl. No.	Name of Trade Associate	Address
1)	A Bibliography of Market Surveys by Products and Countries International Trade Centre	UNCTAD/GATT, Geneva 1967.
2)	Basic Commodity Statistics-International Trade Centre	UNCTAD/GATT, Geneva 1967.
3)	Commodity Trade Imports/Commodity Trade Export Services	OECD.
4)	Compendium of Sources of Basic Commodity/Statistics	UNCTAD/GATT.
5)	Compilation of Basic Information of Export Markets International Trade Centre,	UNCTAD/GATT, Geneva 1968.
6)	Concise Guide to International Markets	International Advertising Association.
7)	Croner's Reference Bookto World Traders,	Croner Publication, N.Y., USA
8)	Export Marketing Research for Development International Trade Centre,	UNCTAD/GATT, Geneva 1967.
9)	International Customs Journal	International Customs Tariff Bureau.
10)	OECED Year Book	OECED
11)	Trade Directories of the World,	Croner Publications, N.Y.
12)	World Trade Annual	UN Statistical Office.
13)	Year Books	Target Countries.

9

Preparation of a Project Report

Good research reports begin with clear thinking on the part of a researcher. The researcher should carefully analyze the readers needs and prepare a detailed outline prior to writing the first draft. The first draft should be considered just that a first draft. Few of us write well enough to produce a polished draft the first time. The writer should plan on at least one major rewrite.

The only reason for writing a research report is to communicate something to someone. The someone is the most important aspect of the communications process. The entire research project is performed to generate information that will aid one or more decision makers. The research report must convey that information to those decision makers. Several facts must be kept in mind:-

First, most mangers are busy.

Second, they are generally much less interested in the technic and logical aspects of a research problem that the researcher is.

Third, they are seldom well versed in research techniques and terminology.

Fourth, if there is more than one reader, and there usually is, they are likely to differ in terms of interests, training and reasons for reading the report.

Finally, managers, like everyone else, prefer interesting reports over dull ones.

With these facts in mind, a number of general guides to writing are offered here.

General Guidelines

Focus on the objectives of the study. The research is initiated to help make a decision. The report should be built around the decision and how the resultant information is relevant to the decision. This is what the manager is interested in. Researchers are often more interested in the research problem and the methodology used to solve it. Unfortunately, many research reports reflect the interest of the researcher rather than the manager. This can result in uncured (and perhaps unreadable) reports, an "ivory tower" image, and a resulting slow erosion of the effectiveness of the research department.

Minimize the reporting of the technical aspects of the project. Researchers have an unfortunate, if natural, tendency to attempt to convince management of their expertise and thoroughness in the research report. This leads to detailed discussions of the sampling plan, why it is superior to alternative sampling plans, and so on. Yet, few executives are interested in this level of detail. However, the research department should keep such a detailed report internally to serve as a guide for future studies and to answer any questions that might arise concerning the methodology of the study.

Use terminology that matches the vocabulary of the readers. As Britt expresses it: "Few (managers) can balance a research report, a cup of coffee, and a dictionary at the same time." Terms such as skewed distribution, correlation, coefficient, or even significance level are not necessarily familiar to all managers. It is often, necessary to utilize the concepts that underlie these terms in many research reports. Three strategies are available for dealing with this problem. The term can be used, followed by a brief description or explanation, the explanation can be provided first followed by the term, or the technical terms, can be omitted altogether. Which approach, or combination of approaches is best depends upon the nature of the audience and the message.

Develop an interesting writing style. Research reports should be interesting to read as for as possible. There is no inherent reasons for a research report to be dull, tedious, or boring.

The use of the analytical techniques of the behavioral sciences will gradually revolutionize the communication arts by predicating their practice upon a body of demonstrably general principles which will be readily available to creative people for increasing their knowledge of consumer response to advertising communications.

Can you imagine reading a report composed of such statements ? No, unfortunately most researchers have not been trained in effective writing. Self-instruction is, therefore, often necessary.

In general, the researcher should strive for simplicity and conciseness. Simplicity does not mean that the report necessarily be short. However, unnecessary complexity in sentence structure and long wideness in reporting should be avoided.

Use visual aids whenever practical. As a general rule, a sentence in the text of a report should contain no more than two or three numerical values. Sentences containing more numbers than this are difficult to read and understand. For example, the pie chart contains the same information and provides a quick, strong impression of the relative sales by each department.

Again, the advantage of graphics is apparent. A wide array of graphic techniques are available and the advent of computer graphics is greatly expanding their use. Descriptions of several of the more common graphic techniques follow.

A pie chart is a circle divided into sections, such that each section represents the percentage of the total area of the circle associated with one variable. Since there are 360 degrees to a circle, 3.6 degrees comprise 1 per cent of the circle.

Another useful visual aid is the bar chart, which may be either vertical or horizontal. Because the same principles apply in either case, we limit our discussions to be vertical bar chart. A vertical chart is constructed by placing rectangles or bars over each value or interval of the variable of interest. The height of the bar represent the level of the variable on the vertical exist. Vertical bar charts are often used to represent changes in a variable over time. The bar chart is somewhat less complex in appearance and may be more suited to those unaccustomed to dealing with figures.

Line chart are generally superior under the following conditions:

1) When the data involve a long time period.
2) When several series are compared on the same chart.
3) When the emphasis is on the movement rather than the actual amount.
4) When trends of frequency distribution are presented.
5) When a multiple-amount scale is used, and
6) When forecasts, interpolations, or extrapolations are to be shown.

A histogram is a vertical bar chart in which the height of the bars represents the relative or cumulative frequency of occurrence of the variable of interest. For example, assume that 730 respondents rate the service provided by a restaurant on a six-point semantic differential scale bounded by 'poor' in the left and 'excellent' on the right. The number of respondents marking each response from left to right is 154, 79, 50, 112, 198, and 146. Stated in percentages the responses from left to right would be 21.2, 10.8, 15.3. 25.9, and 20.0.

The histogram makes clear at a glance the bimodal nature of the response (that is, the fact that responses are clustered in two groups). A textural presentation of the raw data and/or a comment on the fact that the responses were bimodal would not have the same impact on many readers as the histogram.

It is often necessary to present numerical data that cannot be converted to graphic format. When this is the case or when the data underlying the graph need to be presented in numerical form as a supplement to the graph, tables should be used.

Rounding of Numbers

All too often one reads statements in research reports. Such statements are usually the product of a computer analysis having been made in which all calculated numbers were routinely rounded to two places following the decimal point. The analyst then simply copies the data as they are given on the printout and that is the way they appear in the report.

The reporting of data to a number of decimal places that is either unwarranted or unnecessary is a practice to be avoided. There is a spurious accuracy implied by the last two digits for the ages. There are almost certainly errors in the reporting of ages by buyers when the data are collected that would have made the calculated mean age questionable to an accuracy of more than one year. To imply that the data are accurate to one-hundredth of a year is thus both inaccurate and misleading.

Reporting data to several significant digits is often unnecessary, even when accurate.

A general appearance of the project report communicates how tidy or untidy the researcher is. Neat reports cause favourable impressions in the mind of the evaluators. A well arranged report gives the impression of:

1) Completeness of the work,
2) Competency of the researcher, and
3) Professionalism.

Guidelines for Report Presentation

You should follow the general guidelines for laying out different type of contents:

The inclusions in the physical representation of the report are given in flow chart illustrated in Fig. 9.1.

Some of the guidelines for the physical presentation of the report are:

1) Page Layout

There are two types of page layout:

(a) Special page layout.

(b) Conventional page layout.

i) Special Page Layout

This is normally considered when laying out for the following purposes:

(a) Synopsis or executive summary

(b) First page of the chapter

(c) Table of contents

(d) Preface

(e) Letter of transmittal.

(f) Letter of authorisation.

The sample page layout for the above are illustrated in Figure 9.2.

ii) Conventional Page Layout

All the pages following the first page of the chapter should be laid-out in such a way that they look attractive. A proper binding margin should be provided and no letters should get covered by the binding. Normally the reports is left bound therefore an extra margin in addition to suggested margins should be provided for binding.

Generally the recommended margins provided are:

(1) Top, left and right margins are equal and uniform.

(2) For double spaced the margins are generally 25mm.

(3) For single space the margins are generally 1½ times of the double spaced page *i.e.,* 32-38 mm. approximately.

(4) Customarily the bottom margin in kept about 10mm. more than top margin. If you are using DTP (Desk Top Publishing) ensure that the page alignments are proper.

Figure 9.3 shows the margin arrangement for a double spaced page and Figure 9.4 shows the margin arrangement for single spaced page.

Presentation of a Project Report

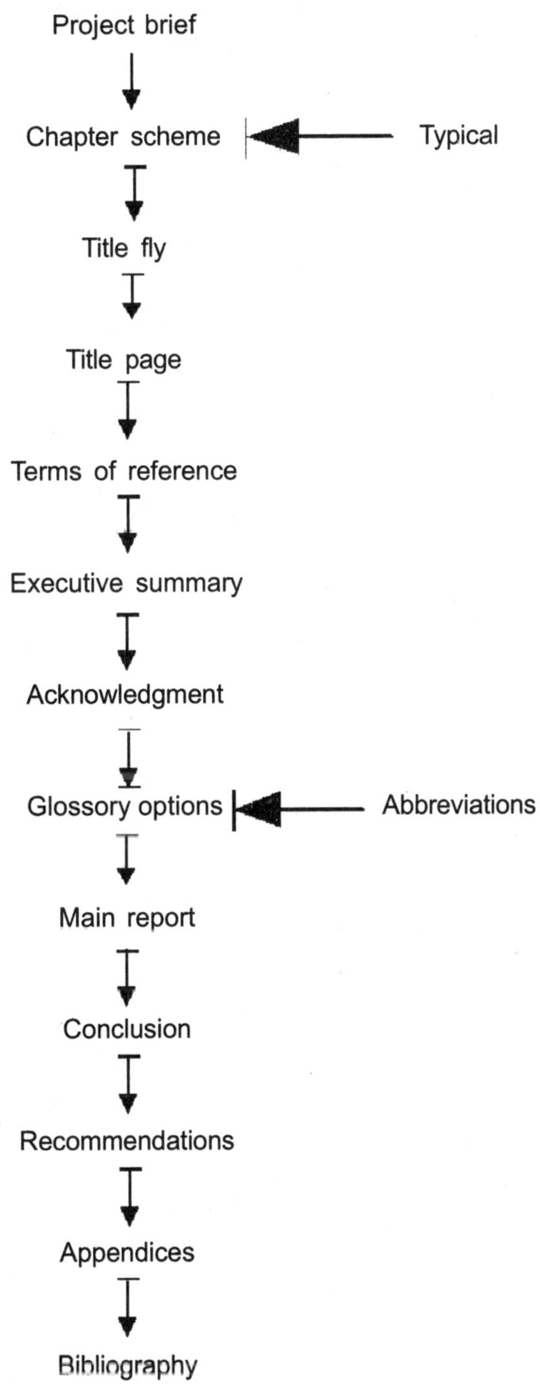

Fig. 9.1: Physical Presentation of a Project Report

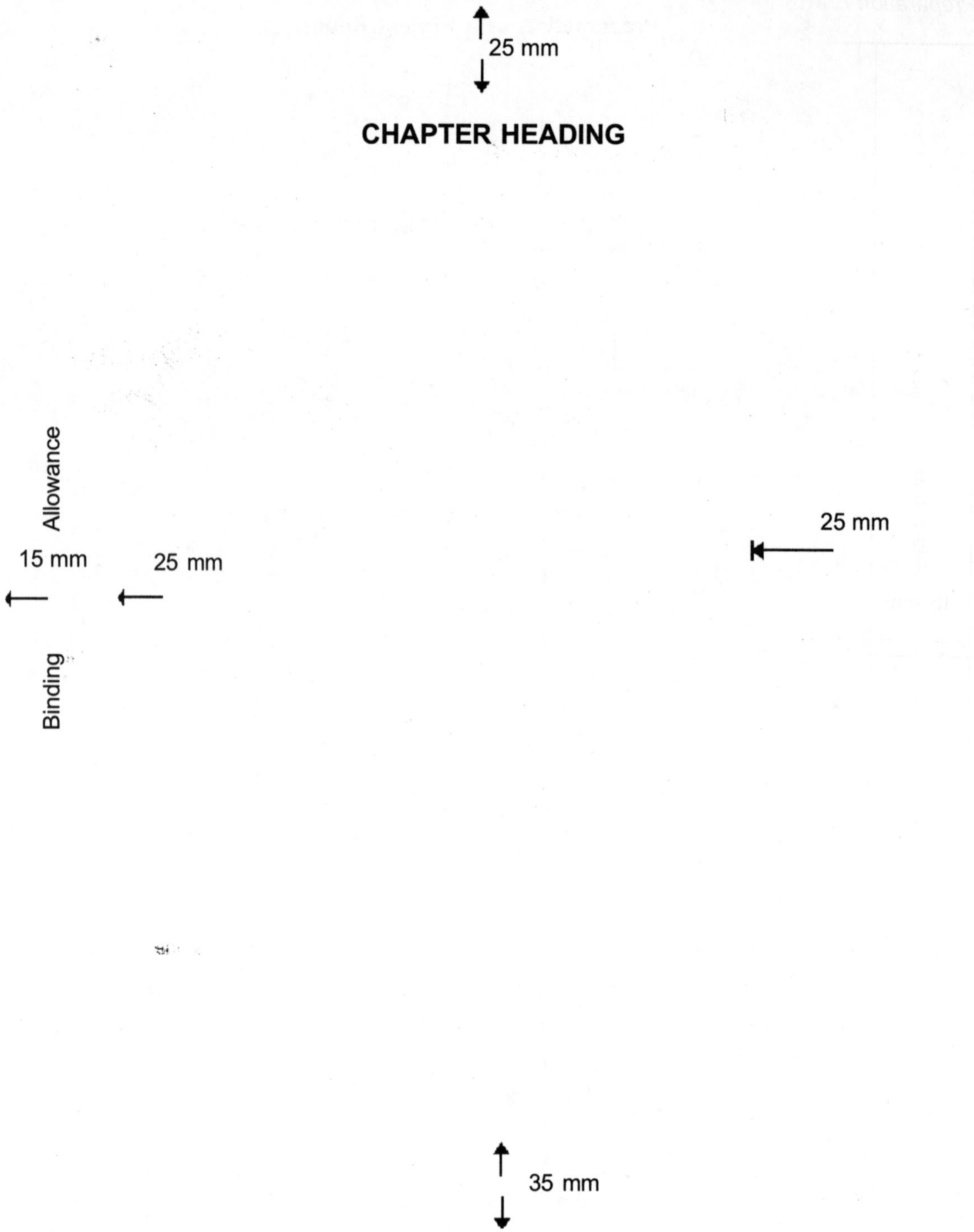

Figure not to scale.

Fig. 9.2: Specimen Layout for Double Spaced Page for Starting Page of the Chapter (Size of Paper A4.)

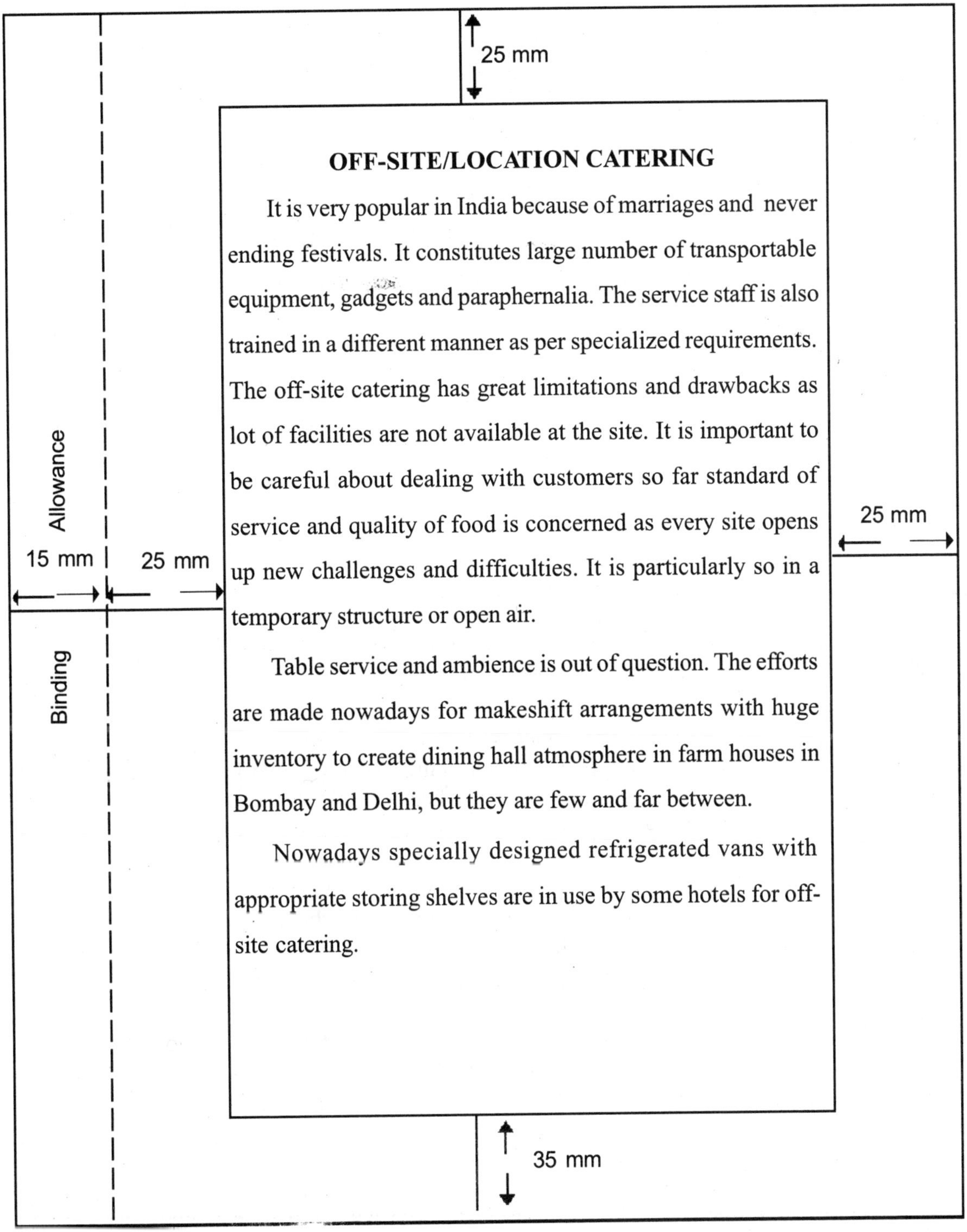

Figure not to scale.

Fig. 9.3: Specimen Layout for a Double Spaced Page

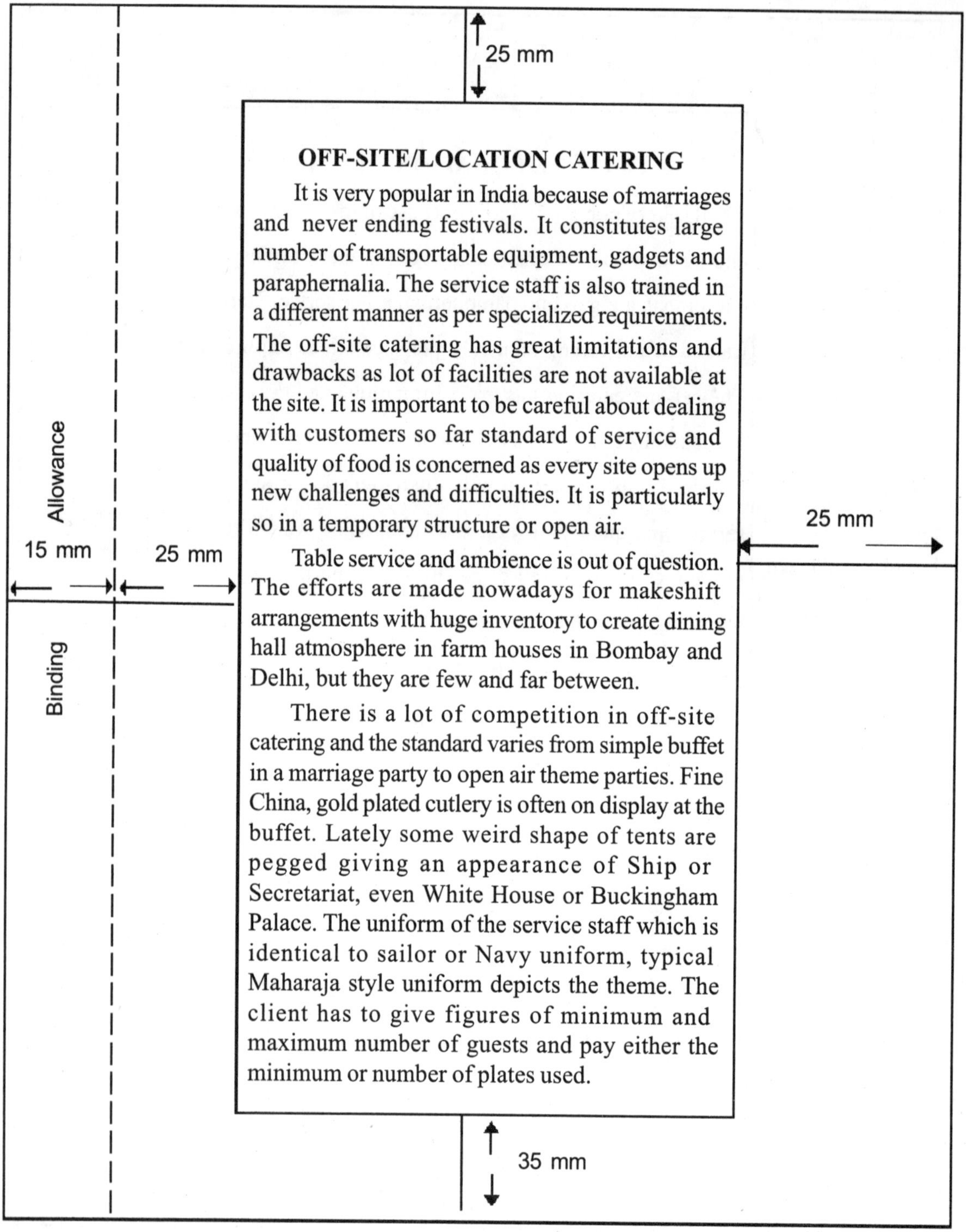

Figure not to scale.

Fig. 9.4: Specimen Layout for a Single Spaced Page

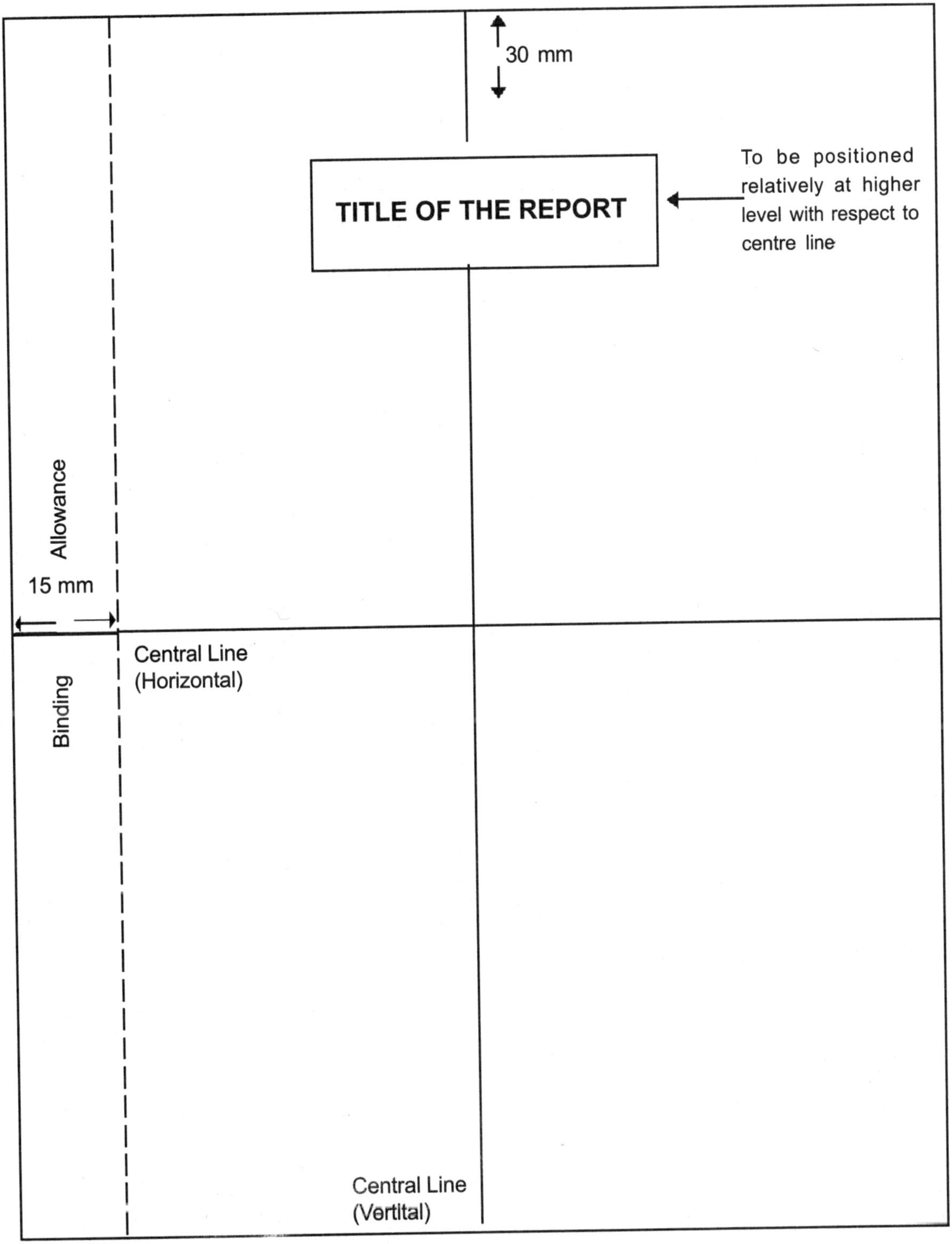

Figure not to Scale

Fig. 9.5: Specimen of a Title Fly

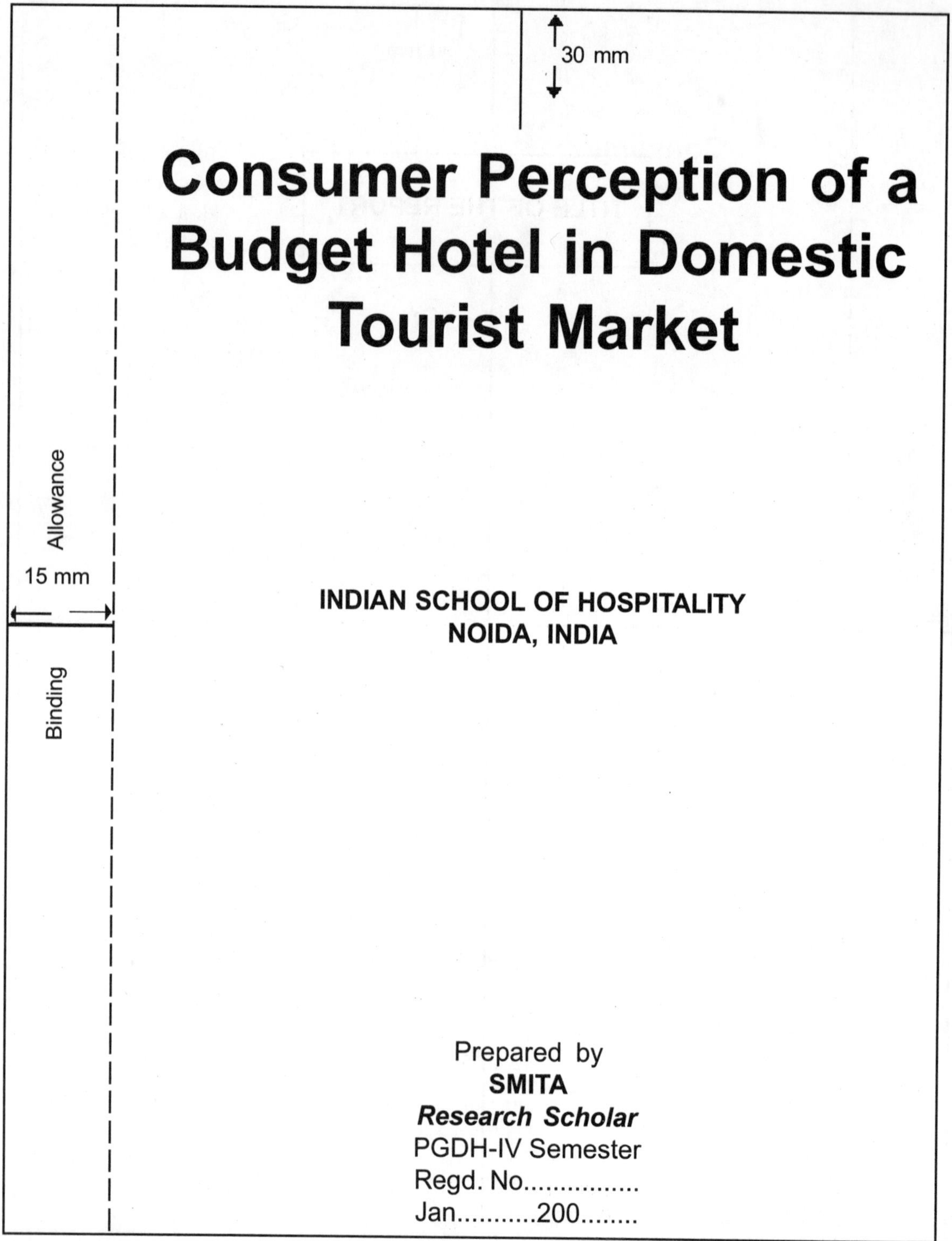

Figure not to Scale

Fig. 9.6: Specimen of a 3 Spot Title Page (A4 page)

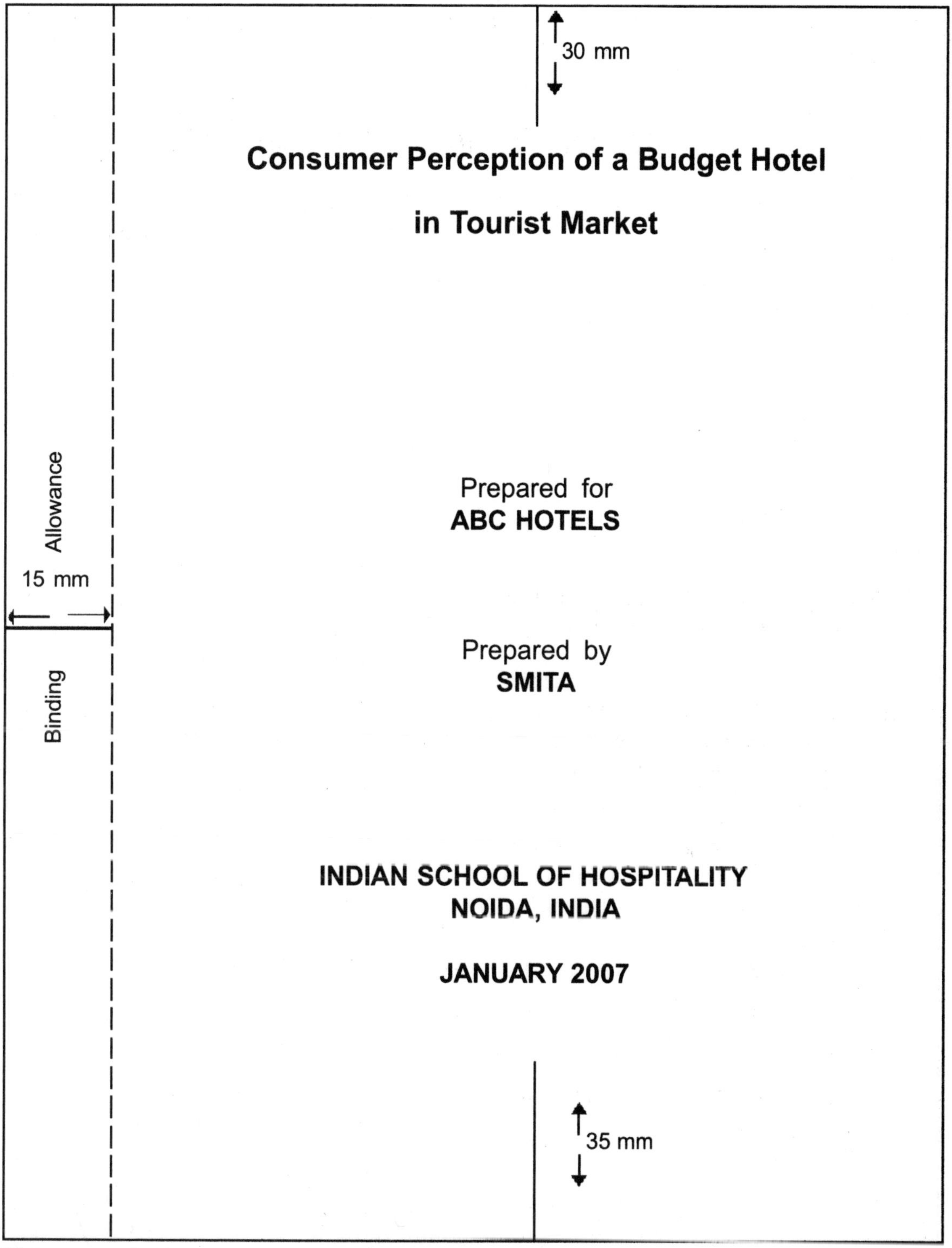

Figure not to Scale

Fig. 9.7: Specimen of a 4 Spot Title Page (A4 page)

Indian School of Hospitality

Noida

January 2006

....

....

....

....

Dear Sir,

The Indian School of Hospitality has approved your projected title under the guidance of Prof..

You may procced on this project as per the framework given in the synopsis approved by the Indian School of Hospitality. The copy of approved synopsis is enclosed for your references.

Thanking you,

Yours faithfully,

Co-ordinator (Project work)

Allowance

15 mm

Binding

Figure not to Scale

Fig. 9.8: Specimen Letter of Authorization

10

Writing Techniques for Research Report

Research and development is a public venture. Therefore, one of the essential skills of the researcher is to be able to communicate ideas and research results effectively. This guide is an attempt to make the style of writing clear to you. It summarizes a lot of the material available in the publication manuals research and is oriented toward undergraduate students. For example, it includes numerous hints to avoid common mistakes students make. Note the examples appearing in a teletype font to distinguish them from the normal text. Finally, the document is organized in an outline format for at least two reasons. *First*, it should make it easier for students to quickly locate the information they seek. *Second*, it should make it easier for an instructor to grade students papers. In most cases, the student can simply be referred to the outline item that addresses the problem rather than writing the comment repeatedly on multiple papers.

Develop a well throughout plan for writing the thesis. Set aside specific hours each week. Initially there will be a considerable amount of library research, later on less time will be spent in the library and more timed will be spent in writing and correspondence. The guidelines set by your research professor will assist you in moving from one task to next until the thesis is completed. Finish the assignment several days in advance.

Two main attitudes you must cultivate for preparing to write a project report are:

1) Adopt fresh mind approach (FMA)
2) Adopt 'kiss' approach (keep it short and simple)

Fresh-Mind Approach (FMA)

It is a general tendency of all human being to proceed with a preoccupied mind as if the solution is available and report is to be made suiting that solution. It is essential that as a researcher you must clear your mind of all precautions about the solution to the problem. If the data collection, investigation and analysis are done properly, the interpretation and recommendations may be quite different from what the you expected. Developing the fresh mind approach will help you in avoiding the mind-set about a situations which is too common when dealing with a familiar work situation. We are always able to find fault with someone else's work, while we fail to see what is wrong with our own. In light of this, the person who is going to assess your work will adopt the above strategy of evaluating your work if sufficient originality, genuineness and fresh approach has not been adopted by you. The project assessor certainly possess the skills of assessing whether the work is done with FMA or otherwise.

Keep it Short and Simple Approach (KISS)

The project work submitted by you is going to be read and evaluated by some one, such as,

1) One who is outside your organisations.
2) One who will not be quite familiar with the field of study.
3) One may not be conversant with technical terms.

You must know this fact and write the project in such a style that it is:

1) Understandable
2) Simple
3) Provides sufficient background information
4) Creates a clear picture in the mind of your work environment
5) Helps the reader to understand the problem under study.

Therefore, you must

1) Use short sentences
2) Use simple sentences
3) Use logic.

Short sentences will help you in avoiding grammatical mistakes, thus creating a good impression of the researcher. Avoid use of technical jargons. If you feel the use of technical terms is unavoidable, it is desired to include glossary of terms in the project report. Sometimes you may use abbreviations. It is recommended that a page explaining the full form of abbreviations may also be included. In a nutshell, short sentences and simple language should be used by a you throughout. Then follow the valuable tips given below:

1) Use of friendly and informal tone
2) Explain things clearly
3) Avoid overloading with information
4) Use relevant anecdotes
5) Keep sentences, and paragraphs, short
6) Choose simple and familiar words
7) Avoid long phrase. Say 'although' rather than "In spite of the fact that".
8) Explain jargon and technical terms clearly.

Size of Report

The size of report will depend upon the subject matter and what is involved in the study.

(1) 125-175 pages

Indian World Hospitality Research and Development Centre suggests that the report should be covered between 125-175 type pages (double spaced without appendices. Each page must be typical only on one side leaving a wide margin.

(2) 100-150 pages

Faculty of Management Studies, University of Rajasthan suggests an average size the report between 100-150 typed pages in 3/2 space.

(3) 60-100 pages.

All India Management Association, Centre for Management Education, suggests that the report should be covered between 60 to 100 typed pages (double space). Each page must be typed only on one side leaving a wide margin.

(4) 50-60 pages

School of Management Studies, Indira Gandhi National Open University (IGNOU) suggests that the length of the report may be about 50 to 60 double-spaced typed pages not exceeding 18,000 words (excluding appendices and exhibits). However 10 per cent variation on either side is admissible.

Bearing in mind the time available to students to complete the report, and to facilitate the understandable anxiety of students who are doing this exercise for the first time, the size of the report is fairly good.

In practice, there is no mandatory length and the students should take guidance from their project guides. The researcher should deal with the report without regard to its length ensuring that all the information is recorded and the report produced conforms to the requirements of the objectives of the study.

Check the following points:

1) Whether all essential information included?
2) Proper structure
3) Clarity
4) Completeness
5) There is no unnecessary pending
6) It essentially contributes to the objectives
7) If anything can be curtailed (if it has too volume notes).

Write everything about the subject under study, structure it with the help of your guide. It is desirable to get the first draft typed in double space with two inch margin on the right hand side of the page. This will give the opportunity to see:

1) What the report looks like?
2) What modifications are necessitated?

The margin and the spacing helps in entering corrections and additional information if desired. This also facilitates editing of the report.

Basic Steps in Writing the Report

The method of carrying out the study, assembling of data and compiling of a report should be carried of in the following stages:

Stage 1. Preparation

Stage 2. Gathering and collecting the information

Stage 3. Sorting, selecting, arranging and recording the material

Stage 4. Writing the introduction

Stage 5. Recording inferences

Stage 6. Writing recommendations

Stage 7. Preparing the report presentation

Stage 8. Typing the report.

STAGE 1. PREPARATION

Keep ready yourself mentally for the task of project writing as explained in Fresh Mental Approach (FMA). Be sure you accurately understand the purpose of your report and its objectives as defined in the project synopsis or terms of reference.

Put yourself in the position of evaluator and ask yourself these questions:—

1) What information, *i.e.*, evidence and justification, would I require to arrive at a logical inference and make the right decision

2) As evaluator, how much, if anything, do I already know about this subject. Decide on the following issues/questions:

   (a) Method of study

   (b) What information you need ?

   (c) Who is going to be involved ?

   (d) Who are you going to carry out your study ?

   (e) When are you going to carry out your study ?

   (f) Project Plan – Time schedule to complete the task.

It is extremely useful for you to relate the plan to a time schedule so that you know what to do and when, in order to complete the report by required deadline (Prepare a CPM by breaking down the project activities in sub tasks and allocate duration to each sub task).

STAGE 2. GATHERING THE MATERIAL

At this stage, don't attempt to write the report. Collect all the information *i.e.,* facts, figures and ideas, about the subject by whatever means available. Some of the means used in gathering the information are briefly given as under:

1) Observation

Don't rely totally on your memory. While observing an operation or coincidence or a situation record the sequence in detail. Look at it, watch it, time it and record everything you see.

2) Reading

Published work of other researchers on similar issues, factual documentation produced within the organisation (if the study is about an organisation), documentation of professional bodies will often provide enough information relative to your subject. Give credit in your report to all such sources.

3) Interviews

Interviews can be formal or informal depending upon their nature and the person being interviewed. Keep the following points in mind:

1) Plan your interview
2) Give your interviewee notice of your subject
3) Prepare your questions before hand
4) Don't rush an interview
5) Focus on substance
6) Be accurate.

4) Discussion

Hold discussions with your colleagues, guide, and any interested person in the subject. Respect their views.

5) Surveys

Surveys are carried out to assess customer opinion and reaction. These are also useful in understanding people's attitudes. Questionnaires are the useful instruments in carrying out surveys. Care must be taken in preparing the questionnaire and, if in doubt, seek advice of your guide. Include copies of the questionnaires and of their analysis in your report.

6) Secondary sources

Secondary sources have been discussed in detail at Chapter 6.

7) Enquiries

Enquiries can be made from service industry through letter, fax or telephone.

Explain the following:

(a) Who you are ?

(b) Purpose of your enquiry.

Be polite while asking for their help. Generally you will receive a favourable response and these sources of information can be most valuable. Give credit to such informants and always thank them for their help. Acknowledge their support in your report.

Use your own knowledge and experience

(a) ***Experiment:*** Try something and see if it works. Record the details and verify the results. If there is any doubt on the accuracy of the information, try and check and verify it from another source.

(b) If it is not possible to verify the information, discard it or quote it as uncorroborated. Always be sure of the facts.

(c) Make liberal use of visuals *i.e.*, CDs, diagrams, maps, charts, photographs, statistical tables. Even sometimes it may be appropriate to attach sample products to illustrate and explain your text. This will make your report visually attractive and interesting.

(d) You should avoid using memory and prejudice. These can often lead to distorted facts. As a report writer always carry a note book with you and note down pieces of information or ideas of things to do at the time they come to you, instead of relying upon the memory. Once you have written it down you can concentrate on something else.

(e) At this stage you will have a sufficient information in the form of notes, collections from various published data, survey data and so on. The next step is to sort it all out.

STAGE 3: SORTING, SELECTING, ARRANGING AND RECORDING MATERIAL

(a) After you have assembled all material, check to ensure that you have all you need to support your arguments.

(b) Arrange it in logical sequence, start to finish, ensuring a natural flow.

(c) The questionnaires, surveys and any other similar document should be explained properly.

(d) To ensure clarity to the readers adequate notations should be used for visuals, *i.e.*, diagrams, maps, charts, photographs, statistical tables.

(e) Illustrations are used to explain a particular part of the text to, Insert them in the appropriate position in the text.

(f) The evaluator needs to refer to these illustrations several times. They form a supportive material. It should be put in the appendices section at the end of the report.

(g) Clear your mind and go through what you have written. Clarify the following questions to yourself:

i) Is your material clear?

ii) Does the material make any sense?

iii) Does the material clearly specify or indicate problem areas?

iv) Does material lead you to the "conclusion" section logically?

STAGE 4: WRITING THE INTRODUCTION

In writing introduction following points need to be count.

1) Create a background of the organisation and work situation for which the project work is being done
2) Describe the purpose of study
3) Describe the method of study
4) Explain difficulties encountered in the preparation of report
5) Introduce yourself, your institution/organisation briefly
6) Ensure continuity between all section

STAGE 5: RECORDING INFERENCES

All conclusions or findings should flow from the outcome of the investigations. These findings should lead to concrete recommendations. While writing conclusions, the objectives of the study should be kept in mind. This will facilitate in understanding the quality of investigations and gauge the success of work. Summary of the problem areas followed explanation of the various alternative solutions to the problem should be undertaken and reason for accepting or rejecting the possible alternative should be explained logically.

STAGE 6: WRITING RECOMMENDATIONS

Adopt a positive attitude and enlist those points first which you really want to be done. You must adopt a constructive approach. This section may be started as follows:

It is recommended that (provide a list of recommendation or action you feel should be taken)

1) ....
2) ....
3) ....
4) ....
5) ....
6) ....
7) ....
8) ....
9) ....
10) ....

If the recommendations involve statements containing financial figures, these should be shown against each item.

Don't repeat matter. In conclusion, you may give a cross reference of relevant paragraph if you want include something in this section.

Bring your report to a positive ending.

At this stage the text of the report is complete and you are ready to go to the next stage i.e. presentation of the report.

STAGE 7: PREPARING REPORT PRESENTATION

Now, stitch together all the different threads of information into a coherent whole. Present the data in a systematic form as suggested in the chapter plan. Write the first draft. Discuss with your guide and incorporate the suggested modifications. If required revise the document and type it finally. The graphics play a significant role in report image and can must be taken about the visual aspects of the report.

STAGE 8: TYPING THE REPORT

For report typing generally A4 size of paper is used. It is universal standard size and will present no difficulty with covers, binding, photocopying and dividing cards between the sections. The margins should be kept as suggested earlier in this chapter. You must ensure the following:

1) Start each section of the report with a new page.
2) Indicate where capitals, italics and underlining are required.
3) If using DTP indicate bold, capital, front type and font size required.
4) All headings and sections and sub-sections are clearly indicated.
5) Indicate clearly where any indentations of the text are required for the ease of reading.

A clear system of identification is used for sections, sub-sections and paragraphs for the speed of reference. An example of a clear system of identification is given in Table 10.1:

Table 10.1: Identification of Sections, Sub-sections and Paragraphs

Selection Pages	Identification		
For Section Headings	1	2	3
For Sub-sections	1.1	2.1	3.1
	1.2	2.2	3.2
	1.3	2.3	3.3
For Paragraphs	1.1.1	2.1.1	3.1.1
	1.1.2	2.1.2	3.1.2
	1.1.3	2.1.3	3.1.3
	—	—	—
	1.2.1	2.2.1	3.2.1
	1.2.2	2.2.2	3.2.2
	—	—	—
For Sub paragraphs	1.1.1 (a)	2.1.1 (a)	3.1.1 (a)
	(b)	(b)	(b)
	(c)	(c)	(c)

Specimen Project Reports

The specimen sample report given in the book in Chapter 14 is the main report with appended parts. This is only a typical report to support the report writers in understanding the principles of report writing. Each report will be unique depending upon the topic of research.

To submit the report, the prefatory parts should be added in the main report.

Check the four points for project report before final binding (typical) the report:—

1) Ensure the prefatory parts are enclosed in the following sequence after the title page:
   (a) Approved project proposal proforma
   (b) Synopsis

(c) The certificate of originality of work

(d) Letter of authorisation

(e) Letter of transmittal

(f) Acknowledgements.

2) Ensure the main report contains:—

(a) Table to contents

(b) Table of illustrations

(c) Glossary of terms

(d) Abbreviations

(e) Executive summary

(f) Introduction

(i) Main report with chapter plan

(h) Recommendations and limitations.

3) Ensure appended parts contain:—

(a) Bibliography

(b) Appendix

(c) Any other source of Information.

Final Remarks

Once your project has been typed, read all print outs carefully and correct any errors. Therefore, carefully consider following questions about your report:

1) Does it look a presentable document ?
2) Does it make sense ?
3) Does it meet objectives of study ?
4) Is it clear and understandable ?
5) Is it factual, logical, conclusive ?
6) Will the evaluator/reader be stimulated to read it ?
7) Are you satisfied with it ?
8) Is your guide satisfied with it ?

Now you should get the report signed by the guide. Determine the number of copies required before going for photocopying. It is preferable, but not necessary, to reproduce photographs and other illustrations in original. The original copy which goes to the assessor and the copy which goes to the library must be neat and presentable. The library copies in all probability may be referred by your juniors.

Advice and Guidance

Your research guide is supposed to be with you throughout the preparation of the report. Bring your problems to his notice. Seek his help and advise. Be guided by him. Respect him. Involve him.

Role of Guide and Completion Certificate

Guide role and involvement of guide is very important during the whole process of research work. His basic roles are:-

1) To direct the author
2) To provide guidance through discussions
3) Guide the researchers in preparing detailed work plan including introduction/outline, methodology for carrying out task, time schedule and other relevant issues
4) To authenticate the mid-term progress report, suggest improvements, variations, changes etc.
5) To check the first draft and suggest changes if any in line with objectives of the study
6) To check the final report for incorporation of changes, suggestions, variations
7) To issue certification of satisfactory completions. After assessing the final report, the research guide issues a certificate of satisfactory completion (For certificate refers Figure 10.1)

Certificate of Completion

This is to certify that the project report titled "..

...." (write the title of the project)

has been accomplished by...(write the name of the author)

under my guidance and supervision.

This project is being submitted by him/her in the partial fulfilment of requirements for the award of the...(Write the name of the degree/diploma) from ....(Write the name of institute/university)

All sources of information and help have been duly mentioned and acknowledged.

Signature of the Guide ....

Name and address of the Guide ....

Date ....

Fig. 10.1: Specimen of a Certificate of Completion from the Guide

Documentation

While writing project report you are likely to use some information which is not your own information. The information which is developed through secondary sources must be foot-noted. It should also be listed in the bibliography. Acknowledge the referred material. For acknowledging the sources a standard reference system should be selected. It should be followed throughout the report consistently.

Getting information

Determination is a major work which you should keep in mind when looking for facts. If you don't find what you need in one reference, look for other sources. Never give up and stop with one or two tries.

Below are some guidelines for getting information

1) Scan material to find out if it is relevant to your project study.
2) Check the credibility of the material by considering its text; source, publisher; author; and currentness.
3) Everything in print is to be necessarily true. Check for genuineness.
4) Look for several viewpoints on a subject. Don't depend on one.

Recording Information

You may find considerable information on a subject. The real test of your research ability comes in getting the important facts down in a form that is easily understandable. Volume of inconsistent information collected do not yield adequate information for preparing reports. The guidelines for recording information are given below:

1) Use separate sheets of paper or help cards for each source.
2) Make a tentative bibliography by writing down the titles which appear to offer the information you require.
3) Keep the papers or help cards in alphabetical order.
4) Write in ink.
5) Use a consistent bibliographical form.
6) Prepare an outline that will give direction to your investigation.

   Usually, bibliography material is recorded on 3×5 inch help cards, and notes are made on 4 × 6 inch help cards. Cards are made from thick sheets of paper
7) Place a heading, keyed to your outline, on each help care.
8) Use direct quotations only when they are significant. Enclose quoted material in quotation marks, taking care to copy each word exactly as written.
9) Use footnotes to give credit for another person's idea which you are using.
10) Arrange your notes in the order of the outline to facilitate their use for the basis of the report.

Footnotes

Footnotes are single spaced and indented five spaces with footnote numbers typed slightly above the line. The names of authors are given in normal order. Use 'Commas' to separate main items. Each footnote ends with a period. All data that has been taken directly or indirectly from another source should be identified in footnotes. Concept also may be footnoted when concept come from reference and publication.

Guidence for footnotes are given below:

1) Acknowledgement

Footnotes are used to acknowledge and document material taken from other sources. Failure to give credit for borrowed material is plagiarism.

2) Placement

Footnotes may appear at the bottom of the page on which the quoted material is used at the end of each chapter or at the end of an entire work.

3) Numbering

Footnotes may be numbered consecutively throughout the entire work or numbered consecutively by chapter.

4) Printing

Footnotes appear in print as single spaced with double spacing separating one footnote from another. However, in manuscript copy, footnotes are double spaced with triple spacing separating one footnote from another.

5) Referencing the same source

Use ibid., (in the same place), to indicate that the source is exactly the same one as the immediately preceding footnote.

Example

(First reference)

1. Negi, Jagmohan, *Hospitality Management: Current Trends and Practices*, Indian University, Noida.
2. Negi, Jagmohan, *Professional Hotel Management*, (New Delhi: S. Chand & Co. 2004), p. 80)
3. Ibid., p. 75.

   (Note: If the page number is not different, simply use *Ibid.)*.

These examples to write footnotes are given in Fig. 10.2 below.

Footnotes

Books

(One Author)

1) Vinson, S. B. 1976. *Host selection by insect parasitoids*. Mittal Publications, New Delhi, pp. 109-133.

(Two Authors)

2) Stinner, B. R. and G. J. House 1990. *Arthropods and other invertebrates in conservation tillage agriculture . Aman Publications, New Delhi*. pp. 299-318.

(Three Authors)

3) Yadav, D. N., R. C. Patel and T.M. Manjunath 1973. Seasonal activity of *Apanteles plutellae* (Kurdj.) a laral parasite of *Plutella xylostella* (L.) a Anand (Gujarat), Oxford IBH, New York, pp 111-115.

(More than Three Authors)

4) Stapel. J. O., A. M. Cortesero, C.M. De Moraes, J. H. Tumlinson and W. J. Lewis 1977. *Effects of extrafloral nectar, honey dew, and sucrose on searching behaviour and efficiency of Microplitis croceipes* (Hymenopterae:Braconidae) in cotton, Oxford IBH, New York, pp. 617-623.

(Corporate authorship)

5) American Chemical Society, Washington, DC., *Insecticides of Plant Origin,* ACS Symp.Ser. 387. pp.110-135,

(An editor)

4) Arnason., J.T., B. J. R. Philogene, and P. Morand (eds.), *Impact of nectariless cotton on plant bug and natural enemies*. Tata-McGraw, NY, pp.110-135.

Magazines and Newspapers

(Article in a weekly magazine with no author given)

1) "*Trends in Office Equipment*", *Office Equipment*, January 1977, pp.88-90.
2) Rajni Rampal, "*Motivating Executives", Marketing News*, 20, No.5(1999), 52.

(A news story with author given)

3) Ashok Galgotia, "*Current Legislation Affecting Business", Delhi Monitor*, 16 Feb 1998, p. 8, col.4.

(A news story with no author given)

4) "Coping with Income Taxes, "The Daily News, 4 July 1995, p.3, col.1.

Encyclopedias

(An article in a reference work with author given)

1) "*Facts About the Bureau of the Census", Trinity Encyclopedia*, 1970, VII, 493.

(An article in a reference work with no author given)

2) Ben Miller,"*Secretarial Skills for the Seventies", Modern Encyclopedia*, 1972, X, 477.

Bulletins and Pamphlets

1) *Guidelines for Managers* (washington, D.C.: Associated Managers of the United States, 1977) p.17.
2) *Highlights of the Annual Meeting of the Personnel Mangement Association*, Personnel Management Association Publication No.A-22 (Washington, D.C.: Washington University Press, 1970), p.35.

Fig. 10.2: Specimen Foonotes in Books/Magazines

Preparing Bibliography

Bibliography is a list of publications, books or works etc. which the researcher has used in the preparation of the report. In other words, this should be a list of acknowledgements of sources of information other than personal contacts.

The need and usefulness for referencing is two-fold:—

1) It enables researcher and evaluator to identify the source of the information or argument, they may consult that source directly on a future occasion.
2) It helps you to avoid plagiarism, the effects of which may be the exacting of a severe penalty.

Referencing

Reference is required for following purposes:

1) To quote any material. If the quotation is taken from a book or article by a third person, then you need to make this clear in your reference; thus you would cite the original source, indicating that it has been quoted by that third person–identifying also that source.
2) To refer explicitly to the work of a particular writer, even where no direct quotation is involved.
3) To say something which is the most important element in your argument, for which a reference can be given.

Reference is not required to support the following:

(i) Factorial information or general statements which are clearly common knowledge.
(ii) An argument that derives from a large number of different sources.

The Reference Form

Once again there are no common rules, but there are two key principles for every effective form of citation:

1) Whatever system of citation employed in a particular piece of work, it is crucial that you are consistent. Thus, once you have decided on the set of conventions you are going to follow, make sure that you follow it rigorously and consistently throughout the piece of writing.
2) References should be full enough to enable the reader to follow them up with a minimum of difficulty. Thus, it is essential that every reference identifies the particular page number (s). A reference that leaves the reader to find his or her own way to the appropriate part of the book is of very little value, unless of course it is in fact the whole book to which you want to refer.

References

Start by identifying books and project areas from the liabrary listing of published books, some students attempt to locate books from commercial book store references such as

1) Allen, George R., *The Graduate Students' Guidelines to Theses and Dessertations*, San Francises Josey-Bass, 1973.
2) Dillman, Don A. *Mail and Telephone Surveys: The Total Design Method*. New York: John Wiley & Sons, 1978.
3) Leedy, Paul D., *Practical Research Planning and Design*, 3rd ed. New York, Macmillan, 1985.
4) Negi, Jagmohan, *Hospitality Management: Current Trends and Practices*. Indian Univesrity, Press New York.
5) Noll, Victor H., *Introduction to Educational Measurement*, 2nd ed. Bosten Houghton Mifflin, 1985.
6) Sax, Gilbert, *Emperical Foundations of Educational Research*, Englewood Cliffs, New Jersey: Prentice-Hall, 1968.
7) Tuckman, Bruce W., *Conducting Educational Research*, New York: Harcourt Brace Jovanovich, 1972.
8) Tull, Donald S. and Hawkons, *Del I. Marketing Research Measurement and Method*, New York: Macmillan, 1984.

Use of Terms

Abbreviations and Acronyms

The terms and abbreviations used throughout the thesis should be defined in this section. There will be worlds, phrases, or acronyms used throughout the project that may be unfamiliar or may be interpreted in more than are way. Each of them should be included in for definition of terms and definitions. Keep note cards of these. List as you come across them and develop them, write the definition on the appropriate note cards, and reference the sources. A list of same abbreviations is given in Table 10.2.

Table 10.2: List of Abbreviations and Examples of some Terms

Sl. No.	*Abbreviations/Terms*	*Full Form*
Abbreviations		
1)	cf.	compare. Also abbreviated cp.
2)	c.i.a.	The Culinary Institute of America
3)	et al.	and others [et al./aliae]
4)	e.g.	for example [example gratial]. Not in italics; preceded by a comma.
5)	etc.	and so forth. Should never be used in formal writing.
6)	ff.	following
7)	ibid.	in the same place [ibidem]. Used to refer to the book, chapter, article or page cited just before. Not in italics.
8)	idem	the same as; as mentioned before. Use to indicate a reference previously mentioned is generally used to refer to the author's name while 'ibid'. refers to the book title.
9)	i.e.	that is [id est]. Not in italics and preceded by a comma.
10)	inter alia	among other things. In Italics.
11)	loc. cit.	in the place cited [loco citato]. Not in italics.
12)	op. cit.	in the work quoted [opere citato]. Not in italics.
13)	sup.	above [supra]. In italics.
14)	[sic]	thus; so. Used to indicate that a surprising or dubious word, phrase, or fact is not a mistake and is to be read as it stands. With brackets.
15)	vide	see.
16)	vide infra	see before. In italics
17)	vide supra	see above. In italics; abbreviated vs.
18)	vis-a-vis	face-to-face. With hyphens.
19)	viz.	namely. not in italics.
20)	w.c.i.	The western culinary Institute

(Contd.)

Sl. No.	Abbreviations/Terms	Full Form
Terms		
Wine by the glass	:	Those wines offered by the bottle, jug, or box that may be sold as a single glass.
Half-bottles	:	Half a much as the standard 750 ml. bottle, these smaller wine bottles contain 375 ml of wine, or just over two glasses.
Wine list	:	A grouping of wine by colour, region, or style; offered by the restaurant for sale.
Variates	:	A specific grape variety used to make the wine listed on the label. Cabernet or chardonnay rather than red or while.
Somellier	:	A waiter in a restaurant who has charge of wines and their preparation; a wine waiter.

General Guidelines

1) Typing the Material

1) Your papers must be in a print out form.
2) Set the word processor to double space and keep it there throughout the entire manuscript.
3) Use one inch margins on the left, right, top, and bottom of he page. These margins are wide in order to leave room for reviewer's comments.
4) Use normal paragraphs in which the first line is indented five characters for all paragraphs in the manuscript except the abstract, block quotes, titles and headings, sub-headings, table titles, notes, and figure captions.
5) Use a 12 point font. In other words, there should be 10 typed characters per inch.
6) Single space after sentence terminators (i.e., '?' '!')
7) Capitalize the first letter following a colon if the clause following the colon is a complete sentence.
8) On a word processor, make sure the text is left aligned and not justified. With left aligned text, the left margin forms a straight line and the right margin is ragged. With justified text both the left the right margins form a straight line.
9) Do not hyphenate (split) words at the end of a line.
10) Finally, just staple or clip the finished product (do not bother with fancy folders, etc).

2) Writing Methodology

1) You must use complete sentences.
2) The first sentence of a paragraph must be independent (able to stand on its own). For example consider, "While these studies are important", there is................ This sentence would be correct in the middle of a paragraph, but as the first sentence, it should more appropriately read, While studies of the effects of whatever on whatever else are important, there is.......

3) Try not to use slang (e.g.,.... put a damper on...).
4) Do not use contractions. That is, instead of 'it's', use 'it is'.
5) If you are doubtful about the spelling of a word, do not guess. Look up the correct spelling in an appropriate reference source.
6) Proof-read the copy that you submit and do correct minor typographical errors, formatting, spelling, or even the wording, with a pencil. These corrections are inevitable and will communicate that you are serious about your work.

3) Style Details

1) Study this handout. When in doubt about a detail, check with the Research Publication Manual.
2) Assume you are writing the paper for submission to a professional journal.
3) A lot of the formatting details can be learned by carefully modeling journal article. It would be a good idea to acquire a few fairly recent articles.
4) Avoid excessive use of the terms 'I', 'me' and 'my', as well as the phrase personally speaking.
5) Avoid the use of sexist language. For example, consistently referring to a person as a him or she when it is just as likely for the person to be a she or a her, is sexist. However, using (s) he or him/her all of the time can also be awkward. If you phrase it right, you can often use the word 'person' instead.
6) Avoid using 'empty words' or words, which serve no purpose. For example, in the Negi (2003) study it was found that............ Should read more like Negi (2003) found that.
7) Generally speaking, use past tense in the abstract, introduction, and method. Results and discussion sections can be in the present tense.
8) Get friends to read it. If they cannot understand it, then it needs work. If you cannot get a friend to read it, then try to read it yourself making believe that you are naive.

4) Abbreviations

1) When abbreviating any terms, spell them out the first time (in both the abstract and again in the body of the manuscript, if need be). For example, The Service Opinion Survey (SOS) was used to....................
2) Do not use too many abbreviations. Whereas one, two, or three can be helpful, four or five can be confusing.
3) You will often see the following Latin abbreviations used.

cf.	compare	etc.	and so forth
e.g.,	for example	i.e.,	that is
et al.	and others	vs.	versus, against

Note that (except for et al.) these abbreviations are only used in parenthetic material. In non-parenthetic material, use the English translation.

4) Do not use 'E' and 'S' as abbreviations for experimenter and subject. This was done in articles written many years ago.

5) Note the following common abbreviations and note also that you do not use periods with them.

cm	centimeter	s	seconds
mg	milligrams	min	minutes
g	grams	hr	hours
M	mean	IQ	intelligence

For example, the bar is 2.5 cm wide and 1.0 cm high.

Numbers

1) All measurement reporting is done in metric units. In other words, use centimeters and meters rather than inches and feet.
2) The numbers zero through nine are spelled out as one, two, three and so on, (except when it is a table or figure number, or a metric measurement, etc). The numbers 10 and above are written as numbers.
3) Capitalize nouns followed by numerals or letters that denote a specific place in a numbered series. For example, as can be seen in Figure 3, during Block 4 of Session 2 such and such occurred. Note also that this example demonstrates one of the exceptions to the rule noted in item number 2 above.
4) Spell out any number when it is the first thing in a sentence. For example, the sentence '54 students were used' is not appropriate and should read 'Fifty-four students were used.'
5) Try to be consistent with number formats. That is, if you are reporting a series of related numbers, they should all be presented with the same number of decimal places. For an example, see point in Abbreviatons.

Citations in the text

1) If you see someone's words or ideas, you must give them credit with a citation. This is particularly important, since the penalties for plagiarism are severe.
2) There are numerous ways to formally cite a reference in the text. Examples include some fact (last name, year)., Last name (year) noted that.., or in <year>, <last name> reported that. For more ideas, pay close attention to the articles you read.
3) The first time the reference is cited in the text, spell out all of the authors last names. For example, Joshi, Pandy, (2004) suggested that........ With articles that have three or more authors use the Latin abbreviation for "and other" when the reference is cited a second (or third) time. For example, Negi et al. (1975) suggested that... or... some fact (Negi et al., 2004).
4) If the citation is in parentheses and you need to use the word "and", use the ampersand ('&') instead. For example, 'Some (e.g., Estes & Skinner, 1940) have suggested that', as compared to 'Estes and Skinner (1940) have suggested'. Note also that the opposite applies as well, that is, if the citation is not in parentheses, you must use the word "and"
5) Multiple citations in parentheses are placed alphabetically and are separated by a semicolon and a space. For example, Some fact (Negi, 1904; Moon, 1968; Partin, 1980).

6) If you cite something second hand, you must make it clear (e.g. Some fact Chauhan as cited in Bose, Year). Note that in this example, only the Bose reference would be placed in the reference section.)

Quotations

1) You must give page numbers for direct quotes. For example, J. Negi (2002) noted that "the world is round" (p. 1).
2) Three or four quotes in a 10 page paper is about the upper limit.
3) Display a quotation of more than 40 words as free-standing block of text indented 5 spaces from the left margin (doubles spaced as usual). Omit the quotation marks and include the page number in parentheses after the last page. Also, if the quotation is more than one paragraph, indent the first line of the second and any additional paragraphs 5 spaces.

Research Reports

The order of the sections of the manuscript are as follows:

Title Page

1) See an example title page.
2) The manuscript page header is the thing that appears on the title page. It consists of the first two or three words of the title and is followed by the page number. It is used by the editors and reviewers to identify the pages of the manuscript. It is placed in the upper right hand corner of all pages of the manuscript (except for any figures). Thus, the manuscript page header should appear as the first line of the title page, right justified with the number '1' either double spaced below it or 5 spaces to the right of it. If you are using a word processor, you can have it put this manuscript page header on all pages on all pages automatically.
3) The running head comes next and is no more than 50 characters (including punctuation and spaces). It typically consists of a couple of key words from the title. Type this running head flush left and in all capital letters. For example, Running head: Abortion Attitudes in College Students (note that the 'R' in running is capitalized, but the 'h' in head is not.
4) Choosing a title. The title should summarize the main idea of the paper in 10-12 words. A good recipe to work with when reporting the results of an experiment is (Dependent Variable) as a Function of (Independent Variable) or The Effects of (Independent Variable) on (Dependent Variable). With other types of research you should try to include the variables of interest in the title (and be careful not to imply causality). Also, it is a good idea to include the species if you're working with animals or some details about the type of population if you're working with humans.
5) When typing the title, center it on the page and capitalize only the first letter of important the next double spaced line is the author's name, and on the next double spaced line is the institutional affiliation.
6) For the purposes of this class, it would be advisable to include something like in partial fulfillment of the requirements for Tourism and Hospitality, Instructor's Name, and the Datea.

Abstract

1) The abstract page is Page 2.

2) Center the word 'Abstract' on this page, then begin typing on the very next double spaced line (i.e., do not insert any extra blank lines here).
3) Type this section as a single (double spaced) paragraph in block format (i.e., do not use indentation).
4) The purpose of this section is to provide a brief (100-120 words), comprehensive summary of the study. It is very important because it is all that many people will read.
5) If should include a brief description of the problem being investigated, the methods used, the results, and their implications.
6) It is a good idea to write this section last (after all of the other sections are written). You might try taking the lead sentence or two from the introduction, method, results, and discussion sections and integrates them to from the abstract.
7) Avoid citing references in the abstract.

Introduction

1) The introduction begins on Page 3.
2) Start this page by retyping your title (centered), then begin typing the section (on the next double spaced line) using normal (5 space indented) paragraphs. Do not type the word 'Introduction'.
3) The main purpose of this section is to tell the reader why you performed the study. In other words, you have to inform the reader of the research question and indicate why it is important and how it is unique when compared to previous studies.
4) It starts out broad and becomes more and more specific. For example, you might begin by defining any relevant terms. Then go on to review the relevant literature. Avoid an exhaustive and historical review. Then go on to make clear the connection between previous research and the present work.
5) You might include any hypotheses and the rationale for them.
6) The final paragraph usually contains a statement which clearly and explicitly states why the study was performed, such as, 'the purpose of this study was to..... or the present study was designed to investigate the..' Be especially careful not to use a sentence of this type earlier in your introduction.
7) Thus, this section should contain an absolute minimum of four paragraphs: the general introduction, the literature review, the connection of the present study to the literature and the explicit statement of purpose.

Methods

1) Do not purposely start a new page for this section. Simply center the word 'Method' and continue typing on the very next double-spaced line (i.e., do not insert any extra blank lines here).
2) The purpose of this section is to describe in details how you performed the study. Someone should be able to replicate your study based on the information you provide in this section.

3) Make it sound professional, that is, do not make it sound like a class project. Assume you are writing for submission to a scientific journal.
4) Avoid unnecessary details like the data were displayed on the computer screen and recorded on the data sheet(s). This is similar to the empty word problem describ.
5. For an experiment, this section is typically divided into four subsections: subjects, apparatus, design, and procedure. The order of design followed by procedure is arbitrary. In other words, you could have the procedure come before the design. Sometimes researchers combine the design and procedure sections, however, in an experimental psychology or research methods class, a separate design section is typically required.
6. For a survey study (i.e. one in which the participants are simply asked a set of questions), the design section is not necessary (and the survey itself may be included as an appendix).

Subjects/Participants

1) This section is labeled as subjects or participants depending on whether animals or humans are used in the study. If animals are used, use the term 'subjects'. If humans are used, use the term 'participants'.
2) Do not purposely start a new page for this section. Type the appropriate title for this sub-section flush with the left margin and underline it. On the next line, begin typing normal paragraphs.
3) Indicate who participated in the study, how many, and how were they selected.
4) Include any details which are relevant to the study (e.g., gender, age, ethnicity, strain, weight, etc.).
5) If the subjects were human, what type of reward or motivation was used to encourage them to participate.

Apparatus

1) Do not purposely start a new page for this section. Type the word 'Apparatus' flush with the left margin and underline it. On the next line, typing normal, paragraphs.
2) Describe what materials were used and how they functioned in the study.
3) If you use a piece of equipment, you must give the model number, company, and state where the company resides (as a two-letter abbreviation).
4) You must give the dimensions (and perhaps other descriptive details) of any important items used in the study.
5) Standard equipment such as furniture, stopwatches, pencils and paper, can usually be mentioned without providing a lot of details. In fact, you may often simply mention these items in passing as part of the procedure.
6) Be careful not to describe procedures in this section. You should make clear what purpose the apparatus served, but do not give a lot of details on the use of the apparatus at this point. One hint in this regard is to avoid using action verbs in this section.

Design

1) Do not purposely start a new page for this section. Type the word 'Design' flush with the left margin and underline it. On the next line, begin typing normal paragraphs.
2) Describe the design and clearly spell out the independent and dependent variables. Indicate what the levels of the independent variables were, and whether the factor (s) were repeated, matched, or independent.
3) Describe how the subjects were assigned to groups.
4) Describe any control procedures used.

Procedure

1) Do not purposely start a new page for this section. Type the word 'Procedure' flush with the left margin and underline it. On the next line, begin typing normal paragraphs.
2) Carefully summarize each step in the execution of the study.
3) Indicate what a typical test, trial, or session involved.
4) Describe any phases that the study had or any instructions that the subjects received.
5) When referring to groups, try to use descriptive labels. For example, instead of saying 'Group 1' or the experimental group, you might say 'the drugged group'.

Results

1) Do not purposely start a new page for this section. Simply center the word Results and continue typing on the very next double-spaced line (i.e., do not insert any extra blank lines here).
2) Look carefully at the results. That is, take a good hard look at all those numbers you collect. Think of different ways to summarize them, as well as to make sense of them. This section will be easier to write if you make any tables and/or figures you intend to use first.
3) Briefly state the main findings in words. That is, first give a general description, then go into the details.
4) When presenting the results of statistical tests, give descriptive statistics before the corresponding inferential statics. In other words, give means and/or percentages (perhaps referring to a table or figure), before talking about the results of any statistical test you performed.
5) When presenting means, it is reasonable to use one additional digit of accuracy than what is contained in the raw data. In other words, if the raw data consisted of whole numbers, then the means should contain one decimal place.
6) When presenting nominal or ordinal data, give the percents rather than frequencies (since percents are independent of the sample size).
7) The general format for presenting an inferential statistic is: Statistic(df) = value, probability= value. Note that if the statistics are generated with a computer, you can give the exact 'P' values. Also if the computer output says the probability is , 0000, then report it as .001.

Ways to Present Results

Manuscript page header:......................................

Page number:......................................

An examination of the number of hours of use of internet and television viewing and the frequency of aggressive acts for each of the 60 students revealed a positive or direct correlation between use of internet and television viewing and instances of aggressive behavior. An analysis using Pearson's correlation coefficient supported this observation, $r(58) = 63$, $p < 0.05$.

The control group ($M = 14.1$) remembered more words on the memory test than the drugged group ($M = 12.3$)

This difference was tested using an independent groups t test, and was shown to be nonsignificant, $t(18) = 1.23$ $p > 0.10$. Thus, the data fail to support the notion of a drug effect on memory.

The mean scores for the short, medium, and long retention intervals were 5.9, 10.3, and 14.2 respectively.

A one way analysis of variance revealed a significant effect of retention interval, $F(2, 34) = 123.07$, p .001. While 60% of the males agreed that their map reading skills were strong, only 35% of the females did.

A 2 × 2 Chi Square analysis revealed that this was a significant difference $(1, N = 119) = 10.51$, $p < .025$ suggesting that there was a relationship between gender and confidence in map reading skills.

Fig. 10.3: Specimen of Ways to Present Results

8) When actually presenting the results, try to emphasize the meaning of the statistics. That is, clearly describe what it is you are testing and what significance means for the variables involved.
9) See some examples of the correct way to present the results of several common statistical tests.
10) Do not discuss the implications of the results in this section.
11) Do not talk about the meaning of the alpha level or the null hypothesis, and what chance factors have to do with it. Since you are writing for the scientific community, you can assume the reader will have a working knowledge of statistics.
12) If you are presenting a lot of material here, you may wish to employ sub-headings (as is one is the methods section). These sub-headings should have meaning and words, they should not be organized by the type of analysis. Since this is not expected by the reader, it is a good idea to precede the sub-headings with a paragraph informing the reader of the logical organization of this section.

13) In cases where the reader would expect something to be significant and it is not, you should address the issue.

14) Do not provide raw data unless, for some reason, you require a single subject approach.

15) Be careful with the word "prove". Since statistical tests are based on probability and can be in error, they do not really prove anything.

16) You can only use wording that implies causality if you actually manipulated the independent variable (i.e., performed an experiment). For example, suppose you manipulated whether subjects received a drug (while employing appropriate control procedures, etc.) and found a significant difference in memory performance (with the drug users performing more poorly than nonusers). In this case, you would be able to conclude that the drug caused the difference in memory ability; it impaired it. As another example, suppose that you compared drug use (as determined from the results of a survey) with memory ability and found a correlation (greater use went along with poorer memory performance). Since correlation doesn't say much about causality, we could only conclude that there is a relationship between drug use and memory ability.

Discussion

1) Do not purposely start a new page for this section. Simply center the word 'Discussion' and continue typing on the very next double-spaced line (i.e., do not insert any extra blank lines here).

2) The purpose of this section is to evaluate and interpret the results, especially with respect to the original research question.

3) Start off with a brief, non-technical summary of the results. In other words, tell the reader about the main findings without using statistical terminology.

4) Then go on to discuss the implications of the results. In other words, whatever was found needs to be discussed.

5) It is also important to discuss how the results relate to the literature you cited in the introduction. In other words, emphasize any theoretical consequences of the results.

6) You might (or might not) also mention any limitations of the study and any suggestions for future research in this section.

7) Finally, you need an ending paragraph, in which you make a final summary statement of the conclusions you have drawn.

8) Thus, this section should contain an absolute minimum of three paragraphs: the non-technical summary discussion of the results and their implications, and the concluding paragraph.

Reference Section

1) Start on a new page. Center the word 'References' at the top. As usual, double space.

2) Any citations made in the manuscript must be presented in this section and vice versa. That is, if something is not cited in the text, then it should not appear in this section. In still other words, this is not a bibliography.

3) In any of the previous sections, whenever you say something like studies have shown you must provide a citation. This section tells the reader where they can find these citations.

4) This section is alphabetized by last name (of the first author involved in the study).
5) Normal paragraphs (i.e., five-space indented) are employed for each reference.
6) For each author, give the last name followed by a comma and the first (and middle) initials followed by periods.
7) Separate multiple authors with commas (,) and the last author with the ampersand ('&') rather than the word "and".
8) After the author(s) comes the year (in parentheses and followed by a period).
9) For a journal reference, underline the title of the journal, volume number and adjacent punctuation marks with a single unbroken line. Note that issue numbers are typically not included. Also, capitalize the important words of the journal title.
10) For a book reference, just underline the title. Only capitalize the first word of the title. Do include the city, state (as a two-letter abbreviation without periods), and the publisher's name.
11) See the example reference section. It provides several types of references, including: Single and multiple author(s), journal articles, book, and book chapter, web pages, as well as a government document.

REFERENCE SECTION

---

manuscript page header

page number

References

Negi, J., (2000), *Effects of Tourism Development: Economic, social and environmental effect.* Psychopharmacology, 61 (1) 107-124.

Beck, A. T. (1967). *Depression: Clinical, experimental and theoretical aspects*. New York: Hoeber.

Cicero, T.J (1979). *A critique of animal analogues of alcoholism.* In E. Majchrowicz % E. P. Noble (Eds)., *Biochemistry and pharmacology of ethanol* (Volume 2, pp. 31- 59). New York: Plenum Press.

Dorworth, T. R., & Overier, J. B. (1977). On "*learned helplessness*": *The thearapeutic effects of electroconvulsive shocks*: *Physiological Psychology*, 5, 355-358.

Plonsky, M. (1988). *Psychology with style: A hpertext writing guide* (Version 3). Retrieved from the Web 9/1/98.

http://www.uwsp.edu/psych/apa4b.htm

U.S. Department of Health, Education, and Welfare. (1971). *Alcohol and Health*. Washington, DC: U.S. Government Printing Office.

Fig. 10.4: Specimen Reference Section

Other Sections

1) After the above sections many more tables, the page(s) with the figure captions, and finally any figures, respectively. Each belongs on a separate page (multiple figure captions can appear on one page however).

2) Tables and the figure captions page have a manuscript page header and page number just like all the other typed pages. Note that figures are not typed, and so do not have a manuscript page header and page number.

3) Tables and figure should be able to stand-along (i.e., you should not have to read the manuscript to be able to understand a table or figure). A big help in this regard is the table title or the figure caption. Use these wisely to explain what is going on in the table or figure. In other words, do not be afraid to be a little bit verbose in your table titles and figure captions.

4) Tables and figures should not duplicate the same information. Likewise, you should not repeat the data point values in a table or figure in the text of the manuscript.

5) Tables and figures are more expensive to include in the manuscript than text. Therefore, if you include one, it should include a reasonable number of data points (unless it illustrates a particularly complex result). In other words, if you only have a few data points to present, do it in the text of the manuscript rather than in a table or figure.

6) Tables and figures are most often used to present results, but may also be used to present other information, such as the design or a theoretical schema.

7) If you include a table or figure, you must introduce it in the text of the results section (e.g., Table 1 displays the...) and describe to the reader what should be seen it.

Tables

1) See an example 'Table'.

2) Note that "APA" style tables do not contain any vertical lines, so do not draw them in or use your word processor to generate them.

3) Type the table number and then (on the next double spaced line) type the table title flush left and underlined. Note that there are no periods used after the table number or title.

4) When using columns with decimal numbers, make the decimal points line up (see Fig. 10.5).

Figure Captions

1) See an example figure captions page.

2) Start on a new page. Center the phrase Figure Captions at the top.

3. Each figure caption is typed flush left in block format.

4) The word 'figure', the number, and the adjacent period are underline, for example. Figure 10.6. The effect of..

Figures

1) 'Figures' is the technical term for graphs, charts, drawings and pictures.

2) Figures (other than pictures) may be drawn in black and white only (using a ruler and preferably on graph paper) or they may be generated with a computer graphics program (keeping it in two dimensions).

TABLE No. ....

manuscript page header
page number
Table 1

Average ages sexual information was acquired
Compared with the youngest and oldest ages subjects
Believed the information should be acquired

	Age Acquired		Youngest Age		Oldest Age	
Information						
How babies are made ?						
How babies are born ?						
Sexual intercourse						
Menstruation						
Noctumal emissions						
Masturbation						
Birth control						
Homosexuality						
Genital terminology						
Orgasm						
STD's						

STD's = Sexually transmitted diseases

Fig. 10.5: Specimen of a Table

3) Center each figure on the page vertically as well as horizontally and arrange for the figure to use the bulk of the page.
4) If the figure is a chart of graph, verbally label the axes (do not use "X" and "Y") and provide a key if necessary (e.g. explaining what open us. filled circles are).
5) On the back of each figure (with a pencil), put the manuscript page header, the figure number, and the word TOP to indicate how the figure should appear on the page.
6) Do not put the figure caption on the figure, since that is what is figure captions page is for.

---

manuscript page header

page number

Figure Captions

Figure 1. Number of people arrested for drunken driving as related to the day of the week.

Figure 2. Mean activity counts as a function of maternal diet and age of the rat at the time of testing.

Fig. 10.6: Specimen Captions Page

Research Reviews

There are a number of kinds of research reviews. You could describe a phenomenon, review an existing theory or present a new one. You could critically evaluate how one theory accounts for some data as compared to some other theory. Whatever the kind of reviews, the goal is to organize, integrate, and evaluate previous research in order to clarify a particular problem or issue. This type of manuscript does not follow as standard a format as a research report. Instead of the introduction, methods, results and discussion sections, there is an introduction, body and conclusions.

A. Introduction

1) Begins on page 3 (after the title page and abstract).
2) Start this page by retyping your title (centered), then begin typing the section (on the next double spaced line) using normal (5 space indented paragraphs. Do not type the word Introduction.
3) The introduction should clearly define the problem or issue. This section is not unlike the introduction for a research report.
4) It starts out broad and becomes more and more specific.
5) It is often useful to use headings (and perhaps subheadings) in the body of the research report to help communicate the outline and organization of the paper to the reader. It is a good idea to precede the headings with a paragraph informing the reader of the logical organization (i.e., other headings that will be employed). This paragraph should appear at

the end of the introduction just before the actual body of the paper and is important because it lets the reader know the directions that the paper will take.

B. Body

1) If you use headings, the primary main heading levels should be treated like the main heading of a research report, that is, type the main heading using upper and lower case, and center it horizontally on the page Second level headings are flush left and underlined. Third level headings (if necessary) are indented like the normal paragraphs that they start off. Thus, the words of the third level heading lead off the paragraph, are separated from it by a period, and are underlined (including the period). The rest of the paragraph follows the period.
2) This section should present the relevant literature and ideas.
3) Often the instructor will set a minimum number of references that are required. These references will be listed in the reference section and are cited using a particular style which you can see most clearly in the literature you are reading for your review.
4) A common mistake that students often make is to organize the paper titles as the main headings of the manuscript) The paper should be organized around the relevant phenomenon or theory and not by the specific references that one uses in the paper.
5) This section can be lengthy (depending upon how much material is presented).
6) You might try to identify relations, contradictions, gaps, and inconsistencies in the literature.
7) You might suggest possible solutions to any problem(s) identified.
8) You might suggest future directions for research to take.

C. Conclusions

1) Finally, you need an ending section, in which, you summarize the main points you have made.

11

Visual Aspects of the Project Report

One more method of making the data intelligible is to present them by means of diagrams and graphs. The special feature of diagrams and graphs is that they do away with figures altogether and present dry and uninteresting statistical facts in the shape of attractive and appealing pictures and charts. Diagrams and graphs give a bird's eye view of the whole mass of statistical data that have been collected about any problem. Diagrammatic and graphic representations of data are methods of visual aids and are appealing to the eye and the mind.

Tables, charts and graphs are convenient ways to clearly show your data. Consider how to best show your results with appropriate graph forms. You might want to consult with your teacher / guide. Give your charts and graphs an appropriate title that explains what the data measure. On line and bar graphs, the x and y axis must be appropriately labeled with correct unit of measure (in metric when applicable).

The easiest way to create a graph is to enter your data into a spreadsheet program (Microsoft Words, Claris Words, Excel, etc.). These programs will generate graphs from the data you enter. The graphs could be done in Microsoft Words and could easily be replicated in any spreadsheet program.

Graphs and Diagrams

There are three basic graph forms. The bar graph, the line graph and the circle or pie graph.

In preparing the visual that accompany the statistical analysis, several factors should be kept in mind. These include visual clarity, evenness of numerical spacing and labeling. The chart must be clear enough that the reader can immediately see the lines and sections on it. Bar or pie chart that have different types of shading reflecting various data categories can be effective if the contrast or shading is substantial.

The numbers at bottom and side of each graph or chart should be spaced, also be consistent within the graph or chart. Labeling is the most frequently encountered problem in graphs, charts, figures and tables. The title should be clearly identified in capital or bold letters at the top. Many project reports require communication of voluminous and complex information. It is not possible to this job with words only. Graphic portray things that would take volumes to explain through words technical reports in particular, cannot be completed without use of graphics. The main role of graphics in the report is to:—

1) Support text to communicate report content
2) Emphasis key points
3) Make report attractive
4) Add interest
5) Save time
6) Create impact
7) Help the reader to remember main points.

Before organizing the report, you must think and plan the followings:—

1) What graphics to be used ?
2) How many graphics to be used ?
3) Where to use graphics in the text ?

The graphics used in reports are normally:—

1) Charts
2) Graphs
3) Photographs
4) Maps.

How many graphic to be used ?

Graphics selected should serve to communicate specific point of the report. Avoid random use of graphics. There is no set rule to determine the number of graphics. However plan what is required to be some guidelines effectively through graphics and include these graphics only.

What to use graphics in the text ?

The graphics should be placed in such a position that are likely to be seen when they are required to be referred. Conductive for placing graphics in a proper manner are:—

1) Place them close to the related text.
2) If the graphic is large, and is of full size, place it on the page following the text.
3) If the graphic is small, place it appropriately and surround it with the related text.
4) Graphics which are not discussed in the main but support the discussion should be appended.
5) Always make reference of the graphic in the text to invite to reader to refer it, e.g. as shown in Exhibit 3, 4, ... or
6) Always use rules and borders to enhance presentability
7) Use colour if you have access to colour printers
8) Number graphics and title appropriately.

Your illustrations should include:—

1) Appropriate title and units
2) Scales or labels on axes

3) Key
4) Source of data (if from outside source)
5) Caption to the chart.

Types of visual aids / graphics

The common types of visual aids used in communicating data are:—

1) Bar charts
2) Line or area charts
3) Pictogram
4) Pie charts
5) Pictorial diagrams.

The most important advantage of diagrammatic presentation of data is that *diagrams are very attractive*, and interesting, so far as the common man is concerned. Since people see pictures carefully, their effect on the mind is more stable. The impression created by a diagram or a picture is likely to last longer in the mind than the effect created by a set of figures. Moreover, pictures, diagrams, etc., are very catching, and this is the reason why modern advertisements are mostly in the shape of attractive pictures and diagrams. Figures are rarely used for purposes of advertisement. Modern advertisement is based on human psychology and advertisers realize that inherently people have a craving and love for beautiful pictures and they take advantage of this fact.

Characteristics of diagrams

1) Diagrams only represent data
2) Data should be homogenous
3) Diagrams are not substitutes for figures.

Rules for drawing

A good diagram should be neat and clean. It should be appealing to the eye and should be attractive. Diagrams that attract the attention of the common man are said to be good. Extreme care should be excised in the selection of particular type of diagram that would be suitable to represent a given set of figures.

Selection of scale

A very important thing in connection with drawing of diagrams is the selection of a proper scale. In deciding about the scale, the size of the paper on which a particular diagram is being constructed should be kept in mind. The size of the diagram should be such that all the important characteristics of the data are properly emphasized and can be understood merely by looking at it.

The vertical scale is generally shown on the left hand size and the horizontal scale at the bottom of diagram. The scale should always be very indicated in figure, as without it no diagram is considered complete.

Types of diagrams

The following are important types of diagrams in common use:-

1) Dimensional diagrams

(a) *One-dimensional diagrams*

They are in the shape of vertical or horizontal lines or bars. The lengths of the lines or bars are in proportion to the different figures they represent.

(b) *Two-dimensional diagrams*

They are in the shape of rectangle, squares and circles. The areas of squares, rectangles or circles are in proportion to the size of items which they represent.

(c) *Three-dimensional diagrams*

They are in the shapes of cubes, blocks or cylinders. Here the volumes of cubes, blocks or cylinders are in proportion to given values.

2) Pictograms

Here the figures are represented by pictures. The size or the number of pictures is in proportion to the given figures. Pictograms are one where it is number of pictures that represent frequency. A key is used to show how many items each picture represents.

3) Cartograms

Here maps are drawn and the figures representing the phenomena at various places are shown to the given values.

4) Graphs and Curves

Here the figures are shown in the shape of graphs or curves. They can be either on natural scale or ratio scale.

The terms "diagrams" "chart" or "graph" are very often used as synonyms.

One-dimensional Diagrams

Bar graphs are an excellent way to show results that are one time, that aren't continuous - especially samplings such as surveys, inventories, etc. Figure 11.1 is a typical survey asking tourists about their activity. Notice that in this graph each column is labeled - it is also possible to label the category to the left of the bar.

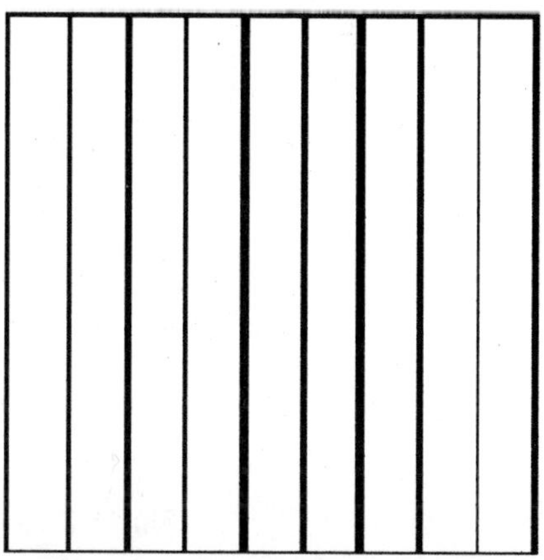

Fig. 11.1: Specimen of a Bar Chart

In this case, the numbers for each category are across the bottom of the chart. A bar chart is marked off with a series of lines called grid lines. These lines typically mark off a numerical point in the series of numbers on the axis or line. In this case, each grid line going up and down marks a multiple of 20 as the graph is divided such. More gridlines can make it easier to be exact with the amounts being shown on the bar graph, but too many can make it confusing.

In these diagrams only the length of the bars or lines is taken into account. Since only one dimension of the figure is taken into account these diagrams are known as one-dimensional diagrams. The bars which are drawn can be any width or thickness. It has no affect on the diagram. However, the thickness should not be too much as otherwise bars would appear like rectangle and give a misleading impression. Such diagrams are also known as Bar Diagrams. Bar diagrams can be three types:—

(i) Simple bar diagrams
(ii) Multiple bar diagrams
(iii) Sub-divided bar diagrams.

Simple bar diagrams

The scale for the construction of simple bar diagrams should be adjusted in such a manner that the longest bar may be easily accommodated on the paper on which the diagram is being drawn. Sufficient space should be left on all sides of the diagram for writing heading, scale, units, etc. Since thickness of bars is not taken into account they should be so constructed that they look attractive and beautiful.

It should further be remembered that whatever the width of the bars it should be uniform for all of them. Bars should further be equi-distant. The space left between adjoining bars should always be equal. Bars can be drawn either vertically or horizontally (Refer Figure 11.2, 11.3, 11.4, 11.5, 11.6 and 11.7).

Bar diagrams can be used in case of discrete series, series of individual observation, spatial and condition series. They cannot be used in continuous series.

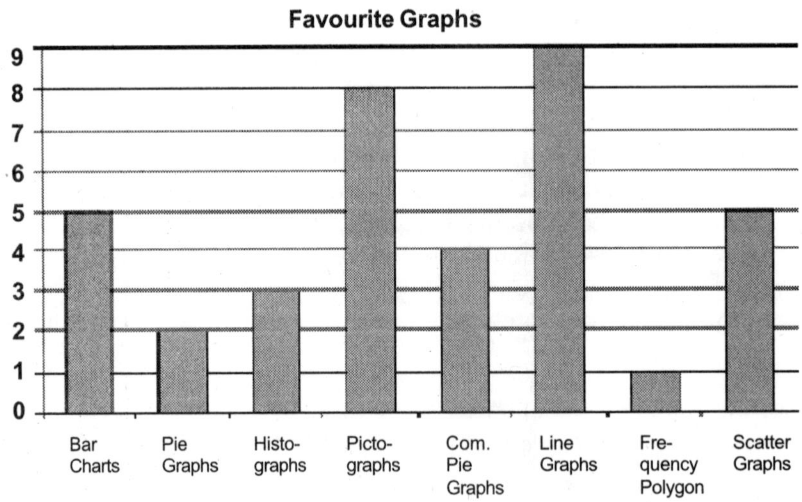

Fig.11.2: Specimen of a Simple Bar Chart

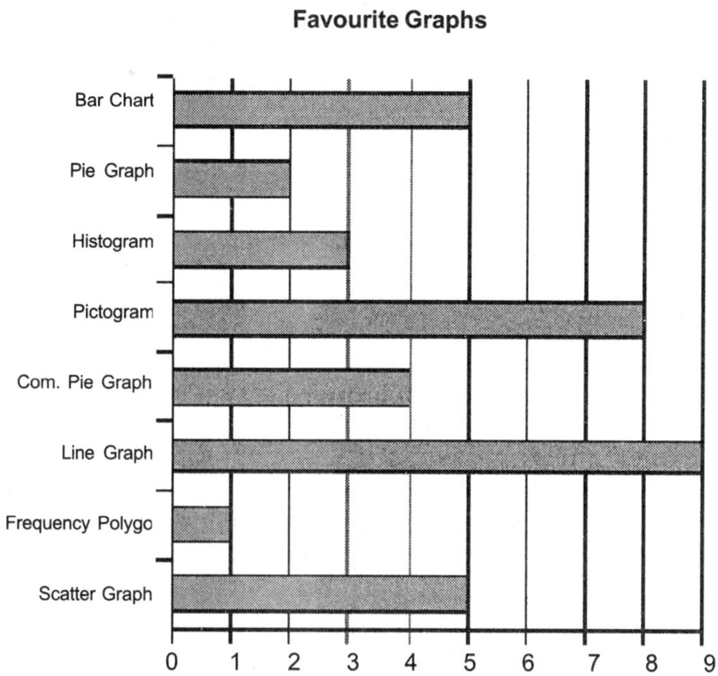

Fig. 11.3: Specimen of a Horizontal Bar Chart

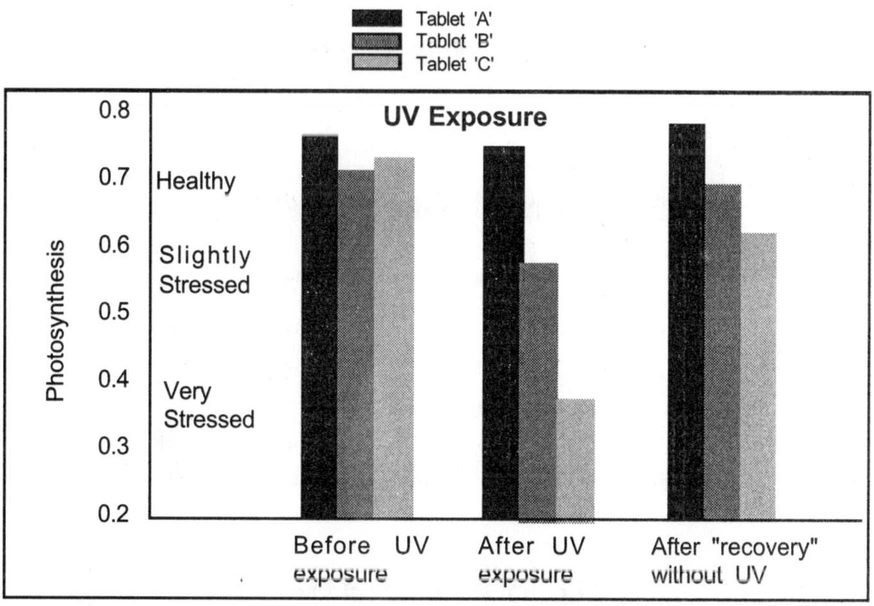

Fig. 11.4: Specimen of a Multiple Bar Diagram

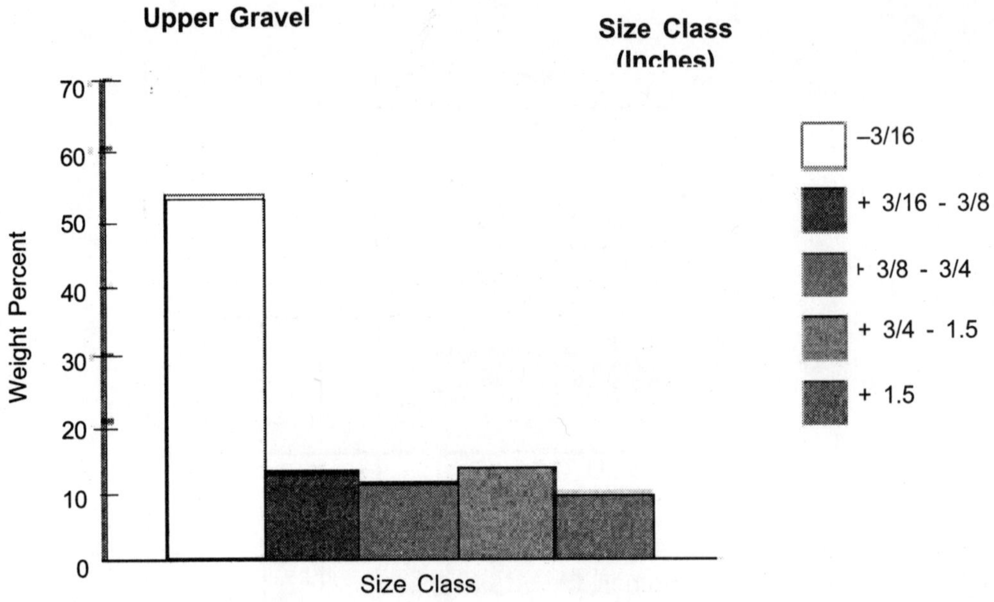

Fig. 11.5: Specimen of a Percentage Bar

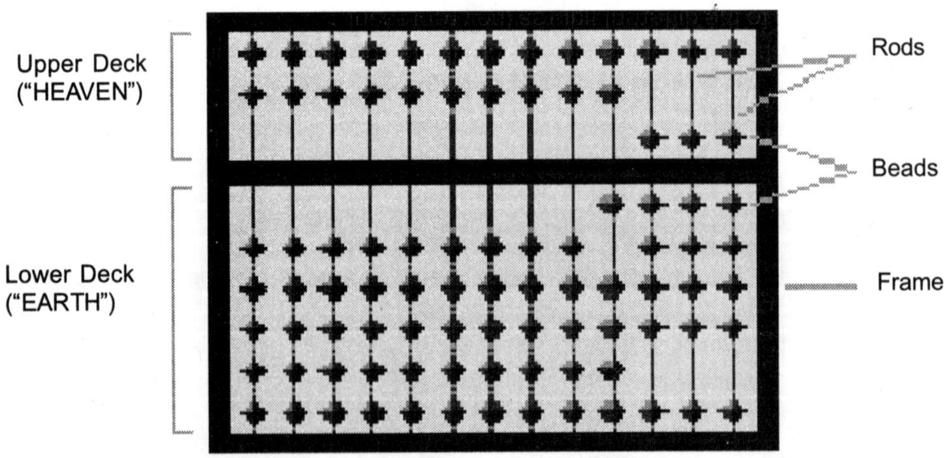

Fig. 11.6: Specimen of a Broken Bar

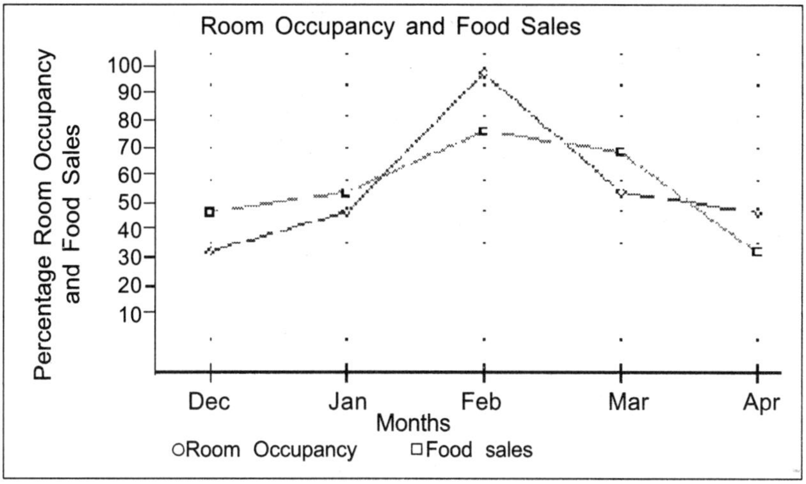

Fig. 11.7: Specimen of a Deviation Bar

A bar graph is used to show relationships between groups. The two items being compared do not need to affect each other. It's a fast way to show big differences. Notice how easy it is to see affect on growth of hotel industry due to different incentives (Fig. 11.8).

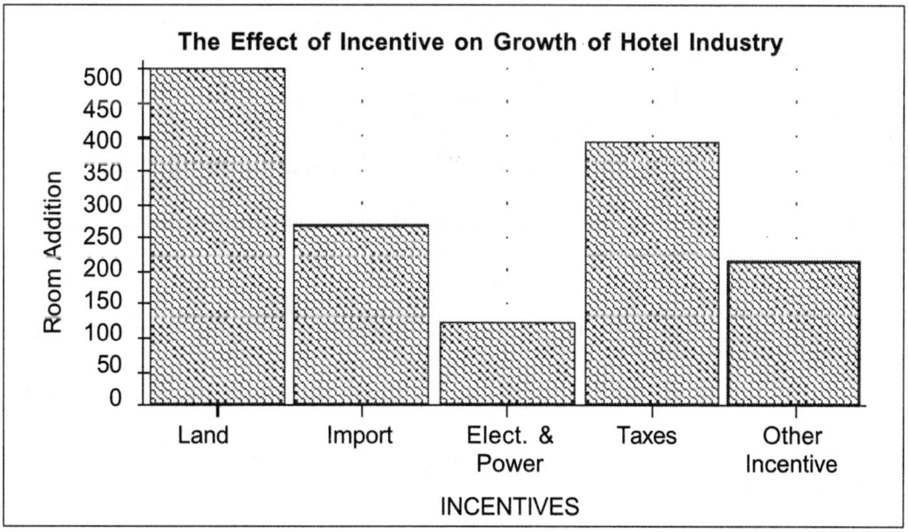

Fig. 11.8: Effect of Incentive on Growth of Hotel Industry

Notice that for data that does not fall evenly on a multiple of 20, the bar is in between two grid lines. Bar graphs are useful to get an overall idea of trends in responses - which categories get many versus few responses.

Table 11.1: Favourite Tourist Activities

Activity	Number
Visit Friends and Relatives	175
Entertainment	168
Excursion Tours	120
Recreation	120
Adventure Activities	65

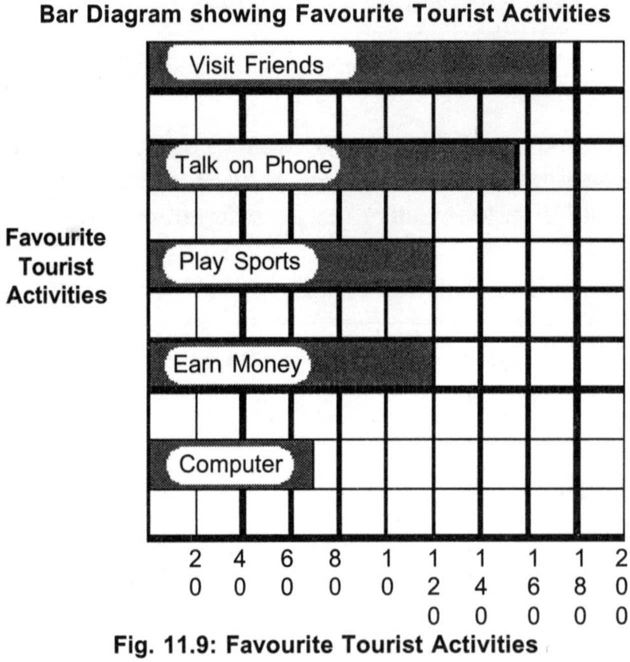

Fig. 11.9: Favourite Tourist Activities

Bar charts

Bar charts are easy to draw, familiar to all, and good for making comparison. While using bar charts ensure:

1) The border of categories should be logical and match any tallies of the same data
2) The width of all the bars should be kept same
3) Start the vertical axis at zero (0), if possible.
4) If it is unavoidable to start at other than zero (0), indicate this clearly by a break in each bar or in the vertical axis, with a zig-zag or wavy stroke across each end of the break.

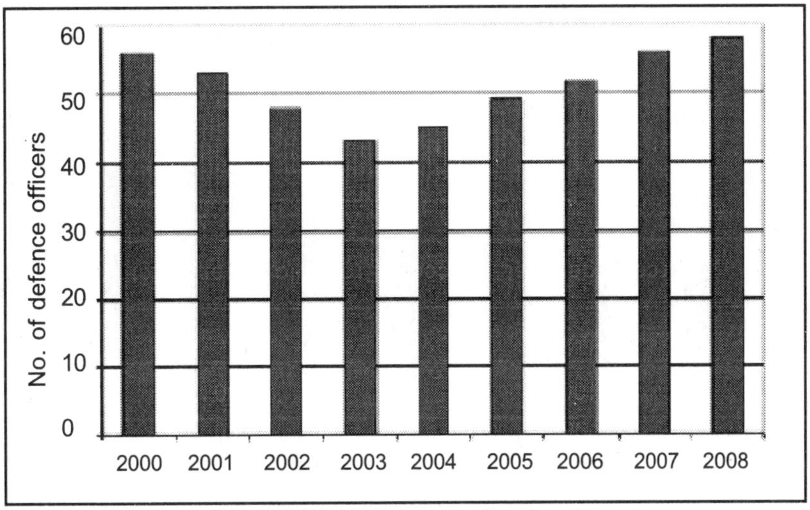

Fig. 11.10: Specimen of a Bar Chart

TABLE 11.2: Number of MBA students in the Indian University during the last eight years (excluding ex-students and certificate examination students) ending 2008-09

Year	Number of students
2001-02	3,737
2002-03	3,897
2003-04	4,183
2004-05	4,447
2005-06	5,066
2006-07	5,740
2007-08	6,199
2009-09	6,474

If the Table 11.2 data are to be represented by simple bar diagrams in Figure 11.11, we should first decide about the length of the biggest bar. The highest figure in the above table is 6,474 and if this is represented by a bar 3 inches in length then the length of other bars can be calculated accordingly. The length of the smallest bar representing figure 3,737 (of the year 2001-2002) would be (3 × 3,737) / 6,474 inches or 1.57 inches. In this way the length of other bars can also be calculated. In the diagram given in Fig. 11.11 the bars are vertical and placed at equal distances. Their thickness is also identical.

If the number of items is very large, bars have to be replaced by simple lines. The technique of drawing such diagrams is the same in the previous case. The only difference is that the bars will have no thickness. The data given in Table 11.3 is represented by lines in the Figure 11.12.

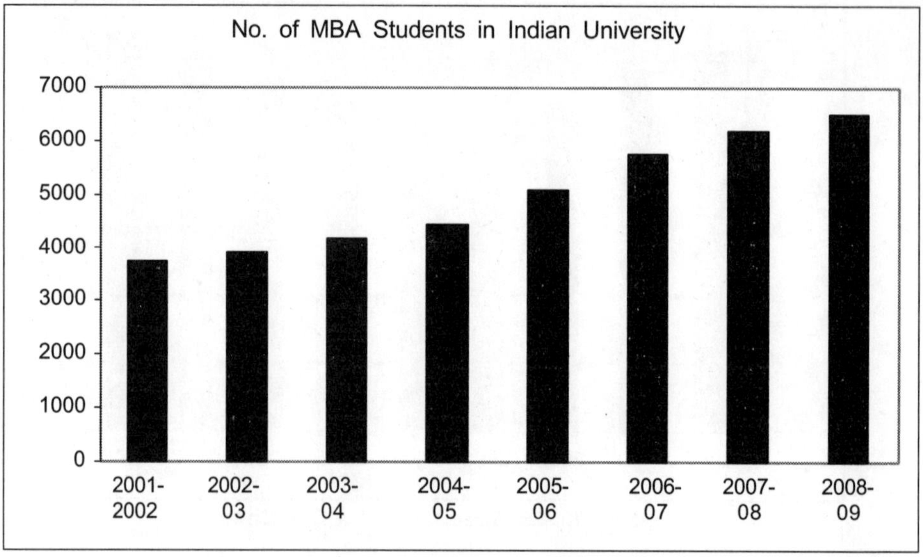

Fig. 11.11: Number of MBA Students in Indian University *(2001-2002 to 2008-09)*

TABLE 11.3: Heights of 32 Students of MBA (Hospitality Management)

Roll Number of Students	Heights in inches
1	4'11"
2	5'0"
3	5'0"
4	5'1"
5	5'2"
6	5'2"
7	5'2"
8	5'3"
9	5'3"
10	5'3"
11	5'3"
12	5'4"
13	5'4"
14	5'4"
15	5'5"
16	5'5"
17	5'5"
18	5'5"
19	5'6"

(contd.)

Roll Number of Students	Heights in inches
20	5'6"
21	5'7"
22	5'7"
23	5'7"
24	5'7"
25	5'7"
26	5'8"
27	5'8"
28	5'9"
29	5'10"
30	5'10"
31	5'10"
32	6'0"

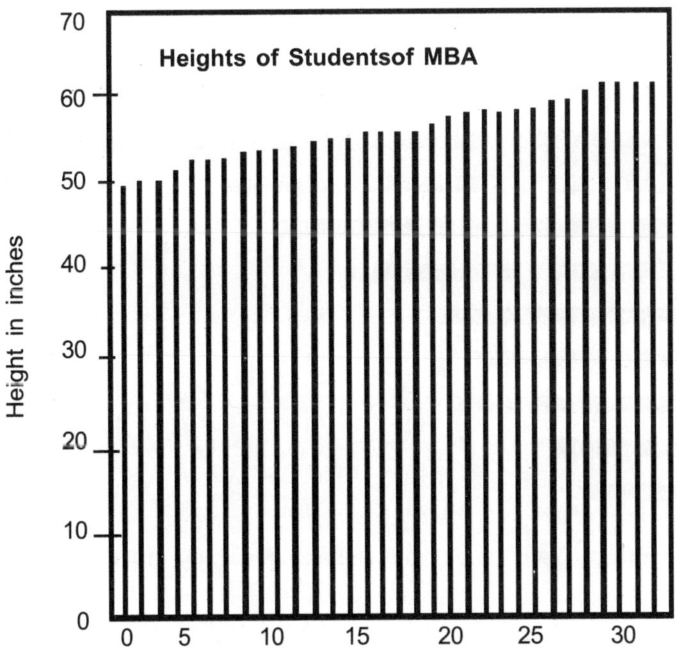

Fig. 11.12: Number of Students

In both of the diagrams given in Fig. 11.11 and 11.12 there is a horizontal base. Base can be on the vertical line also. In Table 11.4 the number of teachers in the Indian University during 10 years ending 2008 have been given. These data are represented in Figure 11.13 which has been constructed on vertical base.

TABLE 11.4: Number of Teachers in Indian University

Year	Number of Teachers
1998-99	1210
1999-2000	1260
2000-01	1320
2001-02	1360
2002-03	1410
2003-04	1500
2004-05	1620
2005-06	1700
2006-07	1880
2007-08	2020

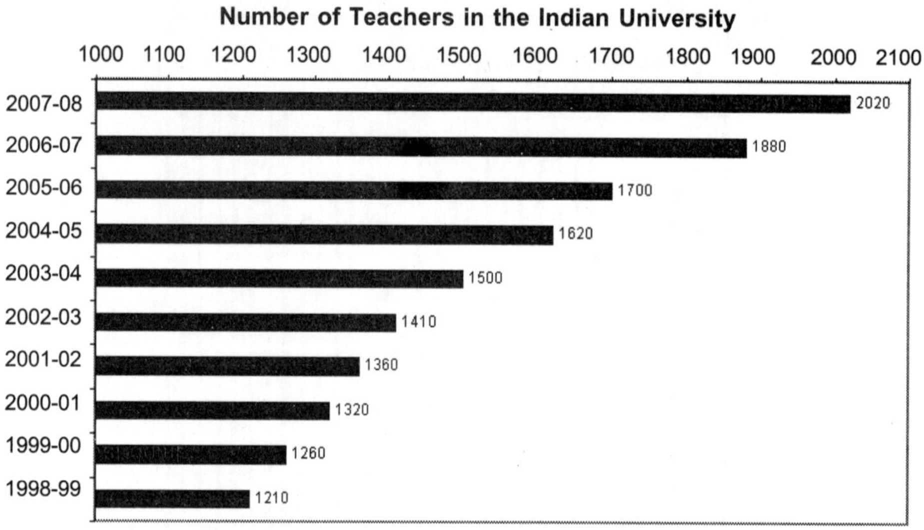

Fig. 11.13: Number of Teachers in the Indian University (1998-99 to 2007-08)

Multiple bar diagrams

Multiple bar diagrams thus supply information about more than one phenomena. In each of the three Figures 11, 12, and 13, the diagrams supplied information about the problem only. Two or more inter-related phenomena can be represented in the shape of multiple bar diagrams.

Table 11.5 and Figure 11.14 gives the data relating to the values of imports and exports in India during four years ending 2008-09:-

TABLE 11.5: Values of Indian Exports and Imports (2005-06 to 2008-09)

Years	Exports (crores of rupees)	Imports (crores of rupees)
2005-06	610.36	624.65
2006-07	955.39	742.78
2007-08	660.65	578.36
2008-09	565.25	527.98

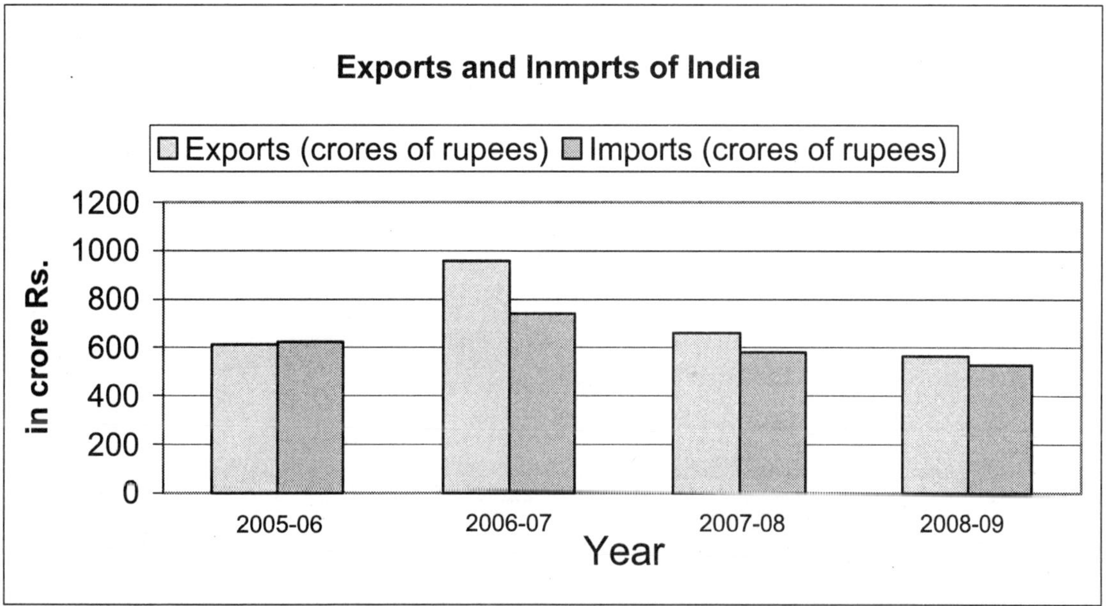

Fig. 11.14: Exports and Imports of India (2005-06 to 2008-09)

Stacked Bar Chart

These charts show the total well. It is difficult to compare heights of sections with stack bar charts. The stacked bar charts should be used if the total height has no meaning (Fig. 11.15).

Sub-divided bar diagrams are use to present such data which are not be shown in the parts or which are totals of various sub-divisions. Table 11.6 and Figure 11.15 gives the number of students in different faculties of the Indian University:-

TABLE 11.6: Number of Students in Different Faculties of Indian University

Year	Engineering	Bio-tech	Law	Management	Total
2003-04	1783	590	391	401	3165
2004-05	2057	650	478	552	3737
2005-06	2096	723	438	640	3897
2006-07	2252	848	364	689	4183
2007-08	2267	900	554	726	4447
2008-09	2613	1218	486	749	5066

These figures are shown on a vertical base in Figure 11.15.

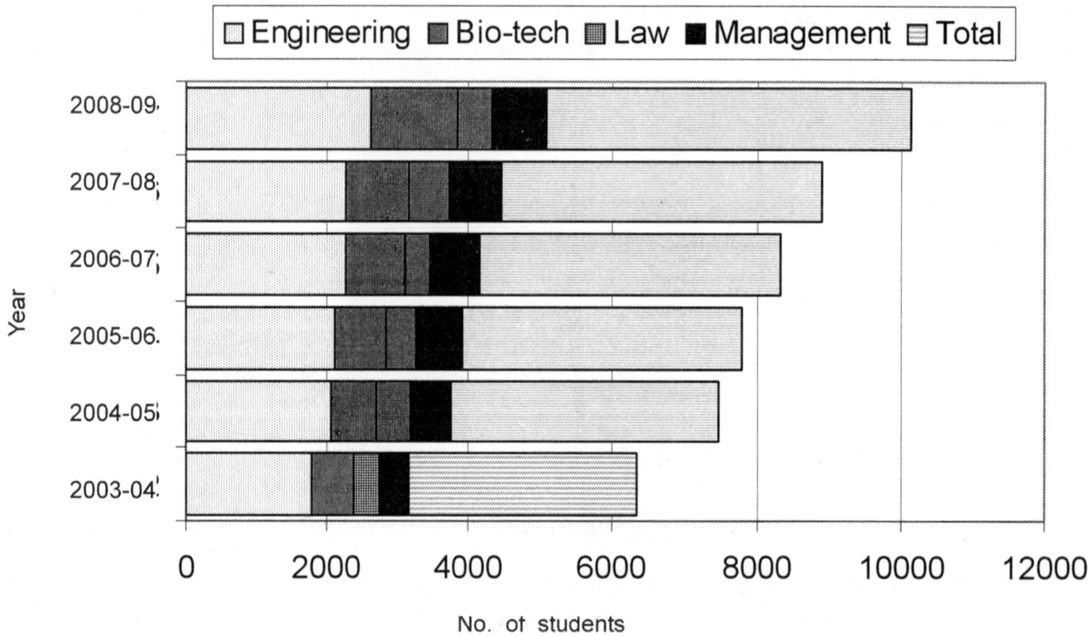

Fig. 11.15: Number of Students in different faculties of Indian University

Table 11.7 and Figure 11.16 indicate the number of hotels in ten different States of India.

TABLE 11.7: Number of Hotels in Ten Different States of India in 2008 to 2009

Name of State	No. of hotels (2008)	No. of hotels (2009)	Difference
A	200	250	50
B	300	340	40
C	400	420	20
D	480	495	15
E	520	530	10
F	300	290	-10
G	400	380	-20
H	280	250	-30
I	750	710	-40
J	570	520	-50

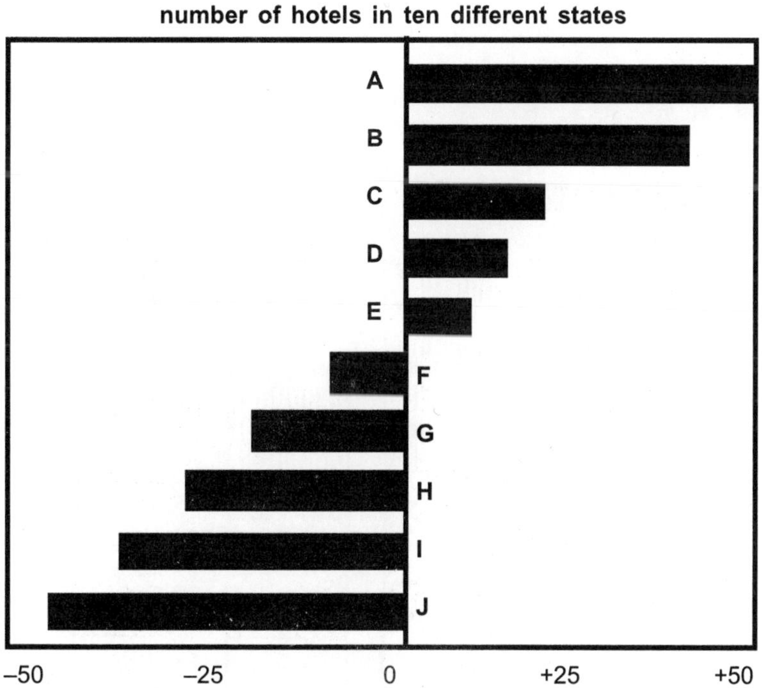

Fig. 11.16: The Number of Hotels in Ten Different States of India from 2008 to 2009

Table 11.8, Table 11.8(a) and Fig. 11.17 show the Cost, Proceed, Profits or Loss per hotel room during the months March, April and May.

TABLE 11.8: Cost, Proceeds, Profits or Loss per Hotel Room During March, April and May

Particulars	March	April	May
Cost per hotel room	(Rs. in lakh)	(Rs. In lakh)	(Rs. In lakh)
(1) Wages	12	10	11
(2) Other costs	8	7	7
(3) Up-keep and maintenance	4	3	3
Total cost	24	20	21
Reciepts per hotel room	25	20	20
Profit or Loss per hotel room	+1	...	-1

TABLE 11.8(a)

Particulars	March (%)	April (%)	May (%)
Wages	48	50	55
Other costs	36	35	35
Upkeep and maintenance	12	15	15
Total cost	**96**	**100**	**105**
Proceed	100	100	100
Profit or Loss	+4	-	-5

Percentage Cost, Preceed, Profits/loss per Hotel

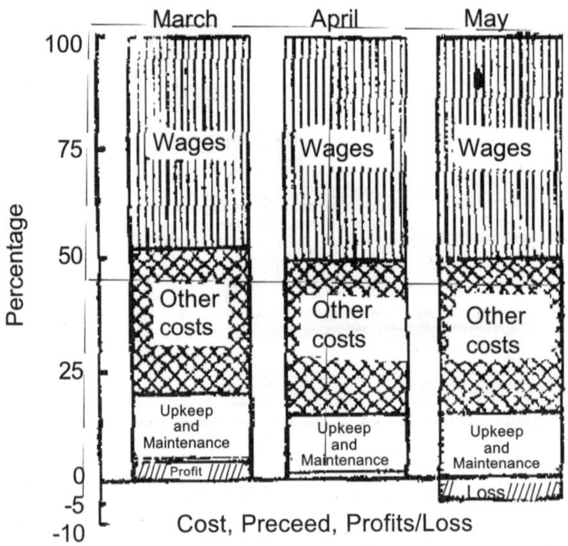

Fig. 11.17: Percent Cost, Proceeds, Profit or Loss per Hotel Room during March, April and May

Two Dimensional Diagrams

These diagrams are very important when illustration of more than one variable is needed. It is of great significance to determine, which variable should be put on which axis.

Rectangle

When two figures are to be shown by the areas of two rectangles, two methods can be adopted: either their breadths may be kept equal and their lengths in proportion to the two figures; or their lengths can be kept equal and their breadths in proportion to the size of the two figures. In both the cases the area of the rectangles would be in proportion to the size of the figures. Generally the lengths are kept equal and the breadth in proportion to the size of items (Refer Fig. 11.18).

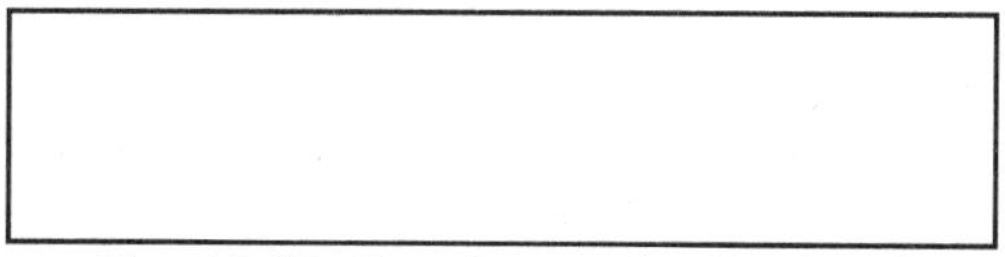

Fig. 11.18: Specimen of a Rectangle

TABLE 11.9 : Expenditure on the Infrastructure (in crores of Rs.)

Sl. No.	Subject	Expenditure Total	Central Govt.	Part A States
1)	Transport and Communication	497	409.5	56.5
2)	Agriculture and Development	361	186.3	127.3
3)	Social services	425	191.4	192.3
4)	Irrigation and Power projects	561	265.9	206.1
5)	Industries	173	146.7	17.9
6)	Miscellaneous	52	40.7	10.0
Total		**2069**	**1240.5**	**610.1**

TABLE 11.9(a): Expenditure on Infrastructure (in percentages)

Subject	Total	Cumulative %	Central Govt.	Cumulative %	Part A States	Cumulative %
1) Irrigation & Power	27.1	27.1	21.43	21.43	33.77	33.77
2) Transport & Communication	24	51.1	33.01	54.44	9.28	43.05
3) Social Services	20.5	71.6	15.44	69.88	31.52	74.57
4) Agriculture & Development	1.75	89.1	15.02	84.9	20.87	95.44
5) Industries	8.4	97.5	11.82	96.72	2.93	98.37
6) Miscellaneous	2.5	100	3.28	100	1.63	100
Total	**100.0**		**100.0**		**100.0**	

The data given in Table 11.9 and Table 11.9(a) are represented in Figure 11.19 in the shape a rectangles.

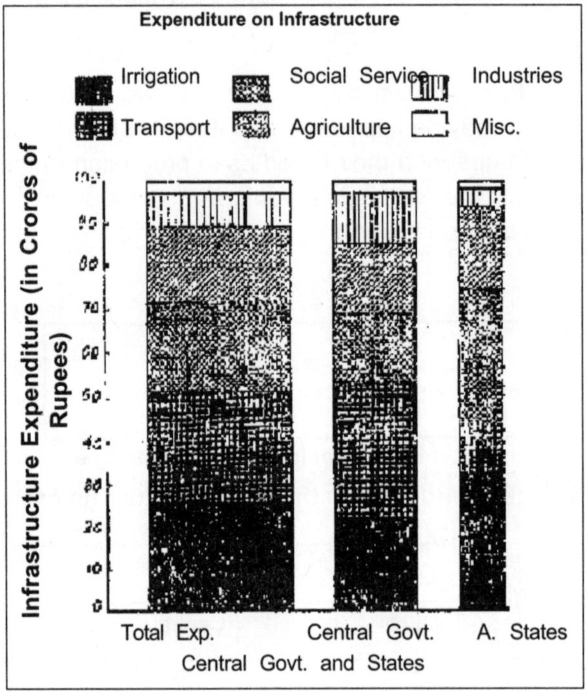

Fig. 11.19: Percentage Expenditure on Infrastructure

If the length of rectangles is kept equal, then their widths have to be in proportion to the figures given in the total column. In other words, the breadth of the rectangles would be in the ratio of 2069:1240.5:610.1: or they would be in the ratio of 3.39:2.03:1. After deciding the widths of the rectangles the percentage expenditures on various items as compared to the expenditure on all the times would be calculated in all the three cases separately. The totals would be taken as 100 and other figures would be expressed as percentages of the total. The percentages would then be divided in accordance with these percentages. Table 11.9(a) gives these percentages for the data given in Table 11.9.

In Table 11.10 sale prices per cakes in case of hotels A and B are respectively Rs. 90 and Rs. 60. Two rectangle would be drawn whose breadths would be in ratio 9:6 and whose lengths would be in the ratio of 100:800. These rectangles in Figure 11.20 would then represent the total sale proceeds and within them various divisions would be made to represent the amount of different items of cost and the amount of profits.

TABEL 11.10 : Cost of Production, Profit and Number of Cakes Produced by Two Hotels 'A' and 'B'

Particulars	Hotel 'A' (Rs.)	Hotel 'B' (Rs.)
Wages	20000	14000
Raw materials	30000	24000
Total cost	50000	38000
Profits	40000	10000
Total sales	90000	48000
Number of cakes produced and sold	1000	800

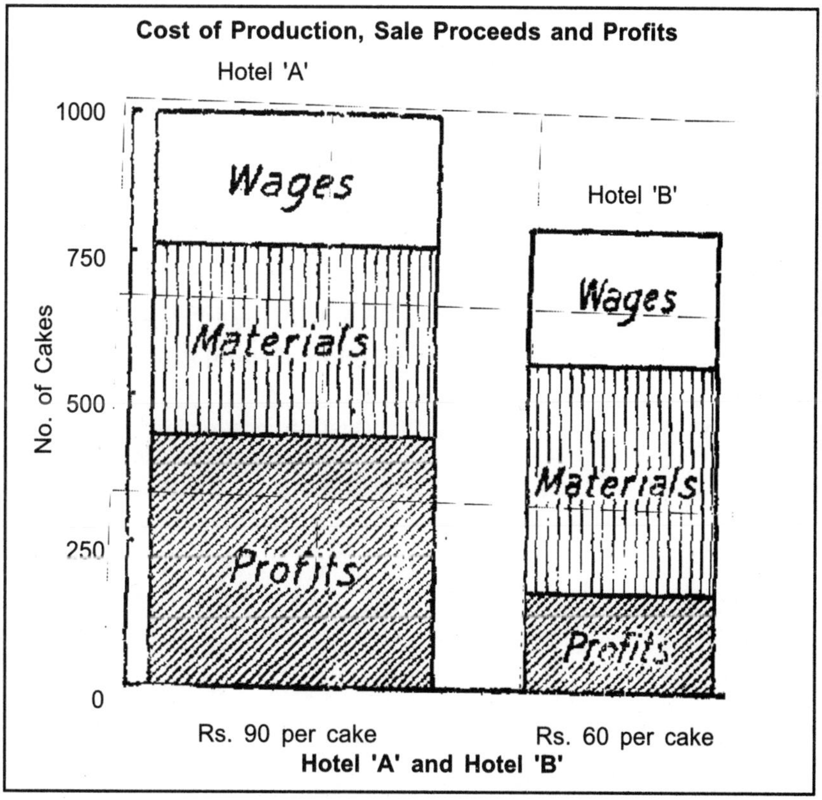

Fig. 11.20: Cost of Production, Sale Proceeds and Profits of Cakes Produced by Hotels 'A' and 'B'

The first rectangle is 3" long and three items (profits, material and wages) whose parts are to be cut are in the ratio of 4000:3000:2000. The vertical scale is divided in this very ratio to get the sub-divisions of profits, materials and wages. Similar calculations have been made in the case of second rectangle representing the profits and the cost of Hotel 'B'.

Squares

They are specially useful when some items of the series have values much higher than others. In such cases if a bar diagram is drawn then the bars representing the smaller figures would be comparatively very small (Refer Fig. 11.21).

Fig. 11.21: Specimen of a Square

Table 11.11 gives the figures of cost of construction of hotel buildings in some countries. These figures are represented in the shape of square in Fig. 11.22.

If, for example, two values are in the ratio of 1600:100 one bar would be 16 times the length of the other. In such cases, squares give a better comparison because in case of squares the area is taken into account. In the above case where two figures are in the ratio of 16:1 the sides of the square would be in the ratio of 4:1 though their area would be in the ratio of 16:1.

TABLE 11.11: Cost of Construction of Hotel Buildings

Country	Cost of construction of hotel buildings (Rs. in crores)
U.S.A.	1301
Russia	440
United Kingdom	164
India	33

TABLE 11.11(a): Cost of Construction of Hotel Buildings

Country	Cost of construction of hotel buildings (Rs. in crores)	Square root of figures of col. II	Lengths of side of squares
U.S.A.	1301	11.4	1.56
Russia	440	6.63	0.91
United Kingdom	164	4.05	0.55
India	33	1.82	0.25

Cost of Construction of Hotel Buildings

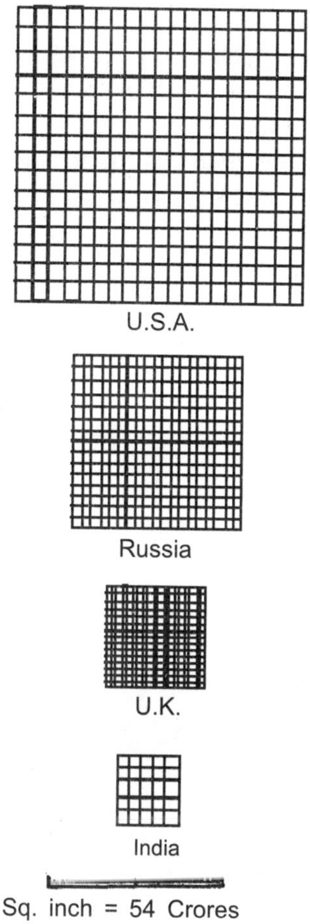

Fig. 11.22: Cost of Construction of Hotel Buildingsin 2008

The square roots of the figures of cost of construction are calculated in Table 11.11(a) and the proportionate length of side of squares is also calculated. The side of the square in Figure 11.23 representing cost of construction of hotel buildings in India which is 1.82" has been taken as .25" and other figures are been calculated on this basis.

The scale in the above diagram is calculated as follows:-

The area of any square is first calculated. Thus the area of the square representing the cost of construction of hotel buildings in United Kingdom is .55 × .55 or .3025 square inches. This represents a cost of construction of Rs. 164 crores. Therefore one square inch would roughly represent Rs. 54 crores.

Circles or Pie-diagrams

The area of a circle is directly proportional to the square of its radius. Thus if a radius of circle is four times the radius of another circle its area would be sixteen times the area of the other circle. The area of circle is always in the ratio of the squares of their radii. Circle can be used at all places where squares are used.

Pie charts are commonly used visual aids. The disadvantages of pie charts are that it is not possible to show any category that has zero (0) frequency. A circle or pie graph is due to show how a part of something relates to the whole. This kind of graph is needed to show percentages effectively.

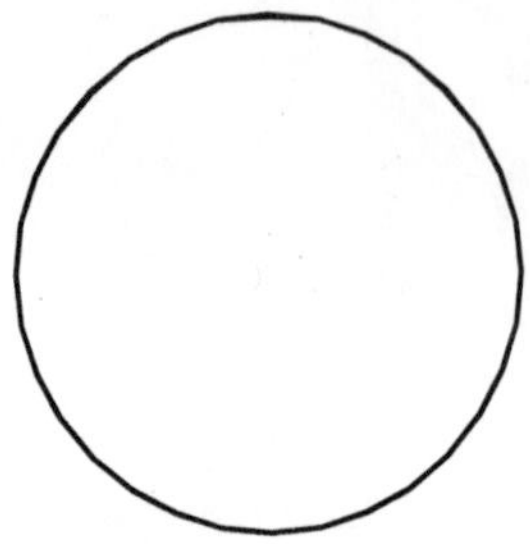

Fig. 11.23: Specimen of a Circle

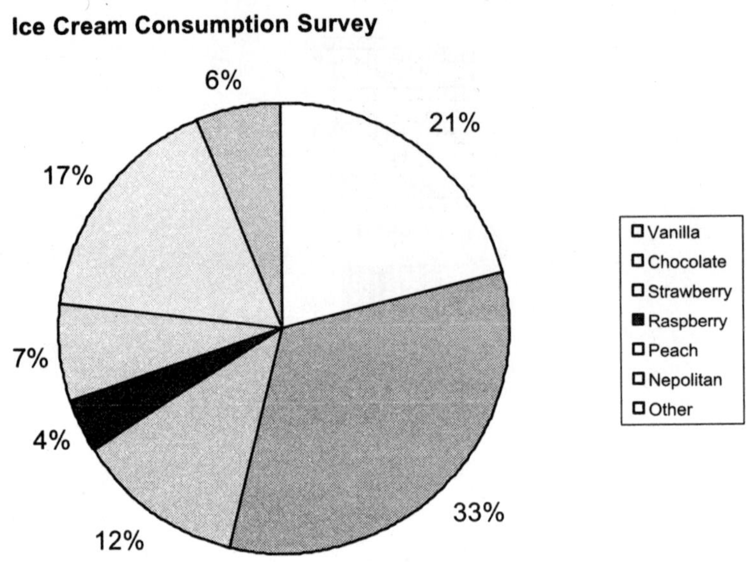

Fig. 11.24: Ice Cream Consumption Survey

A typical chart or table for this graph might look as given in Figure 11.25.

A pie chart is useful when we're dealing with percentages. The chart is a way to visually display what percentage of the total a certain category makes up.

You may use a pie chart when you want to compare a number of elements to each other and in relation to as a whole. If you compare the same information expressed as regular rectangular blocks to a pie graph, you see that a bars are more precise in comparing elements to each other, but that the pie graph is much more effective comparing elements to the whole. One of the fundamental rule of using pie chart in "Never include more than 6 elements." If you have more then only show six main elements and include the other under the diverse heading. If necessary, you can break-down the diverse category in a second pie graph.

The pie graph can be made more attractive by adding pattern to each part, using colours and adding depth (Fig. 11.25).

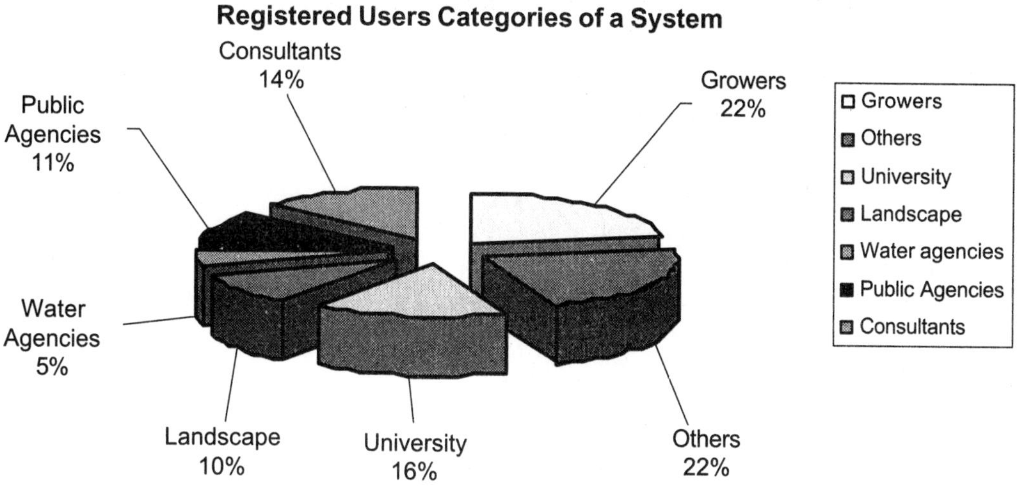

Fig. 11.25: Specimen of a Pie Graph

Circle or pie graphs are particularly good illustrations when considering how many parts of a whole are inception. In the Table 11.12, both the number of hours in a whole day devoted to certain activities is listed as well as the percent of time for each of these activities. The pie chart is then divided very much as a baker's pie would be into slices that represent the proportional amounts of time spent on each activity.

Table 11.12: Percent of Hours of a Day Spent on Activities by a Group of Students

ACTIVITY	HOURS	PERCENT OF DAY
Sleep	6	25
School	6	25
Job	4	17
Entertainment	4	17
Meals	2	8
Homework	2	8

To the right of the pie chart in Figure 11.26 is a legend that tells which colour stands for which category. In addition, the percents are also near the pie slice that stands for that particular amount of time spent.

A pie chart is a graphical way to organize data. All pie charts compare parts of a whole. For example, a pie chart for the time you spend at school could compare the amount of time you spend in each class and at lunch. A pie chart uses percentages or fractions to compare the data. The whole is equal to 100%, which is the same as 1. So if a group of students spends 7 hours at school and 55 minutes of that time is spent eating lunch then 13% of their school day is spent eating lunch. This can be figured by converting 7 hours to 420 minutes (you always

Percent of Hours of a Day Spent on Activities by a Group of Students

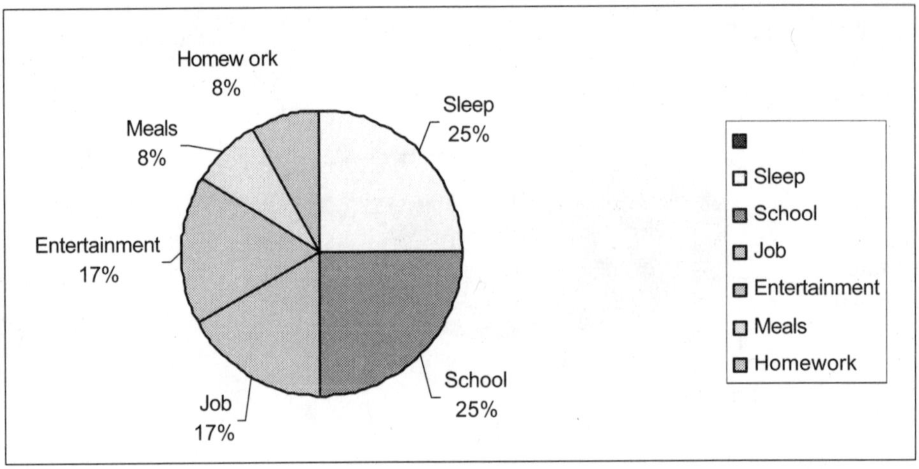

Fig. 11.26 Hours of a Day Spent on Activities by a Group of Students

must compare using the same unit of measure or your numbers are meaningless). Then solve the proportion 55 minutes / 420 minutes = ? % / 100% which works out to be about 13%.

The next step in creating the pie chart is determining what the angle measure should be to represent 13%. Since there are 360 degrees in a circle, multiply 13%(0.13) by 360 to get 46.8 degrees.

Table 11.13 and Figure 11.27 indicate the various categories of tourists visiting a tourist region.

Table 11.13: The Various Categories of Tourists Visiting a Tourist Region

Sl. No.	Percentage	Categories of Tourists visiting a region
1)	36%	Package Tour Groups
2)	25%	Foreign Independent Travellers
3)	17%	Business Travellers
4)	5%	Visit Friends & Relatives
5)	**17%**	**Others**

The year 2008 is another exciting year for Tourism's Industry. Visitors' arrival has achieved another milestone as more visitors come to this region.

From the Month of January to August 2008, visitor arrivals totaled 629,935 as compared to 493,695 previous year, an increase of a whopping 27%! By achieving new records year after year, this shows that the region is on her way to maturing into a premier destination in Asia.

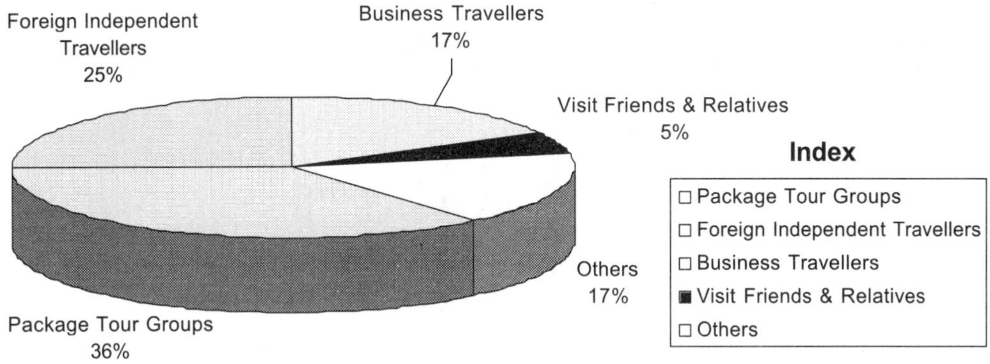

Fig. 11.27: Pie Diagram Indicating Types of Visitors Visiting a Tourist Region

International arrivals comprises of 49% of total arrivals while the remaining are domestic arrivals. Domestic arrivals have also increased by 49% as compared to the same period last year signifying that more Malaysians are coming to the region from other states as compared to traveling abroad for holidays. Visitor from the Asia Region is still the highest at 42% with Europeans being the second highest Region at 4% of total arrivals.

The highest month for arrivals was in the month of January at 104,530 and the lowest month

Total Monthly Visitors to a Tourist Region - 200....

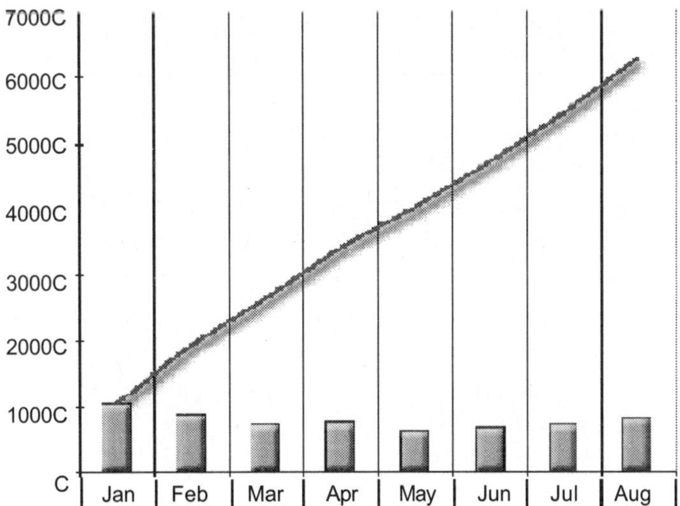

	Jan	Feb	Mar	Apr	May	Jun	Jul	Aug
Monthly visitors	10-530	88086	71986	76105	61887	63805	72994	82632
Total Visitors	10-530	192616	264602	340517	402504	471305	544363	629935

Fig. 11.28: Total Monthly Visitors 200.....

Total Visitors to a Tourist Region (up to April (200. . .) by Region

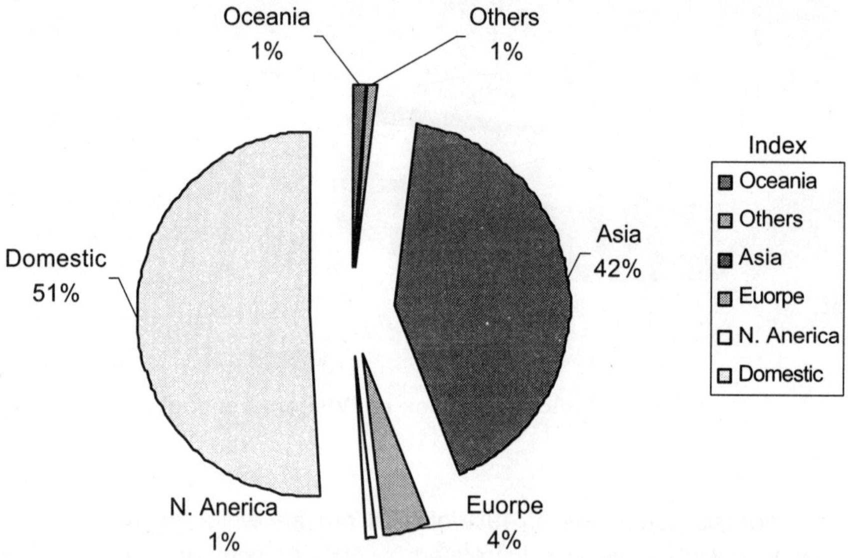

Fig. 11.29: Total Visitors upto April 200. . . by regions

was in May at 61,887 visitors.

The second highest growth rate is from the European region with an increase of more than 56% as compared to the same period last year. European visitors totaled 24,447 up to the month of August which averages more than 3,000 visitors per month. United Kingdom and Ireland remains the top countries from the European Region with 15,483 visitors. Other top countries are Scandinavia with 3,648 visitors, Germany with 1,128 visitors, France with 799 visitors and 3,389 visitors from other countries from Europe.

The Asian Region only registered an increase in 8% as compared to last year and the top country for visitors is Indonesia with 87,033 visitors. Taiwanese arrivals remains the top tourist arrivals with 76,271 which average slightly below 10,000 visitors per month and still remains the critical mass of the industry in terms of number of arrivals. Countries such as Japan with 10,607 arrivals and increase by 46%, Singapore with 9,006 visitor and increase by 30% and Hong Kong with 10,403 visitors and increase by 25%. China is the top growth sector with an increase of 76% with 5,872 visitors.

The Oceania region the highest increase with 65% increase as compared to the same period last year. The region registered 4,782 visitors with more than 80% from Australia with 4,037 arrivals and the remaining 745 visitors from New Zealand.

In the North American region, visitor arrivals totaled 7,472 visitors with more than 60% arrivals from the United States with 4,703 visitors and remaining balance from Canada at 2,769 visitors. This region has experienced a drop in arrivals of 27% as compared to the same period last year.

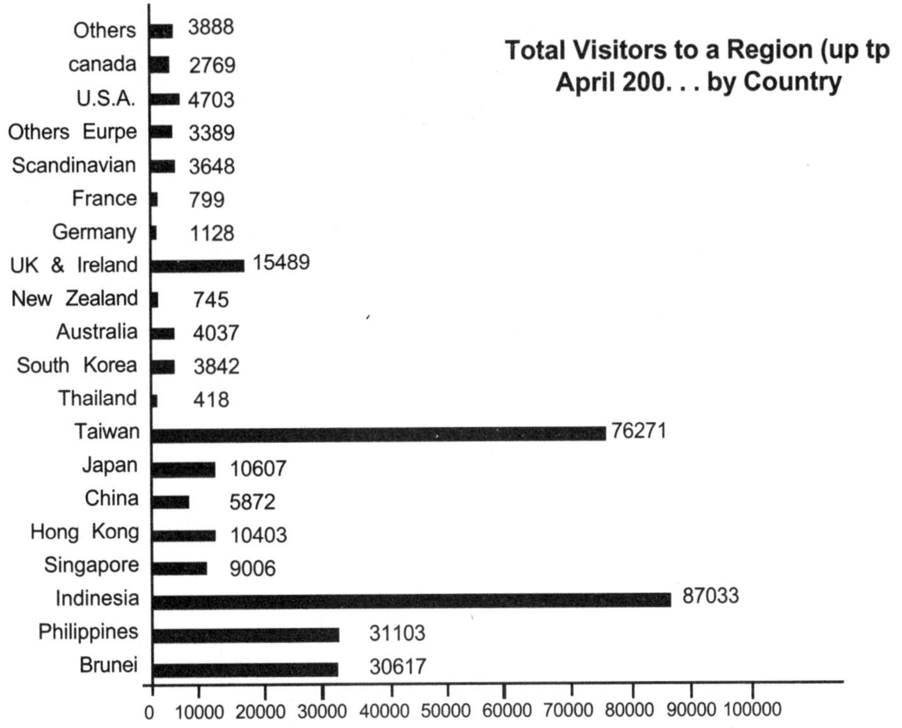

Fig. 11.30: Total Visitor Arrival to a Tourist Region by Country

Constructing a Pie Chart

A pie chart is constructed by converting the share of each component into a percentage of 360 degrees.

Example: 1200 students at Indian University are polled and asked about the number of parking spaces on Campus. Here are the results:

Table 11.14: Parking space in Indian University Campus

Response	Frequency
Too many	300
About right	360
Not enough	540

First determine what percentage of the total each category represents as given in Table 11.14(a).

Table 11.14(a): Parking space in Indian University Campus (in percentage)

Response	Frequency	Percent
Too many	300	25%
About right	360	30%
Not enough	540	45%

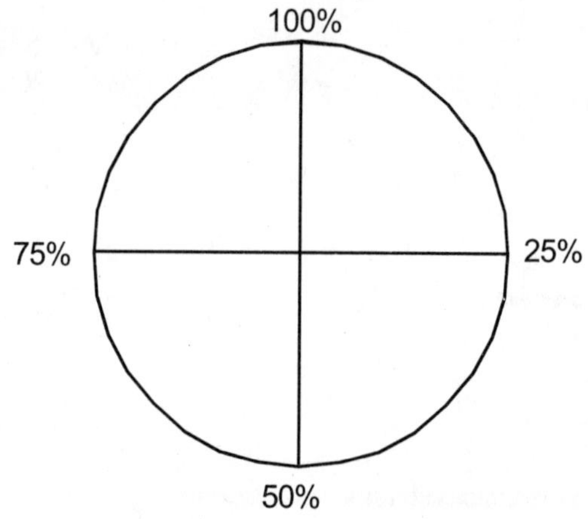

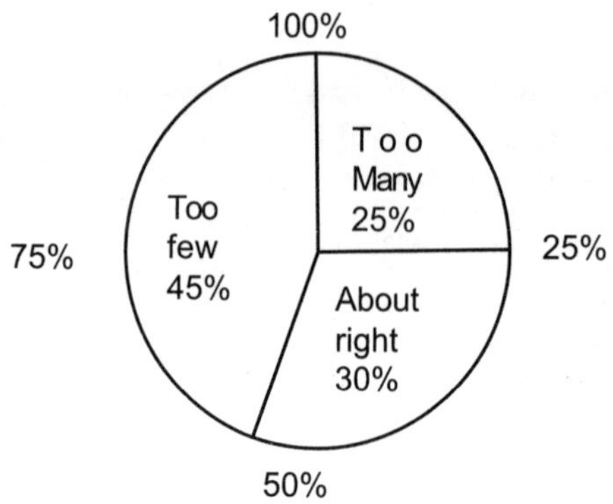

Parking space in Indian University Campus

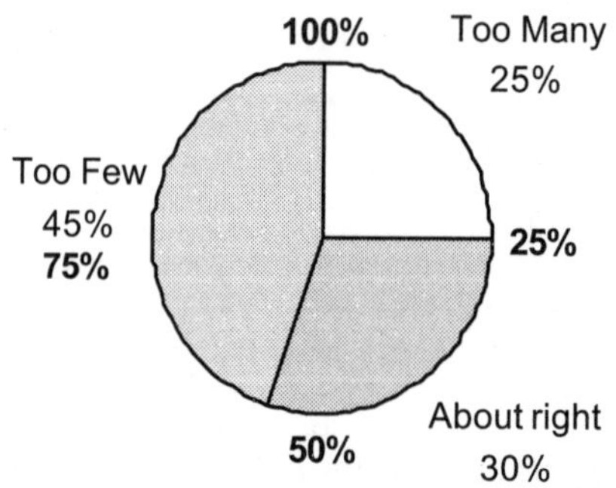

Fig. 11.31: Parking Space at the Indian University Campus

Next draw a circle. This circle will represent 100 % of the value. Place marks every 5%, keeping in mind that one-quarter of the circle represents 25%.

Next starting at the top, move in the clockwise direction until you reach 25%. Then move another 30% (until you reach 55%).

The data given in Table 11.15 are represented by circles in Fig. 11.32.

A little colour could make the circle eye appearing as given in Fig. 11.31 and Figure 11.32.

TABLE 11.15: Total Hotels Rooms in Five Star Hotels in Different Countries

Country	Hotel Rooms
U.S.A.	220000
Venezuela	62200
Russia	30100
Saudi Arabia	26800
Iran	13200

The square root of these figures and the ratio of the radii of various circles have been calculated in TABLE 11.15(a).

TABLE 11.15(a): Hotel rooms in Five Star Hotels in Different Countries

Country (1)	Hotel Room (2)	Square root of figures in column 2 (3)	Length of radii in inches (4)
U.S.A.	220000	46.9	1.02
Venezuela	62200	24.9	0.54
Russia	30100	17.4	0.38
Saudi Arabia	26800	16.4	0.35
Iran	13200	11.4	0.25

In Table 11.15(a) the square roots are divided by 46 to obtain the radii of different circles.

In the Fig. 11.32, for the calculation of scale the area of any circle can be calculated. Thus, the area of last circle representing the hotel rooms of Iran is about .2 square inches. If .2 square inches represents 13200 hotel rooms, then one square inch would represent 66000 hotel rooms. The area of the circle is in proportion to the figures of number of rooms. Circles look more beautiful than squares and are also easy to draw. As such wherever a choice has to be made between squares and circles the latter should be preferred.

Just as in case of squares it is possible to represent the aggregate by one big square and various components by rectangles cut within it, similarly in case of circles the aggregate can be represented by a big circle and the various components by sectors cut inside it. Such diagrams

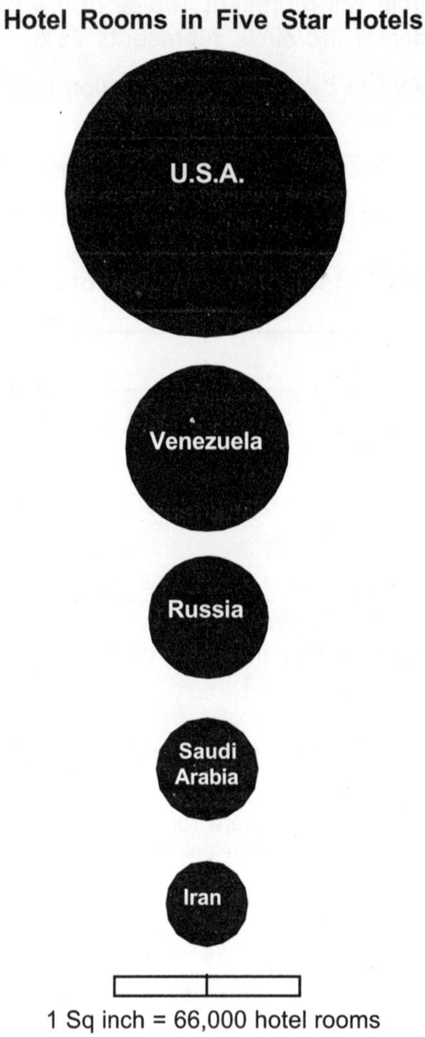

Fig. 11.32: Hotel Rooms in Five Star Hotels in Different Countries

are known as ***Angular Diagrams***. Sectors are not difficult to draw and they look beautiful. This is the reason why they are preferred to squares.

The areas of various sectors are in production to the angles which they make at the center of the circle. The angle at the center of the circle is 360 degrees. This angle of 360 degrees represents the aggregate. It can be divided into a number of smaller angles whose degree would be in proportion to the values of the components.

Table 11.16 gives the total income of the hotel and its distribution amongst various categories.

To represent this data first of all a circle with any radius would have to be drawn. The angle at the center which would be of 360 degrees would represent 2069 crores of rupees which is the total income. The area of this circle thus represents the total expenditure. On this basis of sector which is to represent an expenditure of 1241 crores of rupees would have an angle of

(360 x 1241) / 2069 degrees. In this way we can calculate the degrees of angles which the different sectors should have. The total of the degree of all these angles would be 360.

Table 11.16(a) gives the degrees of angles of different sectors relating to the data given in Table 11.16.

TABLE 11.16: Income of Different Category of Hotels

Hotel Category	Income in crores of rupees
Five star	1241
Four star	610
Three star	173
Two star	32
One star	13
Total	**2069**

TABLE 11.16 (b): Income of the different categories of hotels

Hotel Category	Income in crores of Rs.	Degree of angles
Five star	1241	215.9
Four star	610	106.1
Three star	173	30.1
Two star	32	5.6
One star	13	2.3
Total	**2069**	**360.0**

After the degrees of various angles have been calculated in the manner given Table 11.16, the next thing is to draw any radius in the circle. From this line an angle of 215.9 degrees would be marked and a line would be drawn (passing through this point) from the center up to the circumference. The sectors so framed would represent the income of five star hotels from this second line an angle of 106.1 degrees would be marked and a third line would be drawn forming the second sector representing the income from five star hotels. In this way other sectors would also be drawn. Figure 11.33 represents the above data.

If two aggregates and their components are to be compared, two circles would have to be drawn with areas proportionate to the ratio of the two aggregates. Each circle would then divided into sectors on the basis of the values of its components.

Circles can be used at all places where squares and rectangles are used. Angular diagrams look beautiful but if the number of component is very large it becomes very difficult to show them in this fashion. In such cases smaller components should be merged and then the data should be shown in the shape of circular diagram. It may sometimes create misleading impressions. It should be remembered that various sectors in two or more circles should always be kept in one order to facilitate comparison.

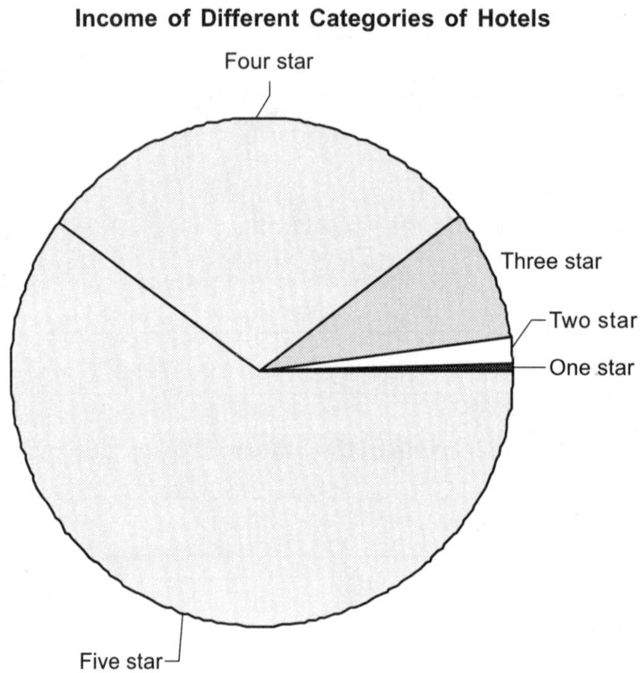

Fig. 11.33: Income of Different Categories of Hotels

Three-Dimensional Diagrams

Cylinders, Spheres, Cubes, etc.' are known as three-dimensional diagrams, as in the calculation of their area three dimensions, length, breadth and depth have to be taken into account. Cubes are very useful in such cases where the difference between the smallest and the biggest figures is very large. Suppose two figures are in the ratio of 1:729. If bars are constructed to represent them one bar would be of 1" in the length and other of 60'and 9". If these figures are represented by squares or circles then the side of one of the squares or the radius of one of the circles would be 1" and that of the other 27". If, however, cubes are constructed their sides would be in the ratio of 1": 9". Thus we find that in cases where the range of the figures is very large, cubes are very helpful in representing the data diagrammatically. Three-dimensional diagrams are *volume diagrams* whereas two-dimensional diagrams are *surface diagrams* and as such the drawing of the cubes, etc., is more is more difficult than the drawing of rectangles or square.

Table 11.17 gives the number of foreign tourist arrivals in four metros in the year 2006.

TABLE 11.17: Foreign Tourist Arrivals in Four Metros

Town	Number of Foreign Tourists
A	5,00,000
B	1,00,000
C	50,000
D	10,000

If the above data are to be represented in the shape of cubes we shall have to find out the cube root of these figures. The cube root of these figures are respectively about 79.25, 46.45, 36.81 and 21.53. The sides of the various cubes have to be in these ratios but since these figures are still very big they can be divided by a common factor. If these figures are divided by 50 they would respectively be 1.58, .92, .74 and .44. We can now have cubes whose sides are respectively 1.58", .92", .74" and .44". The Figure 11.35 represents the data given in Table 11.16 in the shape of cubes:—

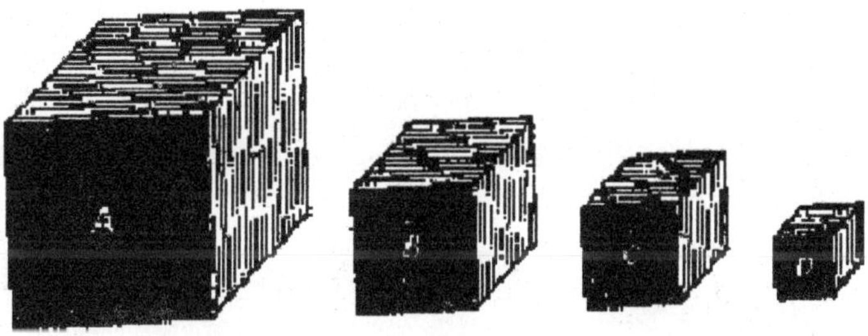

Fig. 11.34: Foreign Tourist Arrivals in Four Metros

Construction of a Cube

Three-dimensional diagrams are more difficult to construct than surface diagrams. Cube root of the figures cannot be calculated very easily and though the drawing of cube is not very difficult, cylinders and spheres require very great care in construction. As such three-dimensional diagrams, in general, and cylinder and sphere in particular are not very popular. But it must be admitted that three-dimensional diagrams look more beautiful than bars, squares, rectangles or circles.

The construction of cubes is not difficult. Suppose a cube with a side of 1" is to be constructed. The following procedure would have to be followed:-

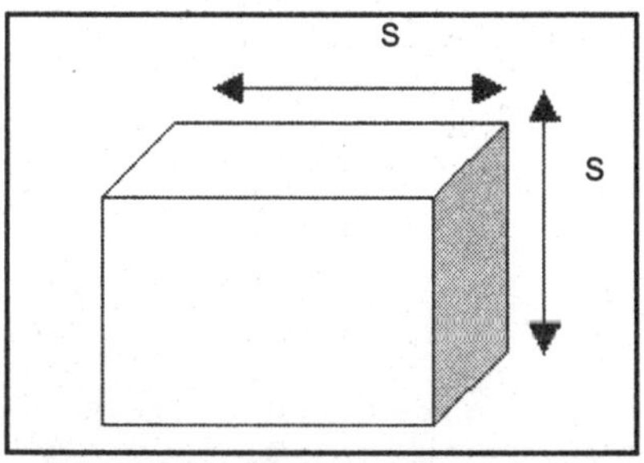

Fig. 11.35: Specimen of a Cube

1) Construct a square with a side of 1". It is represented by ABCD in figure below:

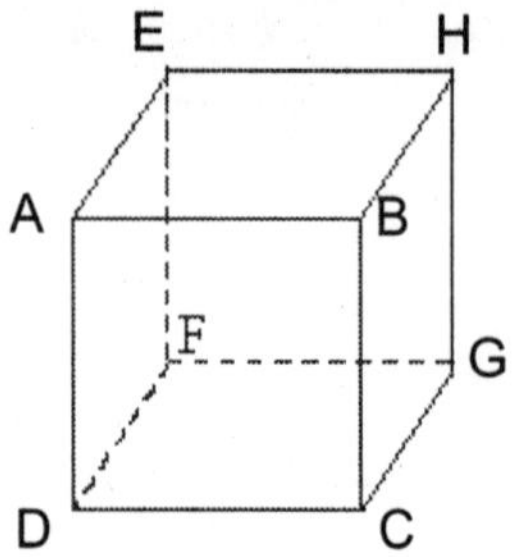

2) Find out the midpoint of the line AB and draw a perpendicular 1" in length, ½" below AB and ½" above it. It is represented by EF.
3) Join AE and from B draw a line parallel to AE and equal to it in length. It is represented by BH.
4) Join EH and from the point H draw a line parallel to EF and equal to it in length. It is represented by GH.
5) Join C and G. rub of line EF and EG. The required cube is ADCGHE.

Pictograms

In pictograms the relative values of items are represented by pictures. The number of picture drawn or the sizes of different pictures are in proportion to the values of various items which have to be represented (Fig. 11.36).

Cartograms

The regional distribution of data is usually shown by the use of maps. The distribution of rainfall in various regions of India or the production of coal in various parts of the country can be shown with the help of maps. Similarly density of population in a particular country can best be studied by drawing a map and putting down dots representing a certain number of people. Thus, one lakh or ten lakhs of people can be represented by a dot and density of population in various regions can be suitably pictured in this manner.

The map in Fig. 11.37 shows the density of the Indian population.

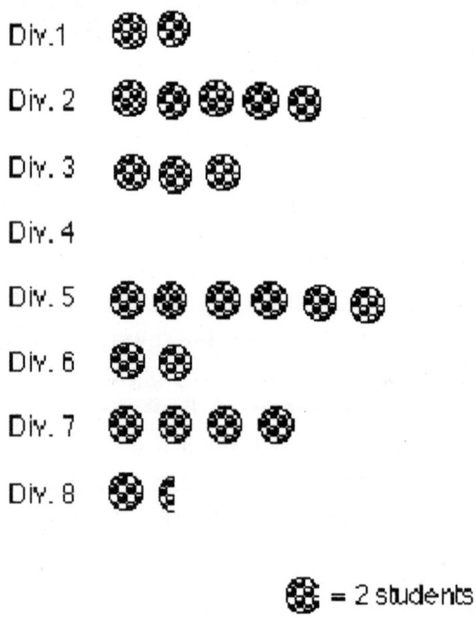

Fig. 11.36: Specimen of a Pictogram

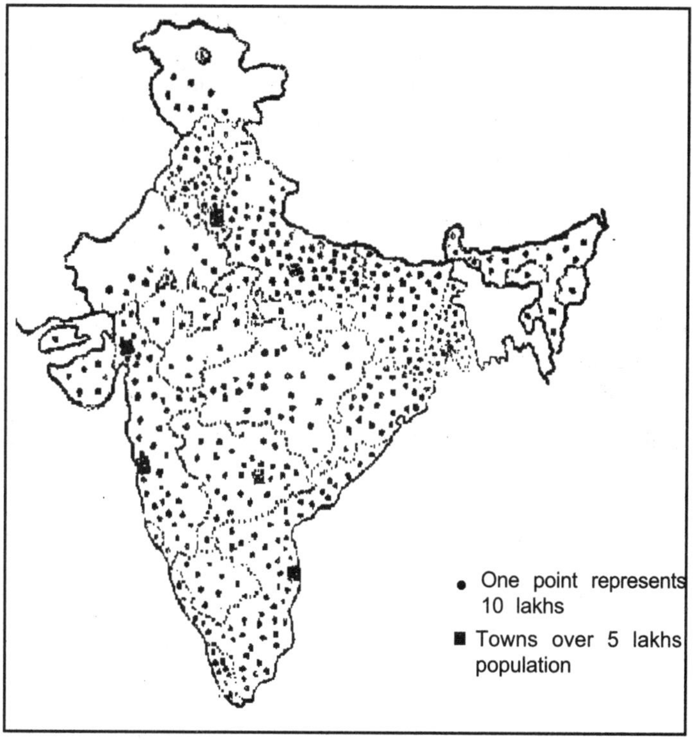

Fig. 11.37: Specimen of a Cartogram

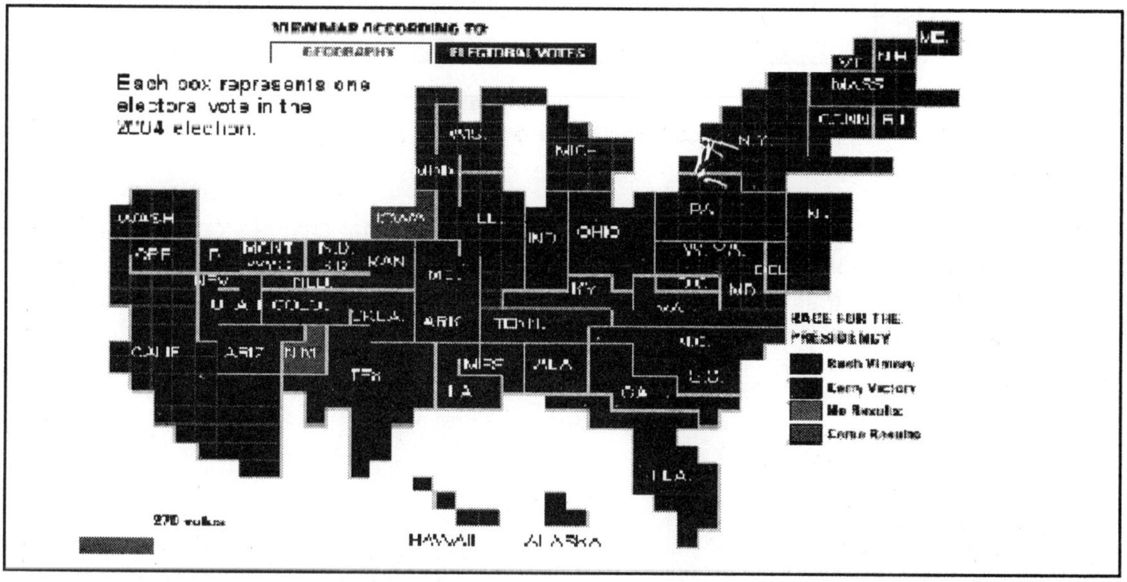

Fig. 11.38: Specimen of a Cartogram

Various methods by which statistical data can be represented by means of diagrams and pictures have been discussed above. Which particular diagram should be chosen for a particular type of data, is a question not easy to answer. The selection of a diagram should be done carefully as an inappropriate selection may misrepresent the data and give misleading impressions. As has been said earlier, in the construction of diagrams and pictures due attention must be paid to neatness and display. Some types of data particularly those relating to time series spreading over long period can best be represented by means of graphs or curves.

Line Graph

A line graph is used to show continuing data; how one thing is affected by another. It's clear to see how things are going by the rises and falls a line graph shows. This kind of graph is needed to show the effect of an independent variable on a dependent variable.

A typical chart or table for this graph might look like given in Fig. 11.39:

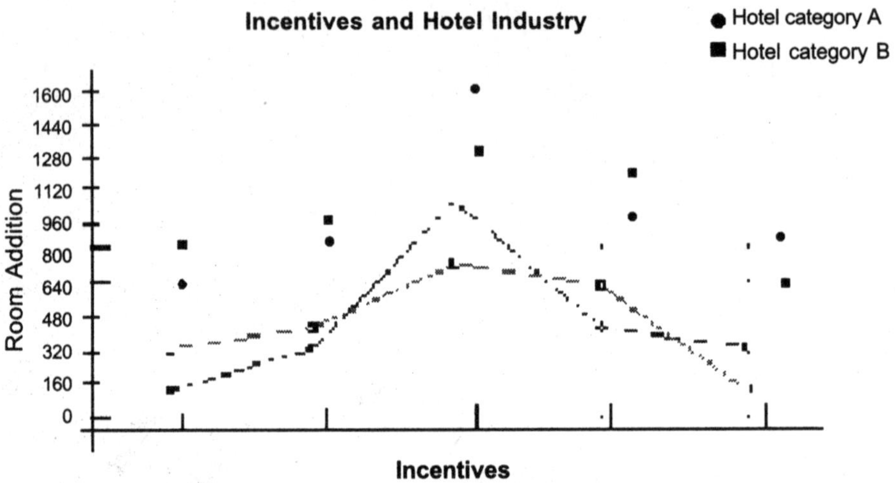

Fig. 11.39 Incentives and Hospitality Industry

A line graph is most useful in displaying data or information that changes continuously over time. The example in Table 11.18 and Fig. 11.39 show the changes in the temperature over a week in January. Notice that the title of the graph is "Average Daily Temperature for January 1-7 in degrees Fahrenheit".

Table 11.18: Average Daily Temperatures for January 1-7 in Degrees Fahrenheit

Date	Temperature
1	10
2	25
3	30
4	42
5	23
6	25
7	40

Table 11.18 shows the date in one column and the corresponding temperature in the second column. The line graph in Figure 11.40 on the right shows the degrees of temperature going up the vertical axis (up and down numbers on the left of the graph) and the days of the week on the horizontal axis (going sideways from left to right). The points for the temperature for each day are connected by a line, thus the graph is a line graph.

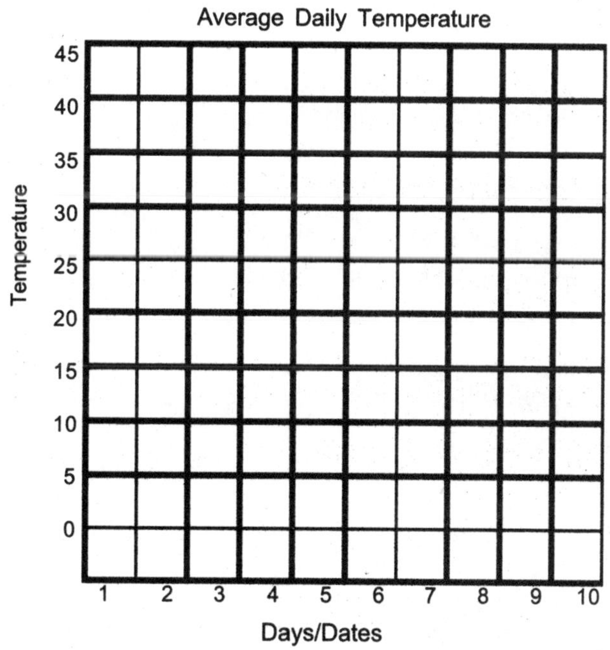

Fig. 11.40: Average Daily Temperature in Degree Fahrenheit for January 1–7

Line or Area Charts

Line or area bar charts are used when there is logical order of points. Area chart illustrate how it stacks the data like a stacked bar chart and so indicates totals.

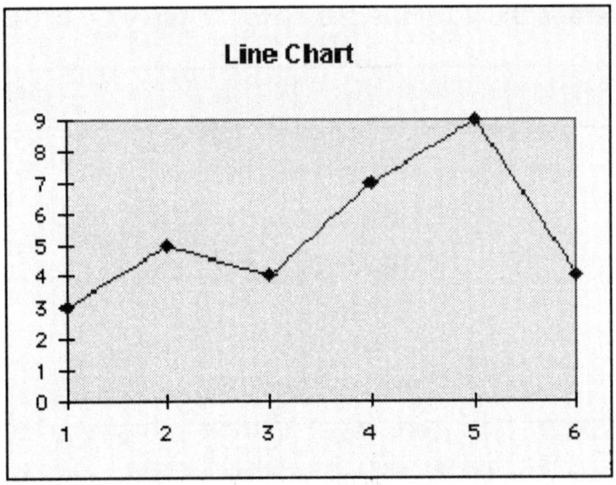

Fig. 11.41: Specimen of Line Chart

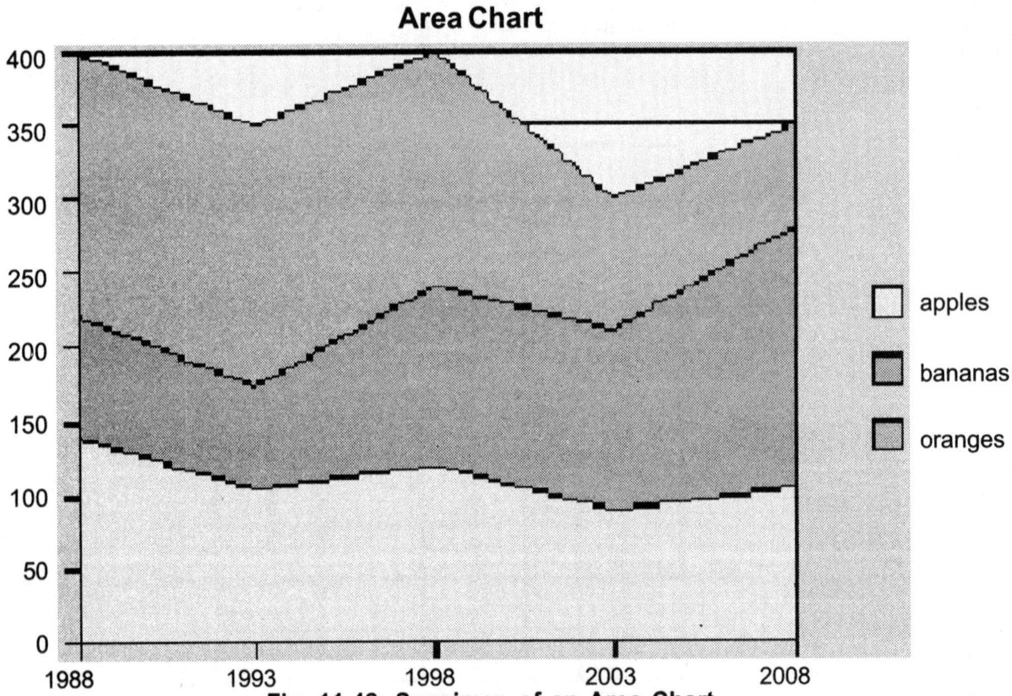

Fig. 11.42: Specimen of an Area Chart

Column Graph

Column graphs are similar to bar graphs and line graphs. All three have grid lines going horizontally and vertically. The column graph is more similar to the bar graph in that it is used more for one time or single events rather than continuous events.

In the column graph the data are literally presented in columns. The category names can be on the graph or underneath the column. It is not necessary to assign different colors to the

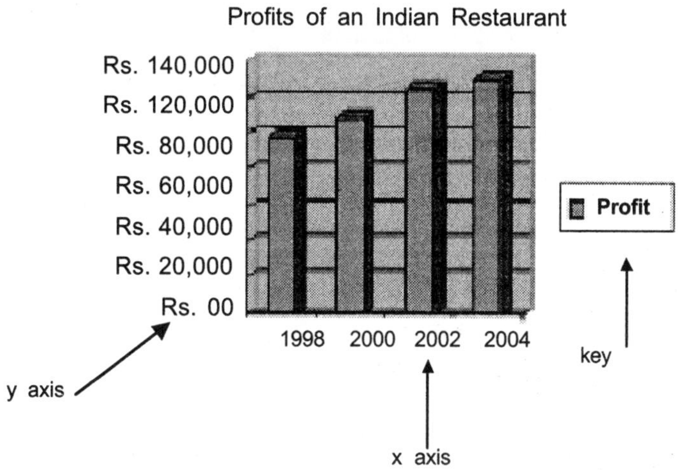

Fig. 11.43: Specimen of a Column Graph

columns although one could do so and then attach a legend that would explain the different colors and which category they stood for.

Table 11.19: Favourite Pets of Tourists

Dogs	Cats	Fish	Birds	Other
820	700	350	320	615

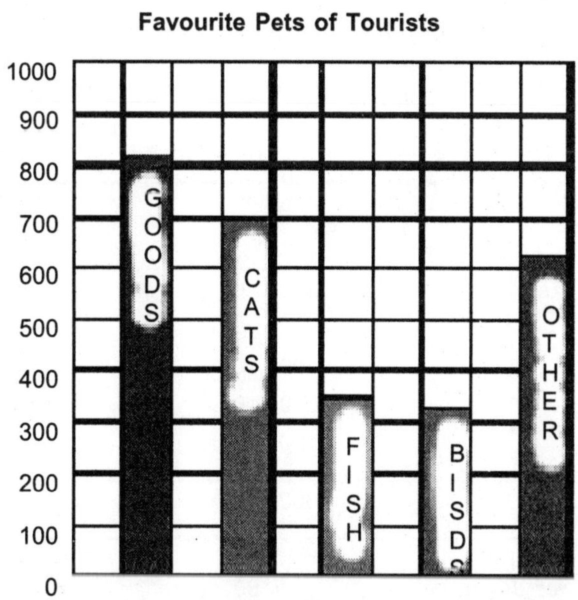

Fig. 11.44: Favourite Pets of Tourists

Questions & Assignments

Q.1. Write a note on the necessity and usefulness of diagrammatic representation of statistical data.

Q.2. Point out the usefulness of diagrammatic representation of facts and explain the construction of any one of different forms of diagrams you know.

Q.3. Write short notes on :-

a) Surface Diagrams

b) Volume Diagrams

c) Pie Diagrams

d) Bar Diagrams

e) Two-Dimensional Diagrams.

Q.4. The following table gives the details of the cost of the construction of a hotel room in New Delhi:-

	Rs.		Rs.
Land	4,50,000	Cement	80,000
Labour	2,50,000	Lime	80,000
Bricks	2,00,000	Stone	60,000
Iron	1,80,00	Sand	20,000
Timber	1,50,000	Other things	1,30,000

Represent the above figures by a suitable diagram.

Q.5. Represent the following data by vertical bars constructed on a percentage basis:-

Proceeds, Cost, Profit or Loss (per dozen of cakes) produced by Indian Petisserie in two different years 20. . . and 20. . .

	Year I		Year II	
	Rs.	Ps.	Rs.	Ps.
Proceeds per dozen of cakes	1,200	0	1,000	0
Cost per dozen				
Wages	400	0	300	0
Raw material	800	0	600	0
Other costs	100	0	0	0
Total	1,300	0	900	0
	Loss		Profit	
Profit or Loss per dozen	- 1	00	+ 0 + 1	

Q.6. Represent the following by sub-divided bars drawn on a percentage basis:-

Cost, Proceeds, Profit or Loss per bottle of wine during 2007, 2008 and 2009

Particulars	2007 (Rs.)	2008 (Rs.)	2009 (Rs.)
Cost per bottle of wine			
1. Wages	450	750	1,050
2. Raw materials	300	510	700
3. Other costs	150	240	350
Total cost	900	1500	2100
Proceeds per bottle of wine	1000	1500	2000
Profit or Loss per bottle of wine	**+100**	....	**-100**

Q.7. The following table gives the employees of various hotels in different countries and the total hotel employees in the year 20. . . :

Country	Employees (-000)
China	4,11,770
India	3,52,370
Russia	1,61,000
America	1,24,070
Germany	64,776
Japan	64,700
United Kingdom	46,077
France	41,860
Italy	40,100
Others	7,05,077
Total hotel employees	20,12,800

Represent the above data by means of circle divided into sectors.

Q.8. Draw suitable diagram to represent the following information relating to food & beverage in two hotels:-

Hotel	Wages (Rs.)	Raw Materials (Rs.)	Profits (Rs.)	Units Produced
A	200000	3,00,000	1,00,000	1,00,000
B	140000	2,40,000	1,00,000	80,000

Show also the cost and profit per unit.

Q.9. Represent the following figures by a simple bar diagram:-

Total Production of bread in a bakery (in lakh)

Year	Total Production
2004-05	54.05
2005-06	5.02
2006-07	51.14
2007-08	57.48
2008-09	65.42

Q.10. Represent the following figures by multiple bar diagram:-

Indices of the quantum of Exports and Imports

(Base 2001-02 = 100)

Year	Imports	Exports
2002-04	100	100
2004-05	194	105
2005-06	83	110
2006-07	100	89
2007-08	74	94
2008-09	64	94

Q.11. Represent the following data by a suitable diagram:-

Imports of various articles for a hotel in India (rupees in lakhs) (2003-04 to 2008-09)

Year	Food, drink and tobacco	Raw materials	Manufacturers and semi-manufacturers	Miscellaneous	Total
2003-04	91.98	126.93	294.52	4.57	518
2004-05	122.36	144.35	288.53	4.79	560.03
2005-06	135.81	125.77	314.78	2.62	578.98
2006-07	262	256.08	351.44	5.35	874.94
2007-08	176	179.16	276.37	4.31	635.49
2008-09	93	169.55	276.03	3.97	542.29

Q.12. Represent the following data by a suitable diagram showing the difference between proceeds and costs in a hotel:-

Receipts and Costs of a hotel (in thousand of rupees)

Year	Total receipts	Total costs
2004	22.0	19.5
2005	27.3	21.7
2006	28.2	30.0
2007	30.3	25.6
2008	32.7	26.1
2009	33.3	34.2

Q.13. The following table gives the profit and loss of a hotel. Represent the data by sub-divided bar diagram:-

Cost, Income, Profit and Loss Account of a Hotel

Particulars	2006 (Rs. in lakhs)	2007 (Rs. in lakhs)	2008 (Rs in lakhs)	2009 (Rs in lakhs)
Cost per unit				
a. Wages	5.4	5.7	6.4	7.0
b. Raw Materials	3.8	2.6	3.0	3.5
c. Salaries	1.0	0.8	0.8	0.6
d. Other Costs	2.5	2.3	2.1	2.4
Total	12.7	11.4	12.3	13.5
Proceeds per unit	11.0	12.1	12.9	13.0
Profit or Loss per unit	-1.7	+0.7	+0.6	-0.5

Q.14. The following table shows the monthly expenditure of three families. Represent the data by a suitable diagram on percentage basis:-

Items of Expenditure	Family A (Rs.)	Family B (Rs.)	Family C (Rs.)
Food articles	4300	8300	12000
Clothing	800	1700	2500
Recreation	300	1000	1200
Education	500	900	1500
Rent	1000	2100	1700
Miscellaneous	600	1500	1100

Q.15. Represent the following data by rectangles:-

Monthly budget of two families

Items of expenditure	Family A (Rs.)	Family B (Rs.)
Food articles	18,000	11000
Clothing	7,000	5000
House rent	9000	6000
Fuel and lighting	3500	3000
Miscellaneous	7500	5000
Total Expenditure	45,000	30000
Saving	2,500	1000

Q.16. Represent the data given in Q. No. 15 above by pie diagrams.

Q.17. Represent the following data by a suitable diagram:-

Main headings of income of a hotel	2006-07 (lakhs of Rs.)	2007-08 (lakhs of Rs.)	2008-09 (lakhs of Rs.)
Telephone	7,274	12,616	12,471
Food sales	5,063	6,785	6,754
Room sales	13,998	11,537	12,571
Miscellaneous	319	360	661

Q.18. Represent the following data by a circular diagram divided into sectors:-

Tourist Arrival in Different States of India- 2009

(in lakhs)

Assam	90
Uttar Pradesh	632
Orissa	146
West Bengal	248.1
Punjab	126.41
Maharashtra	359.56
Bihar	402.26
Tamilnadu	570.16
Madhya Pradesh	212.48

Q.19. Prepare a cartogram and show the concentration of tourists in various regions in India as per data given below:-

State	Concentration of tourists per square mile
Uttar Pradesh	557
Bihar	572
Orissa	244
West Bengal	806
Assam	176
Tamilnadu	446
Mysore	308
Mumbai	323
Madhya Pradesh	163
Hyderabad	227
Rajasthan	117
Punjab	338
Uttarakhand	347
Andhra Pradesh	151
Madhya Pradesh	171
Travancore	1,015
Cochin	

Q.20. The following table gives the breakup of tourists on the basis of religion. Represent the data by pie diagram constructed on the percentage basis:-

Religion	No. in lakhs
Hindu	2031.9
Sikh	62.2
Jain	16.2
Muslim	354.0
Christian	81.4
Other religions	20.1

Q.21. Represent the following data by a pictogram:-

Country	No. of Tourists in lakhs
China	46.4
India	35.7
Pakistan	7.6
USA	15.1
UK	5.0

Q.22. Utilize the following data to represent diagrammatically the *relative* increase in number of tourists towards the end of 2009 in different countries:-

Increase in Number of Tourists (in lakhs)

Country	In 2000	By the end of 2009
Canada	233	1129
USA	7,598	28507
UK	555	1380
Australia	57	200
India	2245	12109

Q.23. Show the details of monthly expenditure of two families given below by means of two-dimensional diagram:-

Items of expenditure	Family A (Income Rs. 50000 p.m.)	Family B (Income Rs. 40000 p.m.)
Food	Rs. 14000	Rs. 12000
Clothing	Rs. 8000	Rs. 8000
House rent	Rs. 10000	Rs. 6000
Education	Rs. 3000	Rs. 4000
Fuel and lighting	Rs. 4000	Rs. 2000
Miscellaneous	Rs. 4000	Rs. 4000

Q.24. Show by suitable diagrams the absolute as well as relative changes in the number of student of the colleges 'A' and 'B' in the different departments from 1999 to2006:-

Subject	College A		College B	
	2006	2009	2006	2009
Engineering	300	350	100	200
Bio-tech	120	500	150	250
Management	200	650	130	150
Law	100	300	100	120

Q.25. Indicate the diagrams you would consider most appropriate to use for representing each of the following classes of statistical data, stating briefly the reason for your choice:-

a) Distribution of large number of candidates according to the number of marks scored by each at a public examination.

b) Marks scored by two selected candidates in each of six different subjects tested at an examination.

c) Total value of Indian exports and imports during the years 2006 to 2009.

d) Distribution of Assets of all Indian Life Insurance Companies put together as at January 19, 2009.

e) Middle class cost of Living Index Numbers in Mumbai and Kolkata during the years 2006 to 2009.

f) Distribution of age, sex and civil condition of person enumerated at the census in 2000.

Q.26. Diagrammatically compare the following statistics:-

Average size of holdings in India as compared to some foreign countries

Country	Acres
India	7.5
Denmark	40
Holland	26
Germany	21.5
France	20.5
Belgium	14.5
Britain	20
USA	145

Q.27. "Give me an undigested heap of figures and I cannot see the wood for the trees. Give me a diagram and I positively encouraged to forget detail until I have real grasp of the overall picture. Diagrams register a meaningful impression almost before we think." ***Moroney***.

Discuss the utility of diagrams and elucidate the above statement.

12

Graphic Representation of Data

Graphs and charts are much better than diagrams. Diagrams can be used only in those places where two or more quantities have to be compared. If the relationship between two variables is to be studied diagrams would be useless for the purpose. Such studies can be made with the help of graphs only. When we study the relationship between two variables the idea is either to study their causes and effect relationship or to study the extent the changes in one variable if the other variable changes by particular amount. Such studies cannot be made by diagrams; graphs are, however, very useful for studying such relationship. The special feature of graphs is that they are more obvious, accurate and precise than diagrams. Graphs are very useful for studying time series and frequency distributions.

Construction of a Graph

In the construction of graphs two simple lines are first drawn which cut each other at the right angles. These lines are called ***axis***. The horizontal line is called ***abscissa or x-axis*** and the vertical line is called ***ordinate or y-axis***. The point at which they cut each other is called the ***Point of Origin***. The Figure 12.1 gives two such lines.

In Fig. 12.1, X'X is abscissa or x-axis and YY' is ordinate or x-axis. The point of their intersection or the point of O. In x-axis on the right hand side of the point of origin, positive values are shown while on the left hand side of the point of origin negative values are recorded. The value at the point of origin is 0. Thus from O to X there are positive values +1, +2, +3, etc. and from O to X' are negative values –1, -2, -3, etc. In y-axis positive values are shown above the point of origin and negative values below it. Thus from O to Y positive value +1, +2, +3, etc., are shown while from O to Y' negative values –1, -2, -3, etc, are shown. Abscissa and ordinate thus divide the graph paper in four parts numbered 1, 2, 3, and 4 as in the figure shown above. In the above figure OX and OY measures positive value and OX' and OY' negative values. If two values (one on x axis and another of y axis) are positive they would be plotted somewhere in part No. 1. If both are negative values they would be plotted in Part No. 3. If the value of x is positive and y is negative they would be plotted in part No. 4 and if the value of x is negative and of y positive it would be plotted in part No. 2. These parts are known as Quadrants.

For each axis a convenient scale is chosen. It is not necessary that the scale of x-axis and y-axis should be identical. The scale indicates the units of a variable which a fixed length of the axis, would represent. Thus in figure above, on the x-axis 1" measures 10 units of the variable

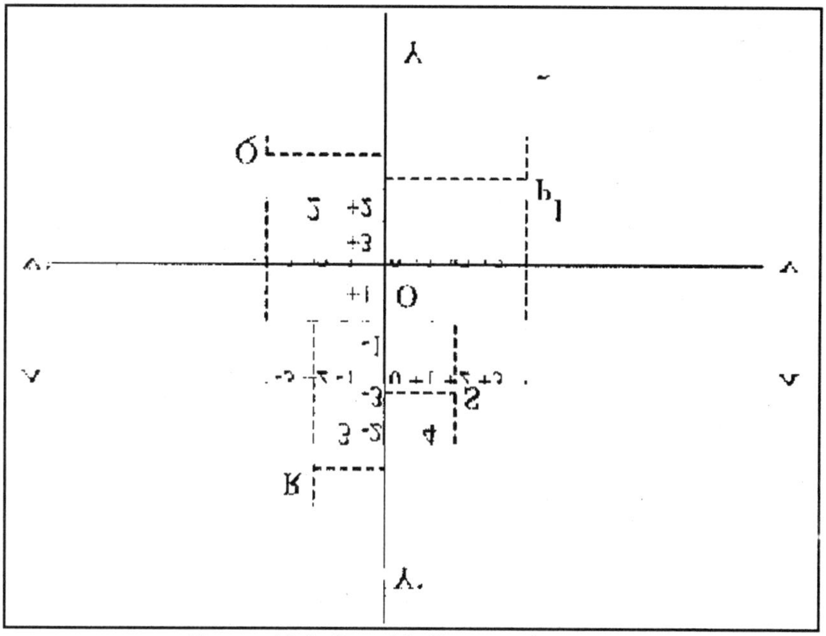

Figure 12.1: Graphic Preparation

and on y-axis 1" measures 5 units only. The values of two variables x and y given in Table 12.1 are plotted in Figure 12.1.

Table 12.1: Values of Variable 'X' and 'Y'

Variable x	Variable y
12	8
-10	6
-6	-6
4	-5

Thus P is plotted at a point where x has a value of 12 and y of 8. The distance of P from the ordinate is 1.2" including a value of 12 of x-variable and its distance from the abscissa is 1.6" indicating a value of 8 on y-variable. Since both the values are positive and point P is in the first quadrant. In x-axis the distance from the point of origin to any other point is known as x-coordinate and in y-coordinate. These two distances are called the co-ordinates of the point which is plotted. Thus the co-ordinates of point P are 12 and 8; x-coordinate is 12 and y-coordinate is 8. Co-ordinates are expressed in terms of x and y, Q, R and S are points in which x and y co-ordinates are respectively –10 and 6, -6 and –6 and 4 and –5. The co-ordinates of these points are indicated by dotted lines in the above table. In actual practice only the points are plotted and lines are not drawn to show the co-ordinates.

Graphs of a Time-Series or Histogram

First we shall study the graphs relating to time series then the graphs representing frequency distributions. Graphs of time series can be either on natural scale or on ratio scale.

Time Series Plot of Sodium Concentration

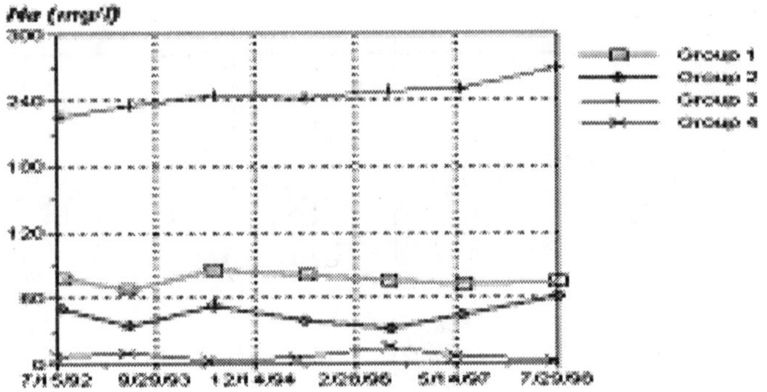

Fig. 12.2: Specimen of a Histogram

If the absolute values of variables are to be represented then natural scale is used. In natural scale equal distances of an axis represent equal values. If for x-axis the scale is 1" = 50 units, then a distance of 1" anywhere on x-axis would represent 50 units. If instead of absolute values the relative values of a variable are to be shown equal distances on the axis would represent portionately equal values of variable. First we shall discuss the graphs constructed on natural scale and afterwards we shall discuss has ratio scale is used.

In graphs relating to time-series values of a variable at different periods of time are shown. In other words, the graph shows the changes in the values of a variable with the passage of time. If absolute values of a variable are taken into account the graphs obtained by plotting them are known as ***Absolute Histograms***. If the values are represented by index numbers and if instead of the actual values their indices are plotted, the graphs so obtained are called ***Index Histograms***. If the changes in the values of two or more variables are shown, there would be two or more histograms and thus a comparative study of the changes would be possible.

Absolute histograms – one variable

In Table 12.2 the number of foreign tourists in a country in the years 2002 to 2009 is given:-

If the data given in Table 12.3 are to be shown by means of graph, first of all x-axis and y-axis would have to be drawn. Since the values of the both the variables are positive we shall draw only the quadrant in which the values of both x and y variables are positive. On the abscissa or x-axis we shall show years and on the ordinate or y-axis the figures of the foreign tourists. In the Figure 12.3, on x-axis 1" represents two year and in y-axis 1" represents foreign tourists in lakhs. Thus against the year 2001 the point of a distance of 2.38" from the point of origin would show the arrivals of 9.54 lakh foreign tourists. Similarly against the year 2009 the point at a distance of 2.22" would represent a tourists of 8.90 lakh. In the same way other points can be plotted. The line joining these points would be the desired graph. It would be as given in Fig. 12.3.

Table 12.2: Number of Foreign Tourist in a Country from 2002 to 2009 (in lakh)

Year	No. of foreign tourists
2002	9.54
2003	8.9
2004	8.93
2005	8.57
2006	8.3
2007	10.04
2008	10.76
2009	11.03

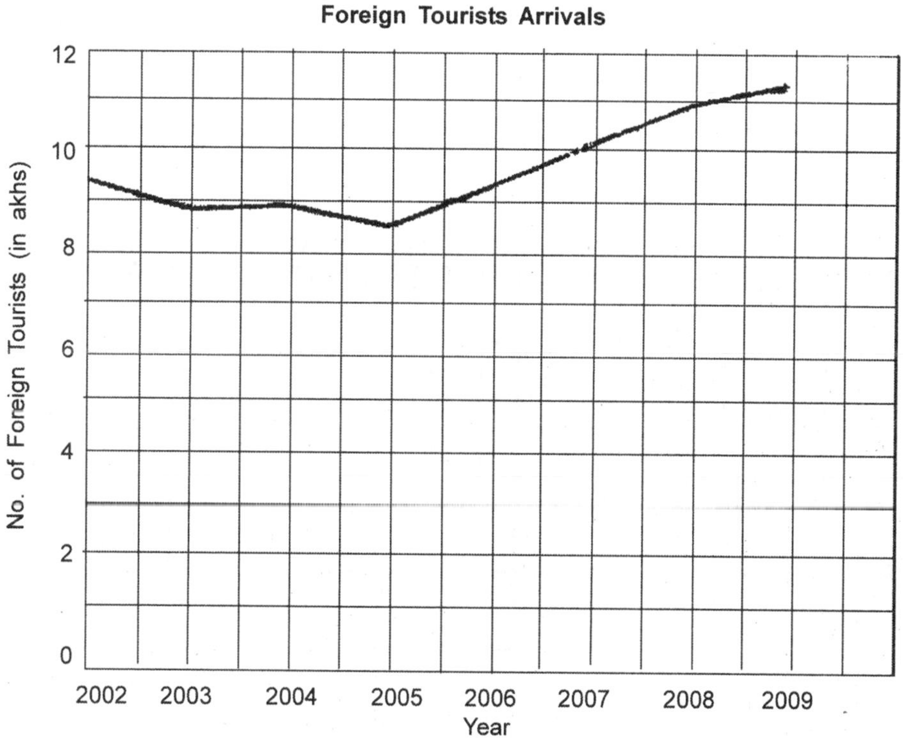

Fig. 12.3: Number of Foreign tourists from 2002 to 2009 (in lakh)

From the above graph the foreign tourists in each year can be known. The graph can also reveal the changes in the production from year to year. If these data were represented by a bar diagram it would not have looked so impressive.

False base line

If the fluctuations in the values of a variable are very small as compared to the size of items, a false base line is used.

Table 12.3: Total Foreign Tourists Arrivals in India (in lakh)

Month	Year	
	2008	2009
January	19.7	18.7
February	20.2	19
March	20.6	18.9
April	20.9	18.9
May	20.9	18.7
June	20.4	18.5
July	20.1	18.3
August	19.4	18.1
September	19	17.9
October	19	17.9
November	18.7	17.9
December	18.8	17.9

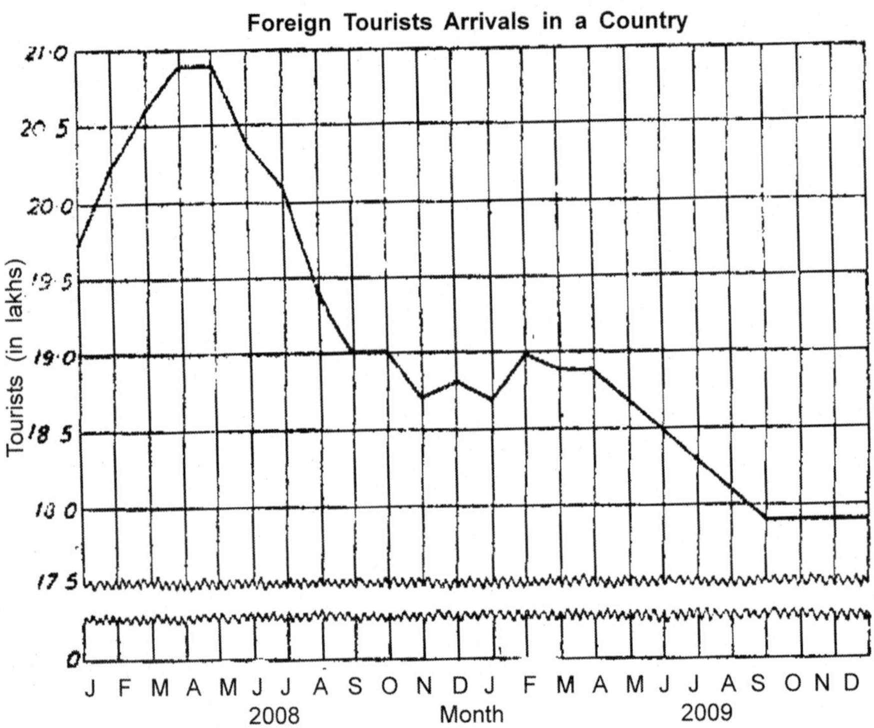

Fig. 12.4: Foreign Tourist Arrivals in India

In the Figure 12.4, 1" on the vertical scale represents 100 lakh tourists. If a false base line was not used the vertical scale would have been 21" long. If 1" was to represent 500 million tourists the size of the vertical scale would still have been more than 4" but then the fluctuations in the supply of money during these two years would not have been very clear from the graph.

False base line should be used only when it is absolutely necessary to do so. It is generally used to save space and to depict small fluctuations sharply. Under such circumstances a graph in which false base line gives very misleading impressions.

Graphs of Frequency Distributions

Frequency distributions of all types are represented by means of graphs precisely for the same reasons for which graphs are prepared for other types of data.

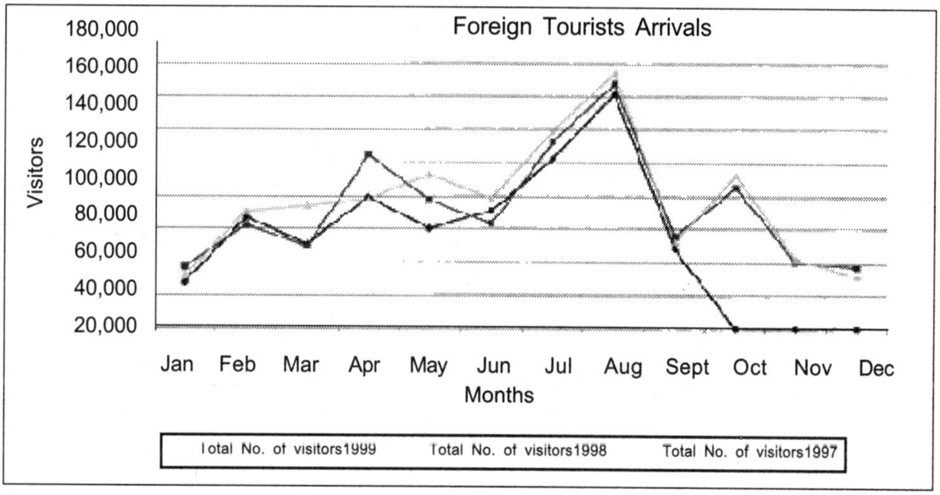

Fig. 12.5: Specimen of a Curve Chart

1) Bar Frequency Curves

Such curves are used to depict discrete series.

2) Discontinuous Curves or Frequency Polygons

In such curves the plotted points are joined by straight lines. The curves are not smoothed. Such curves are also used to represent discrete series.

3) Continuous Curves or Smoothed Frequency Curves

In such graphs the frequency polygon obtained by joining the point is smoothed. Such curves are used to represent continuous series.

In the Table 12.4 the data relates to the number of rooms in star hotels. The series is a discrete one and a bar frequency diagram represents the data as shown in Figure 12.6.

Table 12.4: Number of Rooms in Star Hotels in India

No. of Rooms	No. of hotels
100	170
200	183
300	191
400	146
500	105
600	75
700	42
800	30
900	25

Bars can be horizontal also but vertical bars give better graphs. The data can be shown by a discontinuous curve as well. In this case instead of bars or lines only points would be plotted on various heights representing the number of hotels. These points would be joined by straight lines and a frequency polygon would thus be obtained. In Table 12.5 frequencies of different values of a variable are given. These data are shown in the shape of frequency polygon in the Figure 12.7.

Table 12.5: Value of a Variable and Their Corresponding Frequencies

Value of a Variable	Frequency
1	3
2	11
3	32
4	41
5	65
6	70
7	67
8	53
9	42
10	38
11	31
12	21
13	15
14	9
15	5
16	2

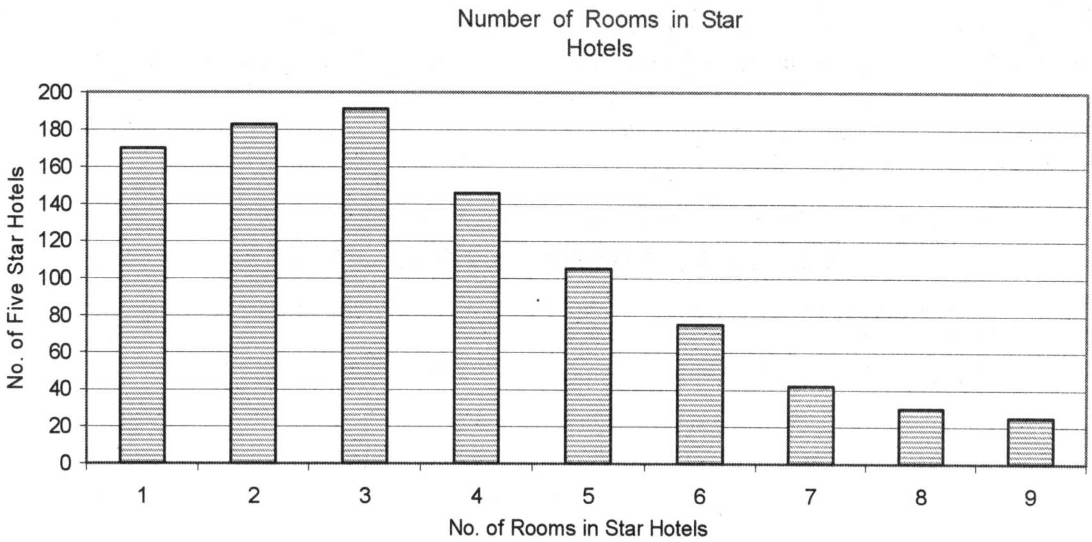

Fig. 12.6: Number of Rooms in Star Hotels

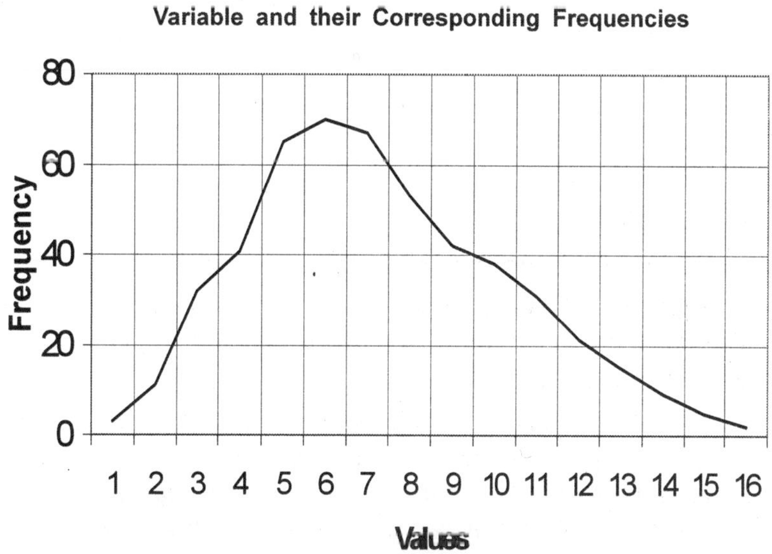

Fig. 12.7: Values of Variable and their Corresponding Frequencies

Continuous frequency curves are used to depict such data which give continuous series and in which a frequency can assume any value of the variable within a particular class limit. In such cases as far as possible, the class intervals should be uniform size otherwise the curves can give a misleading impression. Ordinarily, there should not be more than 25 class intervals though there is no hard and fast rule in this respect. No class interval should be left out for the reason that there is no frequency against it.

The data given in Table 12.6 have to be shown by a smoothed curve.

Table 12.6: Age Distribution of a Group of Tourists

Age (in years)	No. of people
8-10	12
10-12	15
12-14	19
14-16	26
16-18	38
18-20	55
20-22	61
22-24	64
24-26	60
26-28	53
28-30	42
30-32	31
32-34	18
34-36	10
36-38	7
38-40	5

If the data are classified the bar frequency diagram or frequency polygon representing them has to be smoothed for the purpose of getting a continuous frequency curve. The process of smoothing a curve is discussed below:-

The data should firstly be plotted in the shape of a frequency curve or a frequency polygon. Fig. 12.8(a) and Fig. 12.8(b) represents the data in the shape of a bar frequency curve and frequency polygon respectively. The frequency polygon shown in Figure 12.8 (b) can be smoothed by free land. The angularities can be removed and a smoothed frequency curve of the type shown in Figure 12.8(c) can be obtained.

Age Distribution of a Group of Tourists

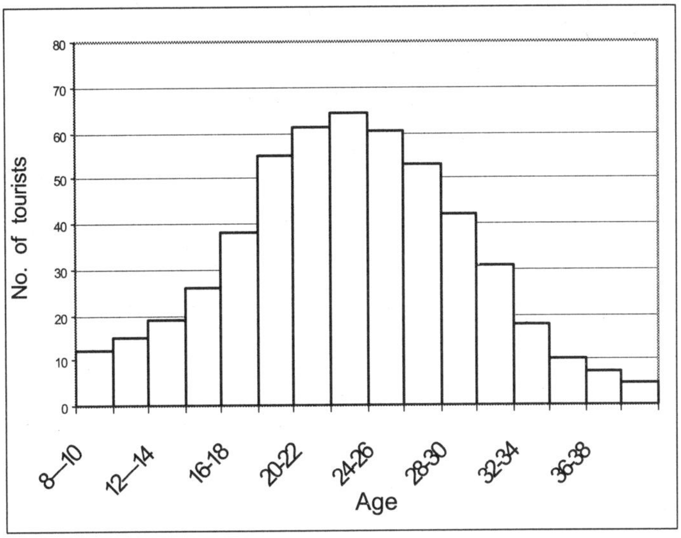

Fig. 12.8(a): Age Distribution of a Group of Tourists

Age Distribution of a Group of Tourists

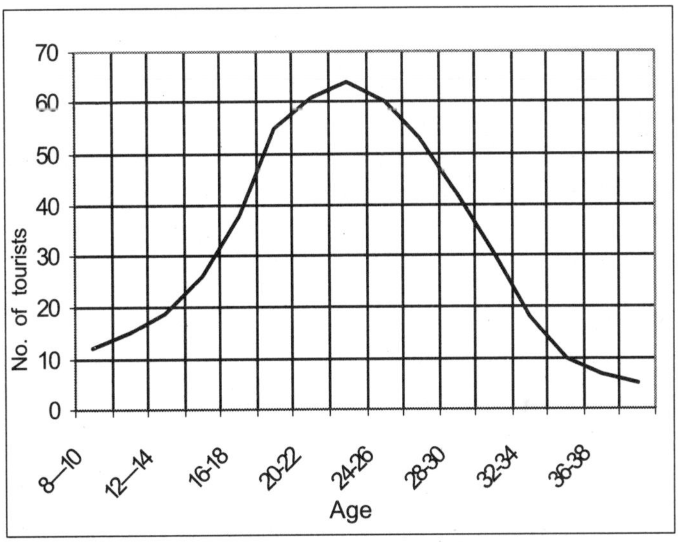

Fig. 12.8(b): Age Distribution of a Group of Tourists

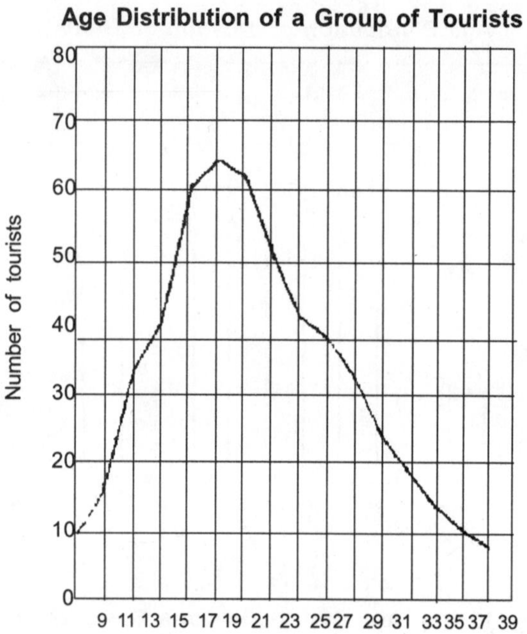

Fig. 12.8(c): Age Distribution of a Group of Tourists

Questions and Assignments

Q.1. What points should be taken into account in the construction of graphs ? Discuss in detail.

Q.2. What is false base line ? Under what circumstance should it be used ?

Q.3. Differentiate clearly between natural scale and the logarithmic scale used in graphical presentation of data.

Q.4. Write short notes on:-

a) Ogive
b) Histogram
c) Frequency Curve
d) Frequency Polygon
e) Zee-chart
f) Band and Zone curves
g) Normal curves of error.

Q.5. What are the advantages of Ratio Scale over the Natural Scale ? Plot the following data graphically on the logarithmic scale:-

Year	Total receipts from a hotel (in crores of rupees)	Receipts from room sales (in crores of rupees)
2000	17.7	16.7
2001	18.6	17.2
2002	19.6	16.7
2003	20.8	19.2
2004	21.4	18.5
2005	20.7	18.7
2006	25.2	23.7
2007	26.9	25.8
2008	42.1	41
2009	65	62.5

Q.6. Describe the Lorenz graph. How does it differ from an Ogive ? Illustrate your answer by fitting a Lorenz curve and an ogive to the following data:-

Percentage of age distribution of foreign tourists in India, 2009.

Age groups	Foreign tourists
0-10	28
10-20	20.9
20-30	17.7
30-40	14.3
40-50	9.7
50 60	5.6
60-70	2.7
70- over	1.1
Mean Age	23.2

Q.7. Represent the following frequency distribution by means of graph. Construct the cumulative frequency curve also.

Class interval	Frequency
0-5	13
5-10	42
10-15	135
15-20	237
20-25	250
25-30	256
30-35	250

(contd.)

Class interval	Frequency
35-40	237
40-45	13
45-50	42
50-55	13

Q.8. Draw a cumulative frequency graph of the following distribution, showing the monthly wages of a group of housekeeping workers in a hotel, and hence or otherwise calculate the values of (a) the mode, (b) the median, and (c) the two quartiles:-

Wages in rupees	No. of Housekeeping Workers
20	8
21	10
22	11
23	16
24	20
25	25
26	15
27	9
28-29	6

Q.9. Represent the following data graphically:-

Hotel Advances granted by Government
(in crores of rupees)

Year	Mumbai	Chennai	All-India
2003	1.7	3.47	9.03
2004	2.22	4.4	10.45
2005	3.29	4.96	14.4
2006	5.29	6.44	17.99
2007	6.9	7.65	22.9
2008	8.12	7.33	24.21

13

Oral Presentations or Viva Voce

Most research projects involve one or more oral reports. Oral reports are also commonly made at the conclusion of the projects. These reports may follow or precede the preparation and distribution of the final written report. Upper-level managers will often base decisions on the oral report. Therefore, we cannot overemphasize how critical this task is. As one successful researcher states: "After working six months or more on a project, the researcher may get thirty to sixty minutes of top management's time. The oral report had better be effective".

The first step in ensuring that the oral report is effective is the same as for a written report–an analysis of the audience. The next step is the development of a detailed report outline or, preferably, a written script for the report. Once the oral presentation is prepared, it should be rehearsed. Even highly trained actors and speakers typically rehearse material prior to making a formal presentation. Researchers, generally with limited training in oral presentations, should plan on several "dry runs" before making a presentation to management.

Visual Aids

The use of visual aids is essential for most oral presentations of research results. The oral presentation of a list of several numbers or percentages simply will not register on many listeners. Even the visual presentation of the numbers in a table will often not have the necessary impact. Many people have to "study" a table to understand it. Therefore, oral presentations should make extensive use of the various charting techniques referred to earlier as well as any other appropriate visual aids. In fact, many research presentations are built around a complete set of visual aids.

A number of kinds of equipment are available to assist in the presentation of visual materials. A chalkboard allows the researcher to write out and manipulate numbers. It is particularly useful when technical questions concerning the findings are anticipated. A magnetic board and a felt board offer some of the same advantages but not as flexible. They do, however, allow the rapid presentation of previously prepared materials.

A flip chart is a large pad of blank paper mounted on an easel. Visual aids are drawn on the pages in advance, and the speaker flips to the appropriate chart progressing through the talk. The use of coloured felt-tip pens can increase the effect of the flip chart. Blank pages can be left at appropriate intervals and the speaker can create new exhibits as the need arises.

Overhead projectors are widely used to show previously prepared images against a screen or wall. The materials presented in this manner can range from simple charts to complex overlay.

An overlay is produced by the successive additions of new images to the screen without removing the previous images. In addition, the speaker can write on the transparency (the acetate sheet on which the image is carried) and the writing will appear on the screen.

Transparent slides of anything that can be photographed can be projected on to a screen. Although these slides are not as flexible as those used on overhead projectors (that is, they cannot be written on while in use), remote-control, magazine-loaded projectors allow a smooth, evenly paced presentation using this technique. Other techniques such as the use of 16 mm film and videotape can be used in specific situations but are not widely applicable.

Post-Study Tasks for Project Report

Once the project report is completed, you would be doubly happy. However the work is yet to be completed. There are several post study tasks that need to be undertaken by you. There tasks include:

1) Prepare the 'addenda' to reproject
2) Package the project report.
3) Writing the synopsis of the report.
4) Writing 'thank you letters', and
5) Mailing the synopsis and thank you leters to those who have contributed to the project, and
6) The optional task getting these published.

The Addenda

Some research guide require students to include in their critical addendum the original response to the quesionnaire. The addenda may include:

1) A copy of the cover letter that acompanied the questionnaire
2) A copy of the mailing list
3) A blank copy of the original questionnaire
4) A copy of the synopsis that were sent to questionnaire respondents
5) A copy of the letter sent with synopsis to questionnaire respondents. Check with your research professor to determine which documents are required as addenda. Each addendum is called an appendex and is labelled as such, ordered and membered sequentially. Identity each appendix sequentially by number or letter. All appendexes are placed at the end of the bibliography. They are placed in the order of their appearance on the table of contents.

Packaging the Project Study

The number of copies required may vary, from only the original, to the original plus one copy, to the original plus as many as five copies.

The form of binding frequently used are three-ring bindinig, velobinding, book-binding and spiral-binding. The inside paper size be no more than 8.5" × 11" and the covers be either the same size or only slightly larger. The front and back covers are usually heavier than regular copy cover. For velobinding and spiral binding, a clear plastic cover, which is placed on top of the cover-light paper stock, may be used.

The order in which documents are bound varies (check you guide). Generally the following order could be as followed:

1) A plastic cover
2) Cover page in cover-weight stock
3) Inside cover page
4) Table of contents
5) Table of graphs, charts, gigures and tables
6) Chapter (one to five)
7) Bibliography
8) The appendixes, each preceeded by an appendix little page.
9) Pack page in cover-weight stock, and
10) Clean plastic cover.

Once the project report and all copies of the report have been bound, they should be inserted into a large mamla envelope. Affix a level on to be outside of the envelope. Type-little number of copies of final bound thesis, your name, your enrolment number, you address, you work and home phone number. All copies of the project report should be turned to your research professor or secretary in one enevelope.

Writing the Synopsis of the Project Report

The synopsis is a summary overview of the study, with the concentration being placed on the outcomes. The synopsis is used to provide results to those who contributed to the project report, completing questionnaire, responded to questionnaires, editors, and publishers and making a presentation to a professional organisation. The synopsis should be short—no more from one page in length in single space with a brief heading at the top, your name on the next line. After skipping two spaces, the synopsis starts with an introduction. The body of the synopsis comes next, and the conclusion is the last part of the synopsis.

In writing the body of the synopsis, revise each chapter, writing one or two sentences summarising each. Each result should be set out clearly.

To write the introduction, the body of the report is reviewed and a few sentences are wirtten to introduce the body. For conclusion again the body is to be reviewed and a three or four sentence conclusion written.

Thank You Letters and Synopses Distribution

At least one copy should go to the each person who contributed to the study. It should be mailed with a cover letter. This letter should be brief reminding the recepients about the study. The letter should state that the study has been completed and that a synopsis of the study, including an cover view of the major outcomes, is attached.

Publishing of Report

The first step is to identify a publication. It is always better to identify two a three potential publications. Once publication has been identified the name of the editor and submit your project report synposis, and/or article concept with appropriate cover letter. A published article or presentation based on you project work present opportunitiese for additional exposure within the industry. Publication credits enhance your additional opportunity in terms of getting a first (a letter) job in the hospitality and tourism industry.

14

A Case Study: Specimen of a Typical Project Report

This topic contains a typical project report titled, '*Impact of Changing Business Environment on Transformation of Owner-Managers in Indian Hospitality Industry*'. This report presents guidelines for researchers. The contents of this reports will facilitate the researcher to follow systematic steps to complete the project report.

However, you are required to make a critical study and analysis of the sample project report and schematically prepare a detailed descriptive note covering all the important points in term of strengthens and weaknesses of this project as per the guidelines given in Chapter 1 to Chapter 13.

Impact of Changing Business Environment on Transformation of Owner-Managers in Indian Hospitality Industry

for

In Partial fulfilment for
Award of Post-Graduate Diploma
in
Hospitality Management

Prepared by

. . . .

. . . .

. . . .

Indian School of Hospitality
Noida

Impact of Changing Business Environment on Transformation of Owner-Managers in Indian Hospitality Industry

for

In Partial fulfilment for
Award of Post-Graduate Diploma
in
Hospitality Management

Prepared by

....

....

....

Indian School of Hospitality
University Campus, Noida

Certificate of Completion

This is to certify that the project report titled .... has been accomplished under my guidance and supervision.

This project is being submitted by Mr/ Ms... in partial fulfilment of requirements for the award of the post graduate diploma in Hospitality Management from Indian School of Hospitality. This work has not been submitted by him/her anywhere else for the award of any degree or diploma. All sources of information and help have been duly mentioned and acknowledged.

Signature of Guide

Name and Address of the Guide
PROF. (DR.) ....
Indian School of Hospitality, Noida

CONTENTS

List of Tables

List of Figures

Foreword

After gaining 10 years experience in international hospitality and tourism development in the Institute of Hospitality Management a cutting edge of the tourism industry; which is highly formal, hierarchical, result oriented, and which places special emphasis on trust, continuous learning, concept of self before service, I decided to have a first hand experience of the fast global changes taking place in the society and prepare myself to meet them headlong in the future.

During this period, I closely interacted with a wide cross-section of young boys and girls working in the industry. They are the leaders of tomorrow, who are going to lead us into the next millennium. I found that they expected everything from their parents, friends, society, education system and employers with least expectations from self. They have a high confidence to subvert the system by overt or covert means through right connections. My observations have been vindicated by studies conducted at various research levels.

Our national education system is under drastic transformation, specially due to the introduction of a new technological in global scenario. We have travelled far since the time when our political leaders were hallowed for their honesty and spirit of public service; and when the civil service was coveted for the respect it commanded. Politics in the public eye is the least respectable of all professions. It is also seen as the one where more money is to be made mostly by corrupt means. Government officials too, rank low with regard to respectability, honesty, accountability and their contributions to society.

The owner-managers who remain today are the struggling corporate chieftains, the university presidents, the city managers, the state governors. Owner-managers today appear to be an endangered species caught in the whirl of events and circumstances beyond rational control. Therefore to examine whether values, ethics, honesty, integrity, courage, knowledge, foresight and all that; the basic qualities of leadership are required or has emerged which will guide Indian hospitality and tourism industry into the future and the next millennium or basic qualities/traits are as valid for tomorrow as they were fifty years ago.

....

ABC

New Delhi: 2008

Preface

With my long varied and rich experience covering both line and staff functions in the hospitality and tourism, it was natural curiosity to view and learn theoretically the present day hospitality management as I am fitting the practical experience into the theories; after all management science had its beginning in the hospitality and tourism industry.

Since the day I joined the academics, I found myself put through constant mental and physical training, knowing more about international hospitality and tourism to be reactive and not pro-active leadership skills. It required a real man of substance to take a decision either way. Globalisation and liberalisation are revolutionizing business world. A product service and industry must have an edge over its competitors. Indian industries which enjoyed protection in the past, will no longer enjoy monopolies and their heads be well advised to initiate appropriate remedial measures urgently to survive and grow.

The corporate leadership in hospitality and tourism have to develop skills for strategic leadership to deal with the ongoing metamorphosis in the economic and business scenario of the world. The time has come when old typologies and classical stereotypes of leadership do not hold the ground. More creative and innovative ways of managing and leading the financial sector and human resources at the political, social and corporate levels have to be discovered. The need for developing countries like India is to increase their capacity to use knowledge, cannot be overstated. Most need to do much more, much faster to increase their knowledge base to invest in educating their people and to take advantage of new technologies for acquiring and disseminating knowledge.

Hospitality and tourism researches all over the world are seeing more and more into the qualities of visionary top managers. The vision depends upon the performance of a leader, who constantly asks himself as to which destination he is taking the institution or the organisation. The future make-up of a top manager would have to suit the changing trends in international business such as more turbulence and openness, more questions of values and initiations, more emphasis on post-quality changes, demanding customers, markets and interdependent partnership.

Therefore, the logic sequence of this research is based on the followings:

1) Study of past, present and future management trends in hospitality and tourism
2) New approaches in the international hospitality market.
3) History of hospitality and tourism in India
4) International business environment and the organisations of the future
5) Case studies and research findings
6) The evolution of successful hospitality leadership likely model of 21st century hospitality managers.

This research paper is laid out in a manner in which beginning is being made with the discussion on general management practices, and instead of looking at these in purely conceptual terms. The endeavour has been made to look at the history of International business environment and the organisations. The number of variables which lead to the ongoing success of an organisation are many– some controllable and some not.

From the study of profiles of selected leading corporate personalities, personal interaction and interviews with over *20 senior* and top leaders in different fields and from *125 replies* to a questionnaire over telephone, fax and internet; targeted at *about 300*, some common points of views have been arrived at. The interaction is carried out at seminars, clubs, offices, and social calls all through mutual acquittances. The area covered is North, Central and West India, while the persons selected are from as diverse areas as education, politics, religions, defence services, government, public and private industries. Few responses are received from abroad through internet.

However this study has not been able to address the objective in depth, due to the constraint of time and shallow base of number of personalities and organisations. The interviews are also not in depth as minimum time is from five minutes to maximum twenty minutes. But despite the limitations of the study, the outcome is still a valuable input in fulfilling the gaps/holes in the development of the model of leadership in Indian hospitality industry.

....

(*Rosorach Scholar*)

Acknowledgments

The author warmly acknowledges the courtesy and prompt response of all those who were asked to contribute their views and readily granted the necessary permission to contact them at the inconvenient hours despite the pressure of time. I must profusely thank those who used their influences and provided their valuables time to make it possible for me to cast my research net far and wide in a short time, especially Chairman, Managing Directors, General Managers, middle level management and lower level management cadre of various hospitality, tourism, airlines, foreign embassies, high commission and many other organisations.

I must also thank my colleagues who gave me moral support and granted me additional funds to push through the work at a faster pace. I would like to record my appreciation for those who helped at one time or other in typing the results, and questionnaires at various places.

Finally I hereby acknowledge my gratitude to Dr. (Prof) Jagmohan Negi, my project guide who encouraged me in selecting the topic and for providing valueable guidance despite the demand made on his precious time. Without his help, I do not think I would have completed the project.

....

(Name of Research Scholar)

CHAPTER 1

An Introduction to Hospitality Management

The concept of hospitality management has undergone various changes over the last three decades. In this chapter an attempt has been made to look at the evolution of methods of manageing the hospitalilty management. Interestingly, these approaches have been revolving around some Ps. The primary consideration of hospitality management in the early 1950s revolved around following four Ps:

1) Purpose
2) Performance
3) Productivity, and
4) Profit.

Every hotel is supposed to have a purpose and get people to perform to achieve the purpose at a high level of productivity influnced which should result in profits. In 1960s Mc Carthy's[1] four 'P's introduced that the hospitality management through marketing strategy for more than three decades.

1) Product
2) Price
3) Place, and
4) Promotion.

The needs of different customers are different and a hotelier cannot satisfy the needs of all the people. However it is possible to identify clusters (segments) of guests (customers) with relatively homogeneous needs and performances. A hospitality should then choose that segment (target) that can be profitably exploited by the company by offering a product needed at a price affordable and make it available in places that are convenient for the target customers and promote/advertise (position) the product as meeting a specific need of the target group. The product, price, place and promotion are the controllable variables that a hospitality leader could manipulate to get the desired result.

Subsequently, Booms and Bittner[2] added the following three Ps to the traditional four Ps of marketing to make them relevant to services sector which was the emerging field during the period:

1) Participants
2) Physical evidence, and
3) Process.

The services and products need to be clearly differentiated. Services are different from products in terms of the following four characteristics.

1) Intangibility
2) Inseparability
3) Heterogeneity, and
4) Perishability.

Basically the production and consumption cannot be separated in the case of hospiatlity services. Additionally the human element posses considerable problems to the markers of services. The problem not only arises due to the service provided but also the consumers. Every time a quality service is offered, the expectation of the customer goes up.

The famous marketing expert, Kotler Phillip[3] added the following two Ps for entry into restricted markets:

1) Politics, and
2) Public.

Companies like Taj, ITC, Oberois etc. had to manage public opinion and local politics to enter into restricted markets like China, Russia and India.

Present Trends in Hospitality

Judd[4], added the fifth P, namely, 'people' to make the four Ps relevant to industrial products. This is similar to participants in the Booms and Bittner model.

In 1990's, the management experts[5] discussed about two others Ps namely

1) People, and
2) Process Reengineering.

All of a sudden, managers started realising that they spend too much time trying to squeeze the last percentage point of productivity out of their capital assets while ignoring the huge untapped potential of the human resources. According to Percy Barnevik, CEO of ABB,[6] "There is tremendous unused potential in our people. Our organisations ensure that they only use 5 to 10 per cent to run their households, lead a Boys Scout trip, or build a summer home. We have to learn how to recognize and employ that untapped ability that each individual brings to work everyday."

Hotel Business-Process Reengineering

Michael Hammer[7] popularised the concept of BPR, basically referring to fundamental re-thinking and radical redesign of work processes so that the company becomes lean and develops the quick response capabilities to face competition and to exploit new opportunities. This led to several organizations de-layering and down-sizing, cutting short through the layers of middle management whose role was to supervise the work of others and transmit information up and down the hierarchy. Re-engineering has been supported by the development of new technologies which have revolutionized inter and intra organizational communication in terms of transmitting information but also resulted in new forms of work organizations where-in the element of supervision and leading the personnel has taken a new form. Though this met with initial success, it also resulted in several problems. It did lead to reduction in costs but it has not brought dramatic improvement in profits and prospects. The delayering has had a negative impact on a large number of employees resulting an increase in personnel problems requiring higher quality of leadership to deal with.

Future Hospitality Management Approach

The future management approach for surviving the turbulence of 21st century should adopt the following:

1) Participative management
2) Partnering
3) Personalized products, and
4) Perpetual learning.

Participative Hospitality Management

It refers to getting the employees to feel a part of the organization so that they can give their best to the organization. Most Japaneses competitors managed to get the involvement of their employees by finding common enemies in foreign companies, which is called 'Strategic intent'. Anita Roddicks of cosmetic business called Body Shop has managed to assemble a set of people who have a common vision, eco-friendly and socially relevant business. The company believes in profit with a principle philosophy. They oppose testing on animals, help third world economies through its trade, contribute to rain forest preservation efforts, is active in women's issues and sets an example for recycling. Robert Semler of Semco Industries in Mexico has passed on the powers even to determine wages and bonuses down the line to the workers and that he is getting the best out of his people. Whatever be the approach, the hotels that are able to share the benefits with its workers and get them united for a common purpose in a participative mode will only survive in the 21st century.

Partnering in Management

Partnering takes up many forms, such as strategic alliances, networking, collaborations and co-operatives. In a complex, knowledge intensive and information oriented 21st century, it is not possible for individual companies to come up with consumers to all their problems by themselves. Comapnies will need to partner with their customers and suppliers. At the further end, comapnies may even partner with competitors, which is called co-competition.

Personalised Products

The days of mass marketing is over in hospitality and tourism. We are getting closure to the era of personalized products. Customisation is commonly followed in both services and industrial products marketing. However, with flexible automation, it has come to be used in consumer products as well. A customer can sit in front of a computer terminal and design his own itinery, car, bicycle or jeans and get the same fabricated and delivered to his house the same day. For example, Japan's National Bicycle Industrial Co-dealers fax a set of specifications based on the customer's requirement for model, colour, components and personal measurements. Computers digest the specifications and print out blueprint from which customer's bicycle is created of cut-to-fit and common parts. Robots do most of the wielding and painting while skilled workers complete the assemble including the silk-screening the customers' name on to the frame. Within a day, this one-of-a kind bicycle (out of 11 million combination of parts) is finished, packed and ready for shipment.

Perpetual Learning Process

The concept of learning organisation was popularised by Peter Senge[8]. In times of drastic changes, it is the learners who inherit the future. It adopts learning as an on going and creative process for its members and develops, adapts and transforms itself in response to the needs and aspirations of people both inside and outside itself. The knowledge so acquired is diffused across the entire hotel organizations and usually it remains embedded in the organisation and it is not easy to copy by its competitors. This has to be a continuous process and hotels that are successful in institutionalising perpetual learning will be more successful in the 21st century.

Summary

The study of past, present and future hospitality management trends show that how the main focus of attention of industry managers shifted from materials and markets to people and back to self. In the last fifty years of business world, with the changing circumstances, the emphasis shifted from mass production, mass marketing to tourist oriented and then to personalised products and specialised and segmented markets and back to hotel industry leaders and the organisations.

(4)

These changes are not evolutionary in nature but were forced upon the hotel business world by the changing scenario. One of the main elements of changing scenario is the successful hotel organisations led by visionary and extraordinary leaders, who choose their path and forced others to follow.

The hospitality industry captains will have to open their minds, educate themselves and innovate new concepts and ideas to lead their hotels and successfully adopt to the changing and demanding situations. The major trends emerging in the international scenario point to more turbulence and openness, more questions of values and institution, more emphasis on post-quality changes and demanding customers market as well as stress on learning and independent partnership. These trends clearly require much more of education and an effective management style.

References

1) Mc Carthy, EJ '*Basic Marketing*, Irwin, Homewood, II, 1960

2) Booms, MH, and Binder, MJ, '*Marketing Strategies and Organisational Structure for Service Firms*, "In Donnelhy, JH and George WR (Eds), (Marketing of Services) American Marketing Association, Chicago, ii, 1982, PP. 47-51.

3) Kotler P, '*Mega Marketing*', Harvard Business Review, vol 64, Mar-Apr 1986, PP. 117 - 24.

4) Judd, VC, "*Differentiate with the 5th P: People*"; Industrial Marketing Management, Vol 16, November 1987, PP. 241-7.

5) Goshal, Sumantra and Bartlett, Christopher A, '*The Individualized Corporation: A Fundamental New Approach to Management* - Great Companies are defined by Purpose, Process, Process and People, 1998.

6) Heil, Puncher, Tate, '*Leadership and the Customer Revolution*, 1994, PP. 92-93.

7) Hammer Michel and Champy James, '*Reengineering the Corporation: A Manifesto for Business Revolution*, Harper Business, New York, 1993.

8) Sengo PM. 'The Fifth Discipline-*The Art And Process of Learning Organisations*, New York, Doubleday, 1990.

CHAPTER 2

Growth and Development of Hospitality Managerial Leadership

The research study of the Indian hospitality managment showed that almost all small hotel units registered with the government are usually run by a sole proprietors or their families. The resources are primarily raised from family and friends. Whatever skills present in the hotel enterprise are usually those of the promoter- there is no attention paid to training or human resource development and skills that are developed on the job. There are of-course some hotels started by chains. They have to some degree inducted a few more skilled people and more accepted techniques of raising finances, management, procurements and marketing.

The overwhelming majority of hotels in India, whether small, medium or large are controlled by family groups. A large number of them tend to be patriarchal in their attitudes to and relationships with the employees.

Perpetuating family hotel business for one more generation is the greatest management challenge. The propensity of most of the business families worldwide to extinguish themselves by the third generation. In India, this is sure, given the Indian business family's missionary tendencies. Then there are a growing number of hotels that are independent and professionally run in the sense that the governance is by people who themselves, are not the related more to their competence than based on their family relationships.

There are many MNCs which have been operating in India, like Intercontinental, Sheraton, Hyatt etc, and others have come to India in recent years. They come from almost every country in the world, though the majority are from Europe, and the U.S.A. They also tend to be diverse in their approach to hospitality management control. Many of them started as joint ventures and some have left control in the hands of Indian partners who usually belong to a family group, and, in some cases are taking back control. Others have generated their own internal management form recruits chosen in India. Yet others are in the hands of nationals of the country to which MNC belongs, and many times, out of touch with their environment.

State owned hotels are found in almost every state. There are some with social functions, but have been corporatised But they are by and large, overstaffed and produce poor returns on capital unless their prices or markets are controlled by government. The management of these public hotel vary a great deal in their autonomy. However, even the best have far less autonomy in every respect than even much smaller private enterprises.

Very few hotel companies in India, whether in the private or public sector, had tried to develop long–term goals and strategies which looked at the emerging context and the way in which their business would exploit opportunities and counter the threats. Even those that tried to engage in long–term planning did little in terms of organizational development to meet their long-term objectives. Planning for successions, skills up gradation, systems and structures to relate the organization to a developing future, human source development and leadership with a vision is a rather uncommon practice in most traditional Indian hotels.

International Environment and Hospitality

The hospitality industry has embark on a journey into the 21st Century. The industry is facing new challenges. In todays scenario no more the hotel manager who used to command and control style of working, will deliver. Technology advance and explosion of knowledge is going to be so great that it would be impossible for any one individual in the, let us say, ten years to cope with the 'changes'. Much global sales of goods and services are being ordered via the internet. Hotels are open 24-hours a day, seven days a week and 365 days in a year, allowing anyone from any part of the world to view the catalogue and buy services at any time of the day.

Managing uncertainty will be primary problem for most senior executives all over the world. Virtually everything in business today is an undifferentiated commodity except how a company manages its information. How you manage information determines whether you win or lose. Fast moving consumer durable and pharmaceutical companies are predominant in the wealth creators list. Satyam Computers was the fastest wealth creator and SAIL became the biggest wealth destroyer in the last five years. In sharp contrast to the wealth creators, the top wealth destroyers of this period are assets intensive businesses with negligible focus on intellectual capital. Wealth destroyers are dominant highly fragmented, low entry barrier businesses provide unique undifferentiated products or services.

The number of multi-nationals is increasing in the wealth creation group. International chains and Indian hotel companies have been able to capitalize on the high growth opportunities and consequently expand their profit margins. The capital productivity of international clains have improved while that of Indian hotel companies have reduced. Wealth creation is the process by which a hotel company increases value of capital entrusted to it by its shareholders. It is a basic measure of success for any commercial venture. From investors point of view the wealth created by the hotel company is the difference between the market value of his holdings and his investment cost.

Peter S. Ducker, eminent business management Guru states: "An organisation composed largely of specialists who direct and discipline their own performance through feedback from collegues, customers, and headquarters. For this reason, it will be what we call an information organization". He further states that the information based organization will pose its own special problems, such as:

1) Developing rewards, recognition and career opportunities for specialists
2) Creating unified vision in an organization of specialists
3) Devising the management structure for an organization of task forces
4) Ensuring the supply, preparation, and testing of top management people.

John Naisbatt in his best selling book Megatrends[1] isolated ten present and future elements of changes as given in Table 2.1.

Table 2.1 Elements of Change

From		To	
1)	Industrial Society	(a)	Information Society
2)	Forced Technology	(b)	High Tech/High Technology
3)	National Economy	(c)	World Economy
4)	Short-term	(d)	Long-term
5)	Centralisation	(e)	Decentralisation
6)	Institutional Help	(f)	Self-Help
7)	Representative Democracy	(g)	Participative Democracy
8)	Hierarchies	(h)	Networking
9)	North	(i)	South
10)	Either/or	(j)	Multiple Options.

Traditional Hospitality Model

In the hospitality model there is a debate between independence in decision making at the level of one or many. The new model has emerged which lays stress on connectivity and inter-dependence. The new model is more appropriate for an ever-changing world and ever-increasing pace of change. Also, certain other factors may just force adoption of this model, such as stricter regulatory norms for more activist investor and community, general rise in level of mistrust of business, and so on (Ref. Table 2.2).

Table 2.2: Traditional and Emerging Hospitality Models

Traditional Hospitality Model	Emerging Hospitality Model
1) Centralized control	1) Centerless organisation
2) Leadership & management	2) Leadership teams
3) Authority based command orientation	3) Personal mastery, shared vision team learning
4) Command and control	4) Empowered
5) Hierarchical	5) Networked
6) Built around assets	6) Built around capabilities
7) Focus on managing numbers	7) Focus on creating value
8) Independent parts/sub-systems	8) Inter-dependent
9) Reactive	9) Proactive, responsive and learning organisation.

Now, Indian hospitality industry is entering a third period of change: there is a shift from the command and control organization of departments and divisions, to the information based organizations, an organism of knowledge specialists. We can perceive, though perhaps only dimly, what this hotel organization will look like. We can identify some of its main characteristics and requirements of its structure system culture.

A New Model for a Twenty First Century Hotel

Structure of Hospitality Industry

A new model for Indian hospitality industry is emerging with full vigour and style. It structure, system and culture is bound to be based on unique characteristics as give below:

1) Non bureaucratic, with fewer rules and employees
2) Limited to fewer levels
3) Organized with the expectation that the management will lead and lower level employees will manage.
4) Characterized by policies and procedures that produce the minimal internal interdependence needed to serve customers.

System of Hospitality Business

1) Depend on many performance information systems, providing data on customers especially.
2) Distribute performance data widely.
3) Offer hospitality management training and support system to many people.

Culture in the Hospitality Business

1) Externally oriented
2) Empowering
3) Quick to make decisions
4) Open and candid
5) More risk tolerant.

Summary

Most hotel in India make little attempt to forecast the future and prepare themselves for it. Instead, they react to situations and events as these arise. The recent wisdom about managing business in India, does buy the old textbooks and concepts already given up by the best hotel in the world. We in India, continue to believe that the essence of management lies in our ability to manage large hotel. Many hotels seem to believe that the best ways to organize a service is to integrate vertically, both backwards and forwards, so that one can retain control over the business. We continue to strongly believe in having well defines organizational hierarchy levels and limit managers span of control.

Reference :

1. John Naisbatt, '*Megatrends*' (New York; Warner, 1982).

CHAPTER 3

Strategic Management and Hospitality Leadership

The successful white-coller workers till now, find reputable hospitality and tourism companies to work with and then moved up narrow functional hierarchies, while learning the art of management. Most successful blue-collar workers find how to do a certain job and then stayed in that position for decades. Union rules have often discouraged personal growth. Narrow job classification in hotels, for examples, are not designed to reduce learning but that has been one of the consequences. In a stable environment hotel could live with these kind of rules but in a rapidly changing globalised market place, hotel probably cannot. The old white collar career path did help people learn, but only in narrow, functional grooves. One had to absorb more and more knowledge about accounting or engineering or marketing, but little else. To progress beyond a certain level one had to learn about hotel management, but not much about leadership.

In the twenty first century successful career in hospital and tourism would be more dynamic. Already hotels are seeing fewer people doing one job the same way for longer periods of time. The greater uncertainty and volatility tend to be uncomfortable for people at first but as they learn to master more volatile career path, they became more comfortable. They change generally and play more useful rules in organisational transformations. They more easily develop whatever leadership potential they have. With better leadership potential they are in a better position to help their employers to face the competition.

Attributes of a Top Hospitality Manager

For decades, researchers tracked their subjects by observing managerial behaviour and interviewing families, friends and colleagues. The description of a personality remained constant like introverts were introverts and extroverts were extroverts. The basic personality trait does not change.

There are some "Managerial attributes" which a hotel seeks in its employees. These attributes are what every single employer is looking for although each one may not have defined and articulated them. Some leadership attribute are given as as Table 3.1.

Table 3.1: Attributes of a Top Hospitality Manager

Category	Hospitality Managerial Attributes
1) Strategic Management	
	(a) Strategic thinking
	(b) Strategic implementation
	(c) Custoner-driven approach
	(d) Inspiring a shared vision
	(e) Decision making
	(f) Quick study
2) Organisational Management	
	(a) Managing operational performance
	(b) Staffing for high performance
	(c) Developing organisational talent
	(d) Delegation and empowerment
	(e) Managing team
	(f) Work cross-functional team work
	(g) Leadership innovation
	(h) Drive for business results
	(i) Use of leadership through quality
3) Managing self and others:	
	(a) Openness to change
	(b) Interpersonal empathy and influence
	(c) Personal drive
	(d) Personal strength and maturity
	(e) Personal consistency
4) Knowledge Base	
	(a) Environment and industry
	(b) Business and financial perspective
	(c) Overall technical knowledge

Modern Hospitality Leadership

A best hotel chain looks at the top ten students of a class because it associates academics with sound conceptual knowledge, prefers to choose from the under 25 age group. These are toppers preferred by most hotel chains. Because their academic performance indicates attribute of personal drive, strength, maturity and consistency. Consistency of results is extremely important in international hospitality.

There are three types of hotel companies: those who make things happen; those who watch things happen, and those that wonder what happened. Most international chains spread world-wide are still family-run business properties. In India, there are enough companies owned by families but not so perceived.

It you avoid the paradox through a model of governance, a model separates ownership from day-to-day management. You can energise and motivate people to rally around the organisation's vision. That is a competitive advantage. Hotel should evolve the corporate centre. Divide your business into rich business sectors, each headed by a vice president, who acts independently. Once a month, have war-room meetings, to discuss ideas and strategy relating to all the business. It is a moment of truth, accountability and transparency for the business. All should share a common vision backed up by shared understanding to achieve the goals. Shared understanding is born out of a shared sense of vision.

Set and maintain an implicit code for managing the hospitality business. Family members who actively manage the business may be chosen by consensus among the families. The role of the family patriarch or the leader is extremely critical. Roles have to be assigned to each family member individually. While shareholding is an inheritable property, the right to manage should not be seen as inheritable. The leader has to take decision by consensus that how many members should be in the business, ideally after assessing the capabilities of each of the members. It is extremely important to send out the right message to the employees of the hotel by forgetting they are the owners and behave like a manager. The leader sets out the agenda, the dream and the big picture and then leaves the professionals to deliver.

Summary

In conclusion, let the family look after the family and the professionals look after the business, but it is easier said than done. Only very few of the top professionals join family run business that too after a lot of homework and like to spend a long time understanding the group before they join.

The search agencies are asked to give their views to a question.

What do top professionals look for in the family run hotel business when they have an offer of joining ?

(13)

May I have your views on the pofile and qualities 21st century hospitality leader who can successfully lead your company into the future.

The prospective managers should quiz the promoters and search agencies about the seriousness of the change process, what exactly the family has in mind, and the reason why they want to professionalise before they take the plunge. Then there are question of ethics. Companies with dodgy or controversial past find it impossible to attract professionals. Clean companies are in demand and even the whiff of a skeleton puts off serious professionals. Next on the agenda is independence and autonomy. Peer group evaluation is high on a professional's checklist. Also professionals like to join companies with proven track records.

In some cases multi-product, multi-business groups can provide career opportunities, but there is no point if one gets caught between feuding brothers and cousins. Therefore even as promoters are deciding that a professional touch is just what the doctor ordered, the professionals would rather stay in multinationals.

(14)

CHAPTER 4

The Modern Hospitality Business Leadership

The significant change one would observe in the modern hospitality industry is that today there is no difference in what promoters or family owned hotel want, and what International hotel chain want, namely:

(a) A leadership which is young and restless but unemotional.

(b) A hands-on manager who thinks for long-term.

(c) Friendly and flexible, but firm and decisive.

(d) He is the public face of the company, but does not dominate it.

In the light of the above profile, the views of the international chains are ascertained based on the type of manager/leader who, would lead a hotel company in the future.

The questions are targeted at the head of human resource development and top man of the hotel organisation through references and direct methods using telephone, fax and internet. Few personalities are quizzed during seminars.

Organizational philosophy normally drives the staffing strategies and practices. Specifically, senior management approach to people/employees and the kind of teams they'd like to build. In the current organizational context, one could definitely say that while one seeks a basic, fundamental skill set for a job roles, the attitude, organisational cultural integration aspect is a key decision factors. The element of attitude and approach is valid at any position in an organisational hierarchy and the weightage of different corporations would be proportionately dependent on the training investment and learning emphasis/opportunities they are willing to provide. At the end of the day one need to recognize that one is not dealing with just a pair of hands. We need to deal with the whole person and get people to bring their head and heart to work.

An Effective and Successful Hospitality Management/Leadership

The king of attitude which one has the essence of one's own life time experiences. It is not easily changeable. Skills are easier to pick up and for a person who wishes to earn, it forms part of personal progress. A hotel prefers to hire people with 'right attitude and 'train for skills'. Attitude with respect to leadership, humility, fire in belly, learning ability, openness, customer orientation, determination to succeed, entrepreneurship among others.

The most important being - a positive thinker, coming from generally happy supportive home, some one who cannot wait to get to work on Monday morning.

The positive attitude will help a person to transform negative situations into positive ones and *vice versa*. The positive/ negative attitudes send vibrations of similar nature, hence reaction is accordingly. If a hotel is not in mainstream business, the required skills are not readily available. Hotel type of job requires total teamwork. Hotel total force is divided into groups. These being the key issues, and guiding philosophy of human resources management is no matter how skilled a person is, what is important is his attitude. So hire a person with right attitude and train him for skills. Accordingly while hiring apart from other traits one looks at these aspects in a candidate: is he keen to learn, how does he update himself in his chosen field, is he a team player, his attitude towards other people.

Many managers in India don't have fire in belly. The fire is made up of a profile that is dramatically different in terms of skills, background, track record, abilities, personality and even looks. Hospitality industry in India is looking for top professionals and the requirement is international mindset, vision, flexibility and agility, multiple skills, customer focus and communication ability.

In the past requirement for managers in hotels was of fixers. He was expected to get licenses and collaborations and know as many officials as possible. People looked for yes-men, now you don't need this. All that has changed. Now managers need to be technology proficient, analytical with a quick grasp of issues, address tasks hands-on, international experience may not be essential but understanding of international trends and the scenario is imperative. His mindset is global not local (Refer Table 4.1).

Table 4.1: An Effective and Successful Hospitality Manager/Leadership Selection Criterion Personalities & Organisations

Leadership

1. **Profile** (as for as possible should have maximum number of following factors) :
   - (a) Adverse & harsh environment during childhood
   - (b) Least family exposure to business
   - (c) Rise by perseverance of self-only.
   - (d) Minimum initial investment
   - (e) Least political & social connections.
   - (f) Spectular performance
2. **Period & Age** (divided in three periods)
   - (a) Past leader
   - (b) Presently top leaders of 40 years and above, and
   - (c) finally young achieves of 35 years and less.

(contd.)

Organisations

	Sectors covered		Views		
		Asked from		Replies received	
1)	Private Hotels				
	Indian	60	80	37	(21)
	MNCs	20			(16)
2)	Public Sector hotel and Goverment Sector hotel		85	30	
3)	Defence Services		15	12	
4)	Educational		10	7	
5)	Political Establishment			5 2	
6)	Religious Institutions			5 1	
7)	MNCs		10	8	
	Total		210	97	

Areas and Number of Organisations

Areas Covered	Number of Organisations
1) Bangaluru	50
2) New Delhi	50
3) Mumbai/Pune	30
4) Kolkata	20
5) Noida (UP)	15
6) Foreign	10
7) Jaipur	10
8) Hyderabad	10
9) Dehradun-Mussoorie	5
10) Ahmedabad	5
11) Chandigarh	5
Total	210

(17)

Progress of successful leaders in hospitality industry need to be judged on the basis of certain criteria, such as

(a) Adverse environment during childhood

(b) Least exposure to hospitality and tourism environment

(c) Rise by perseverance of self-only

(d) Minimum Investment

(e) No political connections

(f) Spectular achievement by single generation only.

A renowed hotelier, Mohan Singh Oberoi[1] was only six months old when his father died. He was educated in a village where there was only one teacher for five classes. The family could not afford to pay the tuition fee. This same young boy within a few decades ended up hosting a dinner for Michael Jackson for Rs 1 lakh a plate at the Oberoi. Few momentous decisions in Manmohan Singh Oberoi's life are worth mentioning:

(a) He took momentous decisions in his life. One was when the decided to shave off his scraggy beard. His orthodox uncle could not accept it and Mohan Singh had to leave his employment of selling shoes.

(b) Once he failed in a PWD typing examination. 'Failures are good for us that is why Americans have said, "It can't over till it's over".

(c) He always dressed well, and said 'Sir' often.

Through his journey Mohan Singh marvelled at his own temerity. Getting Grand Hotel in Kolkata, constructing the Oberoi at Delhi, and then at Mumbai and many more. Again and again and again, 36 times. One can't be lucky so many times - one has to be tough.

The Lives of Conrad Hilton[2] and Mohan Singh Oberoi are more or less the same that is, they had dreams. They had a vision and tried to reach it by sheer hard work. They never wavered from the chosen track. Once Conrad Hilton was refused credit at a petrol pump because he had over stretched himself by making a $ 10 million Hilton Hotel.

Qualities of a Successful Hospitality Professional

A successful hospitality leader is an educated technically qualified, who has gained diverse experiencies and opportunities to mark that such assignment have offered skills such as networking and negotiating with people who are culturally different are vital. He has desire to perform in an alien environment, appetite for knowledge and ability to make tings happen better than others. Some of these qualities are:

1) To take risks
2) To have got to be cut throat
3) Discipline is critical
4) Think out of the box
5) Listen to your people
6) Get a feel of every job
7) Killer instinct
8) Loyalty
9) Suitable family background
10) Promoter's choice
11) Ability to get licenses or collaborations
12) Knowing bureaucrats and ministers
13) Short-term plans
14) Workaholicism
15) Age seniority
16) Autocratic behaviour
17) An image bigger than the company
18) Hyper and exaggeration
19) Others.

Table 4.2: The Resume of a Successful Hospitality Managerial Leadership

1)	Age	: Around 38
2)	Gender	: Male
3)	Address	: Willing to relocate
4)	Work	: 10 to 15 years at least. Worked as unit head and experience
5)	Experience	
		(i) Finance, management and marketing.
		(ii) Personnel/HR,MIS/EDP, strategic planning, cross-functional responsibilities.
		(iii) MNC or overseas experience.
		(iv) Trained at an established large company, preferably one known for its managerial skills.
		(v) Proven track record in varied industries
6)	Education	: Post-graduation preferably MBA Hospitality Management from top institute or post-graduate degree from foreign university. Degree less important than alma mater
7)	Graduation	: Preferably Hospitality Management
8)	Additional	: Courses/training indicating a constant learning curve preferred
9)	Other	: Good to have some and not be one-dimensional
10)	Interests	: Reading.

Summary

Ownership of a hotel and managing a hotel are different fields. There two aspects should be separated to run a successful family business. Visionary leadership aspect with a combination of ethics, values and code of conduct are very important if a family run hotel has to progress beyond third generation.

Money is not uppermost in the mind of professionals, they also seek ethics, clean-image, vision, proven track-record, independence and autonomy before joining a family business.

References:

1. M.S. Oberoi by Negi, Jagmohan, Hotels for Tourism Development, Metropolitan, New Delhi.
2. 'By My Guest' by Conard Hilton.

CHAPTER 5

An Effective Hospitality Professional

The Hospitality Industry is quite distinctive and have effective leadership qualities with many attributes. There are 25 traits attributed to hospitality managers, identified in various surveys. These are arranged in alphabetic order and more than 300 respondents are asked to identify five key traits out of these, which they considered most important and any attribute not required for the manager. They are also asked to include any crucial attribute, which has not been identified.

Hospitality Manager: Tributes and Traits

I Qualities/Traits of a Hospitality Leader

1) Alert
2) Bearing
3) Courage
4) Decisiveness
5) Endurance
6) Enthusiasm
7) Forcefulness
8) Humility and unselfishness
9) Humour
10) Human Relation attitude
11) Intelligence
12) Initiative
13) Integrity
14) Judgement and justice
15) Knowledge
16) Loyalty
17) Maturity

(contd.)

18) Need for achievement
19) Open mind
20) Positive attitude
21) Responsibility
22) Sympathy
23) Tact
24) Vision and foresight
25) Warmth.

II) From the analysis of 125 replies received, following ten traits are considered most important

1) Bearing
2) Decisiveness
3) Enthusiasm
4) Humour
5) Integrity
6) Maturity
7) Positive attitude
8) Responsibility
9) Track and
10) Warmth.

III) Traits which are identified to be out of context for the future top hospitalilty managers

1) Humility
2) Unselfishness
3) Loyalty
4) Sympathy
5) Bearing considered not that important

IV) Crucial traits not included in the list but considered very important by the respondents

1) Authentic and approachable

(contd.)

2) Communication skills
3) Ethics
4) Emotional stability
5) Focus on purpose
6) Flexibility and adaptability
7) Honesty and credibility
8) High tolerance for frustration
9) Physical fitness
10) Resiliency and tenacity
11) Result oriented
12) Risk taker
13) Social skills
14) Team building.

The above traits are collated in relation to the combination of factors in the make-up of a total managerial leader. The profile, which distinguishes between common leaders and exceptional leaders given in Figure 5.1.

V) Summary Analysis: The combinations of following factors make a top hospitality manager

1) General personality traits
2) Task-related personality traits
3) Leadership motives
4) Cognitive factors
5) Physical and background factors
6) Influence of heredity and environment.

Traits for the Future Hospitalilty Managers

The following traits are considered important for the top hospitality managers :-

1) Sound technical competence including computing skills.
2) Dynamic disposition, strong initiative and high level of committment.
3) Creativity on the job which adds value to the product, process or business strategy.

(*contd.*)

4) High on the learning curve, perseverance and strong conviction for success.
5) Willingness to shoulder responsibility and personal accountability.
6) Ability to set moderately high self-goals and work under strict timeframes with a 'no excuse' framework.
7) Strong teamwork, self-effective communication. confidence and
8) Ability to update on changing technologies and new industry norms.
9) Ability to face up to the rigours of high job pressure situations and longer hour of work to stretched project targets and deadlines.
10) Ability to face up to the rigours of high job pressure situations and longer
11) Focus on internal and external customer on whose assessments your performance shall be evaluated.
12) High focus on organisational goals and integration of individual goals to that of the organisation.

Making of a Top Hospitality Manager:
Combination of Factors
Execeptional Hospitality Managerial Skills

Common Leadership Traits	Key Personality Traits	Task Accomplishment Traits	Motives & Needs	Cognitive Factors	Physical & Background	Heredity & Environmeny
1) Alert	1) Authentic & approachable	7) Assertiveness	14) Power motives either personalized or socialised			
2) Bearing	2) High tolerance for frustration					
3) Courage 4) Decisiveness			17) Knowledge of business			25) Synergy of traits Transactional and Transformanal leadership
5) Endurance					22) Energy & physical atamina	
6) Enthusiasm 7) Forcefulness/ assertiveness		8) Team Building				
8) Humility & unselfishness 9) Humour	3) Emotional stability 4) Sense of humour					**Effective leader**
10) Human relation attitude 11) Intellience	5) Emotional Intelligence	9) Flexibility & Adaptability	15) Drive & achievement	18) Openness to experience	23) Bearing	
12) Initiative 13) Integrity 14) Judgement & justice	(a) Self awareness (b) Self regulation (c) Motivation (d) Empathy			19) Creativity	24. Background (a) Education (b) Type of school (c) Company seniority	
15) Knowledge	(e) Social shifts		16) Tenacity	20) Insight into people & situations		
16) Loyalty 17) Maturity 18) Need for achievement	6) Honesty, integrity & creditabiity (ethics)	10) Risk & Initiative				
19) Open mind 20) Positive attitude		11) Resiliency		21) Farsightedness		
21) Responsibility 22) Sympathy 23) Tact		12) Communication skills				
24) Vision & forsight 25) Warmth		13) Vision				

Fig. 5.1: Exceptional Hospitality Managerial Skills

THE HOSPITALITY MANAGERIAL STYLES MODEL I :

Likert's System of Top Management

	System 1	System 2	System 3	System 4
	Exploitive Autocrat	Benevolent Autocrat	Participative	Democratic
Manager's confidence and trust in	No confidence & Trust	Condescending Confidence & Trust	Substantial but not complete confidence & trust	Complete confidence & trust
Subordinates feeling of freedom	Do not feel free at all to discuss things	Do not feel very free to discuss things	Feels reasonably free to discuss things	Feels completely free to discuss
Superiors seeing improve-ment with subordinates	Seldom get ideas and opinions from subordinates	Something get ideas & opinions from subordinates	Usually gets ideas and opinions	Always ask subordinate for opinions

Fig. 5.2 Likert's System of Top Management

He leverages his innate performance for consensus by using a mix of the participative and democrative style of dealing with his people.

Mode II

The business leadership style The Blake and Mouton Managerial Grid

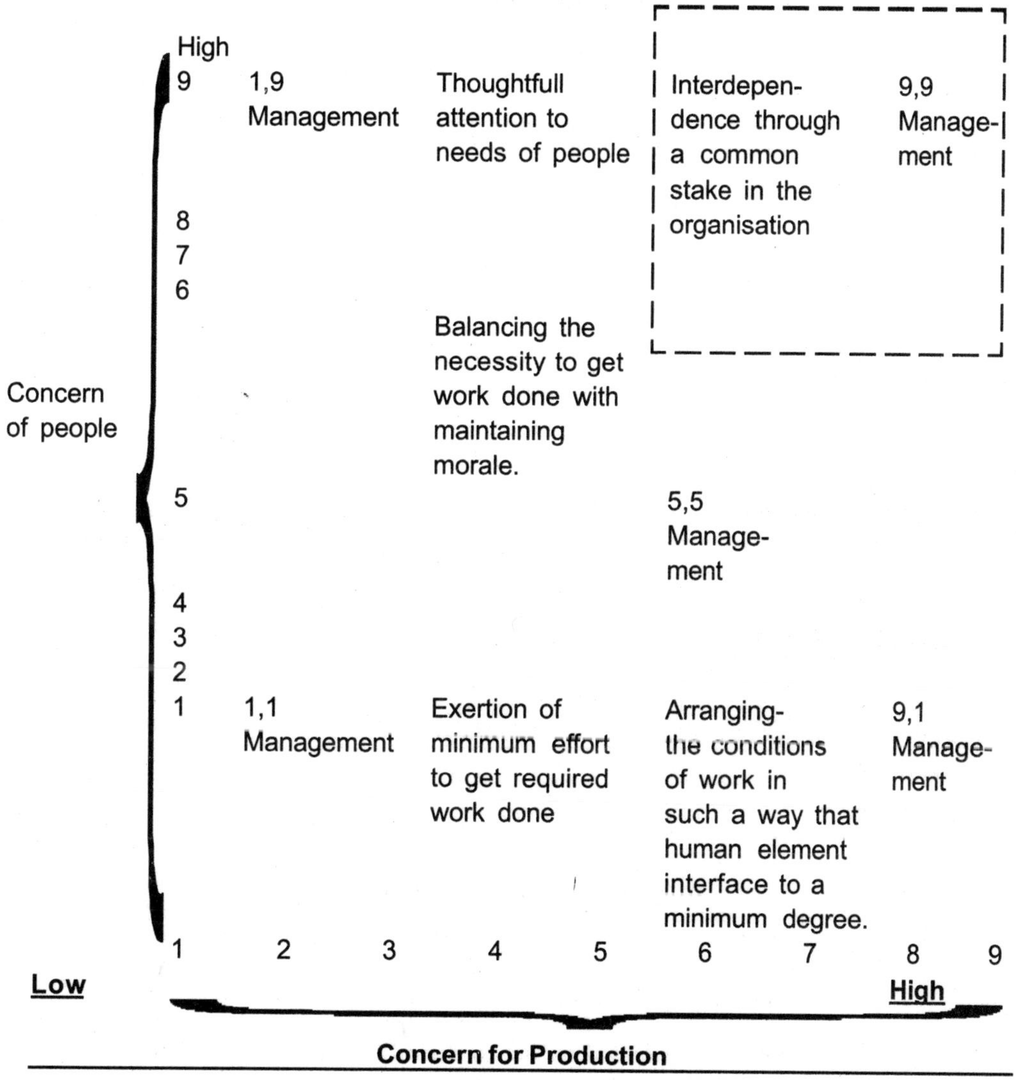

Fig. 5.3 The Business Leadership Style: The Blake and Mouton Managerial Grid

He balances his concern for employees, with whom his sense of identification is strong, with a concern for organisational objectives.

Model III

The Hospitality Managerial Leadership Style
The Situational Top Managerial Mode

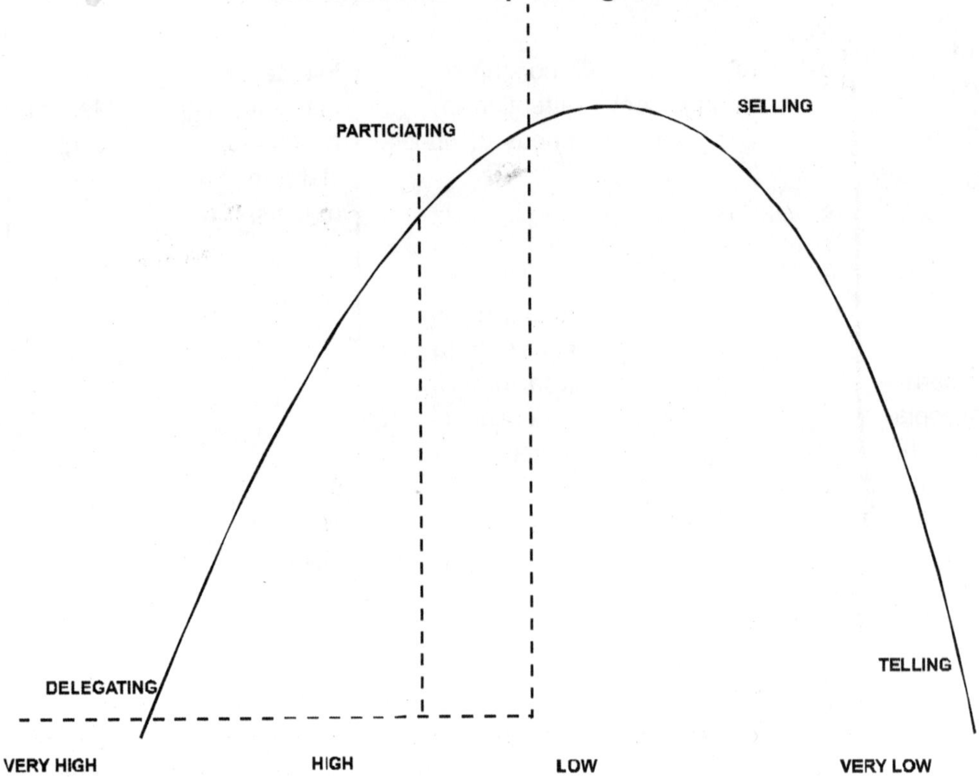

Maturity Level of Followers

Low	Task Oriented	High

Fig. 5.4 The Hospitality Managerial Leadership Style: The Situational Top Managerial Mode

He leads by delegating with knowledge, workers, and by participation when managing the larger workforce.

Model IV

The Hospitality Managerial Leaders Style: a Charismatic Management Styles

Type of charismatic leadership style	Meaning	Example
1) Envisioning	Creating a picture of the future with which people can identify	Articulating a compelling vision and setting high expectations
2) Energising	Directing the generation of energy and the motivation to act	Demonstrating personal excitment and confidence
3) Enabling	Psychologically helping people to act, or perform in the face of challenging goals.	Expressing personal support and empathing with employees.

Fig. 5.5 The Hospitality Managerial Leaders Style: a Charismatic Management Styles

After creating a vision, he leads by energizing his followers with his own excitment, and supports them by empathizing with their problems all the time.

Table 5.1 Transformation Process of top Hospitality Management Style

From 20th Century Manager	To 21st Century Leader
1) Few leaders, many top managers.	1) Many leaders and every fewer managers
2) Leading by goal-setting e.g. near term profits, ROI growth.	2) Leading by vision-creating, new directions for long-term business
3) Downsizing bench marking for low cost, high quality	3) Also creating domains of uniqueness, distinctive competencies.
4) Reactive/adaptive to change	4) Anticipative/future creative
5) Designer of hierarchical organization	5) Designer of flatter, distributed, more collegial organization, leader as social architect
6) Directing and supervising individuals	6) Empowering and inspiring individuals, but also facilitating team-work.
7) Information help by few decision-makers	7) Information shared with many, both internally and with outside partners
8) Leader as loss, controlling processes and behaviours	8) Leader as change-agent, creating organisation.
9) Leader as stabilizer balancing conflicting demands and maintaining the culture	9) Leader as change-agent, creating agenda for change, balancing risks and evolving the culture and the technology base.
10) Leader responsible for developing good managers	10) Leader also responsible for developing future leaders; serving as leader of leaders.

Figure 5.6 : An Ideal and Successful Hospitality Professional

CHAPTER 6

Managerial Leadership Behaviour in Indian Hospitality Industry

The importance of top managerial leadership in hospitality industry, and the continual interest in the concept of acknowledge, however, the phenomenon continues to attract controversy about conceptual and methodological issues. This research note adds to the debate by assessing independent dimensions of hospitality leadership behaviour with an adapted version of an instrument. The results of the study which are obtained from a sample of 50 managers from the hospitality industry, reveal that the respondents indentified 25 dimenstions of hospitality managerial leadership behaviour. These findings are discussed in terms of the consequences and implications for human resource management and development.

Influence of Globalisation

The influence of globalisation has created a world that faces challenges far beyond the comprehension of yesterdays's managerial leaders in hospitality industry. Consequently, contemorary hotel organisations may be characterised by constantly changing dynamics such as:

1) Complexity, customisation and competitiveness of hospitality business,
2) Importance on guest rather than strategies,
3) Reliance on technology and the rise of the knowledge economy,
4) Potential pitfalls of dispersed and virtual working teams, and
5) Increasing interest of investors in 'intagibles'.

These trends and influences demand institutional flexibility, quality service, flatter organisations, interpersonal skills and innovation. Indeed, the growing democratisation and the rapid mobility of labour and capital around the globe has forced hotels organisations to trim their pyramidical frameworks, and to root out cumbersome and bureaucratic structures. As a result of these transformations, hotels are being compelled to adopt strategies and cultures that demand new mindsets, as well as incumbents with skills and ability to operate in fast traumatic work settings of discontinuity. In fact, over the years organisation culture of collaborate individualism in hospitality have replaced property and capital as the source of power and profit.

Contemporary hotel organisations are thus taking steps to adapt their ways and are calling for modern managerial leadership styles that would manage these challenges and yet achieve the holistic organisational goals. Consequently, the strategic management of human resources is being recognised incresingly as the ultimate source of corporate adaptability and competitive owner. Now, more than ever, responsive managerial leadership is seen as a critical factor in hotel's organisations success. Therefore, to be effective, hospitality managerial leaders need to adapt their styles to fit a broad range of individual and team situations.

There raises the need to study managerial leadership behaviour as the leaders face these challenges and cope with the emphasis on guest rather than products. Recognising this need, a study is conducted on managerial leadership dimensions. The findings obtained in the study when managerial responses to a questionnire are factor analysed, are interesting and thought provoking. These study findings have the potential to contribute towards human resource managment policies in the hospitality industry.

Methodology

Respondents for this study are 50 hospitality managerial leaders from various organisations, different background and managerial leader levels. The reason for choosing these hotels is for convenience (because the researcher has direct contact with the chosen hotel and hence, found it comparatively easy for data collection), but more importantly because little is at all is known about the leadership style of these hotels. Indeed there is scant evidence that any research of this nature has been conducted in these hotels.

The research strategy has projected and is designed to follow a pluralist approach. Nevertheless, in this project there is a great emphasis on quantitative methods and the qualitative dimensions. The first objective is to obtain data with a good balance across respondent backgrounds. For example, gender, age managerial level and formal education are examined from data where there are adequate sample numbers in partitioned categories. This is a significant aspect of the study as this is the first time it has been reported that a comprehensive managerial related analysis has ever been undertaken in these hotels. The second feature of the study design is that it is conducted as a cross-cultural analysis. Utmost care is taken to provide clear definitions of the requests and to keep the questionnaire as comphehensible, yet as succinct as possible while not compromising the quality and the validity of the questions asked. An overriding consideration in designing the research stragegy and the instruments is also to enhance the determination of a robust data set that had relevance for the disciplines being examined and to ensure that the chosen sample is representative.

Common techniques of quantitive research uses questionnaires, structured interviews and tests. The main data collection for this project is carried out through questionnaires. The questionnnaire is attached with a cover letter which explains the purpose of the study and also carries full instructions emhasising anonymity and voluntary participation of the articants. All the questionnaires are administered with the support of sponsorers who approved the conducting of the study in their region.

Prior to actual data collection, a pilot study is conducted using 10 questionnaires. They are distributed to the chosen participants of the pilot study which is administered over a period of one week. Since it is important to use carfully constructed instruments that have been tested for validity and reliability, the initial data from the pliot study are thoroughly tested. On completion of the administration of the questionnaire, discussions are then held and interviews are carried out with the resondents, to identify any nomenclature problems that the partcipants may have encountered while answering the questionnaire items in terms of clarity, sensitivity to cultural nuances and relevance to the industry. This is a vital element of the qualitative component of the study design. After careful assessment (quantitative), and particularly of the verbal resonses offered, the questionnaire is modified to enhance better understanding and to accommodate the cultural sessitivities of the study participants.

Final collection of the data is carried out by sending 150 questionnaires to each of the sponsors of the respective hotels. After the questionnaires are analysed, discussions is held with the focus groups. This is carried out to gain qualitative data which is not available on surveys alone. The resulting discussions with the focus groups elicited ideas, opinions and experiences which prompted them to respond to the questions. Hence, these discussions enhance better understanding of the practical aspects of the answers, especially in cases where the answers differed from the exected response.

The degree of initiating structure or task oriented style of management, and consideration or relationship oriented style leadership is assessed with a 15 item scale that is developed using concepts, and values. This instrument is adapted from a sub scale of the Leadership Opinion Questionnaire derived from the same research rogram as the Leadership Behaviour Description Questionnaire X 11, 1963, Cook, Heworth, Wall & Warr (1981). This instrument (LOQ) measures how leaders believe they behave in leadership roles. This instrument is used because of its popluarity in assessing managerial leadership behaviour. Frequent use in recent empirical research has accumulated a wealth of information about the scale psychometric properties and correlates. Respondents addressed each of the 15 items in terms of a five-point scale. The factor analysis produced unexpected and interesting results, highlighting that this instrument has unexplored dimensions.

The study data from the 150 hotel managers are assessed. Multi-variate factor analysis is employed to determined construct validity, and alpha coefficient is used to examine construct reliability.

Managerial leadership styles are studied using questionnaire. It is administered to hotel business leadership managers from various hotels. A majority of the managerial leaders held tertiary qualifications and there is a resonable gender balance that is representative of the study groups.

Findings

The findings from this research provided enlightenment on the used measure. First, this study establishes that the business leadership in hospitality instrument used for the study to espoused leadership behaviour, is applicable in all environments. It also establishes that the instrument has the potential to measure multi dimensions of leadership. In fact, it appears that the employed scale measures independent dimensions of managerial leadership behaviour. This unexpected finding may have many explanations. One possibility is that this instrument is developed in past and leaders/managers of that time are comparatively less educated and knowledgeable than the managers of today. Another possible explanation is that today's hotel managers are empowered and are in a world that is fluid and in constant turmoil surrounded by demands far beyond what managers faced in the past. The reality faced then is diffierent, and hence what may have been conceived by the educated mangers of today (i.e., in the period of this study) may be signficantly different from yesterday's managers' comprehension of the instrument. It is also possible that the instrument is developed for a different level of managers and for a narrowed leadership scope. This raises the possibility that this instrument may have produced a different set of results, if limited to lower level managers.

One of the most salient findings is that the top management scale is extremely versatile as it is able to capture more multi-dimensions of leadership for which it had been designed. This is despite the study respondents being mostly educated senior and executive managers, who are expected to be 'thinkers' and not just administrative mangers. Focus group discussions revealed that in the study contemporary work settings, managers/ leaders are compelled to employ a variety of behaviours that go far beyond the traditional, widely acknowledged activities of initiating structure or task, and consideration or relationship. The context of leadership today is very different from what it is in the past. Consequently, the perception of the study respondents is that leadership by educated and learned executives is not just the few dimensions that are examined. But keeping in line with conflicting demands of their jobs, their style is a mix of many dimensions that is not necessarily fixed or limited to just few types, but a bundle of behaviours that are dynamic, versatile, and in some situations need to be extremely sensitive.

In this context, it is debatable that this instrument is applicable in contemporary work settings. However, the fact that it measured multi independent dimensions may imply that this instrument is still applicable, but that the scope needs widening, thus further refinding the scale to incorporate the trends and influences that drive managerial/leadership behaviours. Nevertheless, finding five independent managerial leadership behaviours has a salient implication in the development and management of human resources. It is presumed that this information is beneficial to staff development and training within hotel organisations in terms of raising awareness and building corporate human resources that will effectively contribute to the success of the business. The findings will thus encourage consensus, cooperation and collaboration rather than competition and conflict and assist overall skill development for human resources. It is likely that these findings may also help shape human resource policies and contribute towards building a more positive and responsive organisational culture to meet the needs of learning organisations and help develop leadership for the new millennium.

CHAPTER 7

Conclusion

In the hospitality management the most desirable managerial attribute is the leadership. This attribute is seriously lacking in most hotels. Through mangers do a good job of maintaining and sustaining existing organisational system, they fail to steer innovation and change in the organisation. They seldom inspire people to go beyond the call of duty. Only effective leaders are capable of producing results beyond the call of duty. They can bring about transformational change. They dare to dream and they share the dream with others and translate it into reality by aligning the energy of people in one direction.

The hospitality management is indeed more about doing and less about knowing. A look at the nature of leadership and the various approaches to leadership development forms the background to understand the primacy of self-empowerment and self-reprogramming in realising one's leadership potential.

There are four signs of effective management style in hospitality industry:

1) A hotels unit (an organisation, a department, or section) attains results beyond established norms. If the hotel achieves usual result, it is being managed by a manager rather than being led by leader. The leader sets stretch goals, i.e. goals that are not considered normal and which require very high efforts from sub–ordinates.
2) Hotel members have a sense of pride in their jobs, which goes beyond mere job satisfaction. Though job satisfaction is important, it is impacted by so many variable that the unit leader has only a marginal role in promoting a sense of pride among the unit members for the sets challenging goals, galvanises them to achieve them, and helps them realise their potential.
3) Hotel members grow at the workplace. Employees growth does not mean promotion or career progression but relates to the development of requisite competencies and horning of existing skills. Effective leaders provide their subordinates with opportunities to help them grow.
4) Finally, a leader also grows while performing his tasks. He develops when all the four conditions are being fulfilled, then one can safely say that effective leadership is in place.

References

Cascio, W.F. (1992). *International Human Resource Management Issues for the 1990s*. Asia Pacific Journal of Human Resources, 30 (4), 1-18.

Clarke, C. (1998). Reconcilling Western Management Ideas with far Eastern Realities. *Long Range Planning,* 31(4), 523-529.

Cook, J.D., Hepworth, S.J., Wall, T.D., & Warr, P.B. (1981). *The Experience of Work: A Compendium and Review of 249 Measures and Their Use.* London: Academic Press, Harcourt Brace Jovanovic Publishers.

Cronbach, L.J., (1951). *Coefficient Alpha and the Internal Structure of Tests.* Psychometrika, 16, 297-334.

Fleishman, E.A. (1953). *Leadership Climate And Human Relations Training.* Personnel Psychology, 6, 205-222.

Gopinath, C. (1998). *Alternative Approaches to Indigenous Management in India.* Management International Reviews, 38(3), 257-276.

Helgesen, S. (1990). *The Female Advantage: Women's Ways of Leadership.* New York, N.Y.: Currency and Doubleday.

James, M. (1997). *A Conceptual Framework for Alignin Managerial Behaviors with Cultural Work Values.* International Journal of Commence & Management, 7, 81-102.

Limerick, D. (1992). *The Shape of the New Organisation: Implications for Human Resource Management.* Asia Pacific Journal of Human Resources, 30(1), 38-52.

Negi, Jagmohan, *Hospitality Management: Current Trends and Practices*, 2009, New Delhi.

Nunnally. J.C. (1978). *Psychometric Theory.* (2nd ed). New York, N.Y.: McGraw-Hill. Palomba, C.A. & Banta, T.W. (1999). *Assessment essential.* San Francisco: Jossey-Bass.

Patton, M.Q. (1990). *Qualitative research and Evaluation Methods.* Thousands Oaks, California : Sage.

Phillips, N. (1993). *Innovative Management.* London: Pitman.

Rampal and Gupta, *Project Report Writing*, Galgotia, Nre Delhi.

Stogdill, R.M. (1963). *Manual for the Leader Behaviour Description Questionnaire-Form XII.* Ohio: Bureau of Business Research, Ohio University.

APPENDICES

APPENDIX A

Research Methodology

Some facts

- Only 5% of people make things happen,
- 15% watch what is happening, and
- 80% have no idea about what is happening.

Sources of data

1) Theoretical research.

(a) Books and journals as given in references

(b) Magazines

(c) Newspaper reports

(d) Annual reports of hotel companies and extract of chairmans' speech

(e) Research reports as mentioned

2) Practical/field research

(a) Interviews

(b) Telephonic views

(c) Fax

(d) Internet

(e) Questions

f) Seminars/workshops/conferences.

3) Books referred but not mentioned in the report

(a) Guest and blackhead-organisational change through effective leadership

(b) Warran G. Benin-Managing the Organisations and Leadership in 21st century

(c) David A-The Achieving Society

(d) SF. Fiddler-Theory of Leadership Effectiveness

APPENDIX B

Profiles of an Effective and Successful Hospitality Manager

Selection Criterion Personalities

Managerial Leadership

1) Profile (as for as possible should have maximum number of following factors) :
   (a) Adverse and harsh environment during childhood
   (b) Least family exposure to business
   (c) Rise by perseverance of self-only
   (d) Minimum initial investment
   (e) Least political and social connections
   (f) Spectular performance.
2) **Period and Age** divided in three periods of: a) past leaders, b) presently top manager of 38 years and above, and c) finally young achievers of 32 years and less.

Organisations

Sector covered	Views Asked from		Replies received	
1) Private Companies				
Indian	100	130	49	(37)
MNCs	30			(12)
2) Public Sector		25	22	
3) Government Sector	25	8		
4) Hotel Schools		10	7	
5) Political organisations		5	2	
6) Religious organisations		5	1	
7) Private Cos (foreign)		10	8	
Total		210	97	

APPENDIX C

Area and Number of Organisatios/Institutes Contacted

	Areas Covered	No. of Institutes/ Organisations
1)	Mumbai/Pune	30
2)	Bangalore	50
3)	Chandigarh	5
4)	Delhi	50
5)	Hyderabad	10
6)	Jaipur	10
7)	Kanpur	5
8)	Ludhiana	20
9)	Meerut	5
10)	Nodia	15
11)	Abroad	10
	Total	210

APPENDIX D

Sample Questions

1) **Search and Placement Agencies**

   "What do professionals look for in the family run business when they get an offer of joining'?

2) **Personalities**

   "May I have your views on the profile and qualities of 21st century business leader who can successfully lead your company into the future"

3) **Questionnaire for Identification of Traits/Qualities of an Effective Top Hospitality Manager of the Future**

   The basic make-up of a managerial leader consists of some of the following twenty five traits. Please identify/mention.

(a) Tick any five traits, which are most important for the future.

(b) Tick any traits out of these, which are out of context or not required by the next future manages.

(c) Mention any other quality/traits, which the future should have and does not exist in the list.

Questions on Traits/Qualities

Traits:

I) Any five essential traits

1) ....

2) ....

3) ....

4) ....

5) ....

II) Any trait out of context (Please Tick)

1) Alert ☐

2) Bearing ☐

3) Courage ☐

4) Decisiveness ☐

5) Endurance ☐
6) Enthusiasm ☐
7) Forcefulness/assertiveness ☐
8) Humility and unselfishness ☐
9) Humour ☐
10) Human relation attitude ☐
11) Intelligence ☐
12) Initiative ☐
13) Integrity ☐
14) Judgment and justice ☐
15) Knowledge ☐
16) Loyalty ☐
17) Maturity ☐
18) Need of achievement ☐
19) Open mind ☐
20) Positive attitude ☐
21) Responsibility ☐
22) Sympathy ☐
23) Tact ☐
24) Vision and foresight ☐
25) Warmth ☐

III) Mention any other trait of you choice

1) ....
2) ....
3) ....
4) ....
5) ....

Index